History of The Next Century
Where is the world headed according to civilizational cycles?

(Histoire Du Siècle À Venir
Où va le monde selon les cycles des civilisations?)

PHILIPPE FABRY

Translated from French
by

JEAN-FRANÇOIS GARIÉPY

First published by JC Godefroy 2015
E-ISBN: 9782865532742

Translated by Jean-François Gariépy, Ph. D.

© JC Godefroy 2015
© Philippe Fabry 2015

© Paul Sheer 2022

ISBN 978 0 578 39649 1

Cover by Marija Tatarinova

Benefactor's Note

Thanks to Dr Gariépy for his careful and true translation of this work.

Thanks also to Léo Portal for his encouragement and enthusiasm for this project.

It is my privilege to have brought this volume to the English-speaking world and my hope that readers can find enjoyment and enlightenment through its insights.

Paul Sheer, Spring 2022

Table of Contents

FROM THE SAME AUTHOR

Rome, du libéralisme au socialisme, leçon antique pour notre temps, Jean-Cyrille Godefroy, 2014.

For my brothers

Introduction

> "Whatever is has already been, and what will be has been before; and God will call the past to account."
>
> Ecclesiastes 3:15

Numerous thinkers of the past centuries have tried to understand the historical developments of human civilization by attempting to uncover general principles, rules, or laws of History. Greek philosophers tried discovering laws that would govern the political history of their cities, notably as it relates to the changes of political regimes: monarchy, aristocracy, democracy… and one finds virtually as many explanatory schemes as there are authors.

The same pursuit, centuries later, motivated jurist Maurice Hauriou, as he investigated the political instability of his country since the Revolution, which he explained by invoking a recurring cycle that alternated between a legislative dictatorship, an executive dictatorship and a softened parliamentary regime.

During the XIXth century, Clément Juglar, who was then contributing to the nascent science of economics, tackled the recurrence of economic crises by invoking cycles. The description and categorization of these cycles would later tempt numerous authors who would look at history through the lens of cycles that differed in various ways. These authors sometimes saw longer or shorter cycles, or applied their analyses to broader or stricter economic sectors. Their goal was not merely to find order in a set of observations that appear, at first glance, quite disordered. More prosaically, they were interested in predicting crises in order to prevent them. This meant using the theory of economic cycles as forecasting tools.

Comparative history, global history, macrohistory… for decades, historians have tried to follow in the economists' footsteps with the purpose of elevating historical science above itself. This research direction has provided an opportunity for geniuses like Fernand Braudel to shine, as he attempted to explain the long term history of Europe with a concept that he refers to as "World-Economy." Braudel identified parallels between medieval Venice, Renaissance Portugal and Modern Times England. In doing so, he uncovered mechanisms of history that were recurring and systematic: Laws of History. Importantly, he was highly influenced by the theory of economic cycles and was fascinated by secular movements[1].

The XXth century was also a period for the apparition of other theories attempting to predict the collective activities of human populations. Technical analysis appeared in this period, a discipline which seeks to anticipate stock market movements through the analysis of graphs displaying price history. One of the most striking concepts coming out of this discipline is Elliott Wave Theory, based on the idea that markets, and more generally, human behaviors, follow a mechanistic progression formed by successive waves. Elliott has defined certain rules regarding the order, nature and duration of his various waves in relation to each other, highlighting cycles of various durations which can be embedded into one another.

In his fascinating book *Study of History*, Arnold J. Toynbee laid out the deepest and most systematic theory of History to date. He showed that there were three important courses in the historical developments of civilizations at the global level. The first course is the Hellenic one, in which a civilization emerges from the unification of rival states fused into a "Universal state," thus encompassing an entire civilization. The second course is the Chinese one, in which a Universal state, after having established its existence, undergoes series of declines and recoveries. The third course is the Jewish one, which applies to scattered civilizations forming diasporas. The ideas of Toynbee are extremely important, but they have unfortunately not attracted the attention of mainstream academia. Most historians have probably been embarrassed in front of Toynbee's conceptual tools, for which they could see no use. This torpor was likely the result of the common repulsion of historians for explanatory systems combined with the embryonic character of Toynbee's results, which require supplementary analyses and further conceptual developments in order to function properly. I hope that the observations in this book constitute a step in that direction.

Economists, historians and financiers are not alone in their fascination for cyclical models that could hold the key to explaining and even predicting crowd behaviors. In his famous novel *Foundation*, the pope of science fiction and biochemist, Isaac Asimov, envisioned a statistical science called Psychohistory. The imagined science allowed one to predict future history by measuring and predicting human psychology at the scale of social groups, with a precision that is evocative of certain physical sciences such as gas kinetics. Physical sciences, he noted, illustrate how one can successfully predict the collective behavior of great ensembles of molecules, in spite of the fact that the movements of the underlying fundamental particles are governed by probabilistic rather than deterministic laws.

All of these examples illustrate in one way or another a tenet of conventional wisdom: History repeats itself. Indeed, I believe that it repeats itself even more than we generally recognize. The goals of this essay are to determine the extent to which History is predictable, to discover the real "Laws of History," and to begin unpacking the possibilities offered by such discoveries for the development of models that can predict the future developments of human civilization.

Finally, we shall present a tentative application of the first results of our work.

---

1. *Civilisation matérielle, économie et capitalisme (XVe-XVIIIe siècles)*, tome III, Paris, 1979.

PART I

Historionomy and the existence, nature and utility of Laws of History

We have begun with observations from numerous authors who have looked at periods ranging from the Greco-Roman antiquity to occidental history after the fall of the Roman Empire. Some of them compared the "Greek Dark Ages" to the European Middle Ages. Albert Thibaudet compared the suicidal conflict of World War I (in spite of not knowing about the second one) with the equally suicidal Greek Peloponnesian War[1], a comparison also made by Arnold J. Toynbee[2]. Jules Isaac, in Oligarques[3], compared the regime of

Vichy to that of the Thirty Tyrants of Athens, established by a victorious Sparta. Oswald Spengler understood that Ancient Greece and Medieval Europe do not constitute a separate civilizations spreading over a continuum but that one has reproduced the trajectory of the other[4]. Chantal Delsol compared the current situation of Europe with respect to the United States with that of Greeks with respect to Romans[5]. The opponents of American hegemony often talk of *Imperium americanum*. Our occidental bewilderment at Islamic terrorism reminds the clash between Roman and Judaic civilization that occurred in the first century of our era[6].

These comparisons are not merely isolated similarities. Taken together, they form a system which demonstrates a true symmetry between the history of Antiquity and global history since the fall of the Roman Empire.

We will thus show the existence of a model of cyclical history over a period of two millennia. The model describes about 40 stages which are embedded or overlap between four cyclic periods that we have termed A, B, C and D. Scheme A applies to Ancient Greece and Occidental Europe. Scheme B applies to Ancient Rome and the United States of America. Scheme C applies to the Judaic Civilization of antiquity and to Islamic Civilization. Scheme D applies to the Assyrian and Persian Empires as well as to the Seljuk Empire and the Ottomans. We will show that certain clues exist allowing us to tentatively superimpose these cycles unto an even older time period, where A would apply to Minoan Civilization, B to Mycenaean Greece, D to the Mesopotamian Empires and where the memories of this era as described by the Hebrews in the Bible seem to point to a similarity with scheme C, despite the absence of precise archeological data for these periods.

Of course, it will be impossible to revisit in full detail the entire history of such vast civilizations. We will limit ourselves to a few historical reminders which, while they may not teach anything new to the educated reader, will allow us to highlight the existence of the common schemes and to define their structure.

Once we have shown the existence of the phenomenon, we will propose certain lines of thought and attempt to provide the beginning of an explanation concerning these recurring civilizational schemes.

---

1. *La Campagne avec Thucydide*, 1922.

2. Arnold J. Toynbee, *A Study of History*, 1934-1961.

3. Jules Isaac (Junius), *Les Oligarques, essai d'histoire partiale*, Paris, 1946.

4. Oswald Spengler, *The Decline of the West*, 1918-1922.

5. "You state that France suffers from being too intelligent, coupled with a lack of will, a situation precisely inverse to that of the United States! [...] It is the history of Rome vanquishing the exhausted Greeks in order to feed on their culture. We may very well be in a similar situation to Greeks in front of Americans." *La modernité contre l'homme intérieur*, La Nef n° 173, July-August 2006. Quote translated to English.

6. Properly analyzed by Martin Goodman, *Rome and Jerusalem: The Clash of Ancient Civilizations*, Vintage, 2008.

Chapter I

The cycles

In this first step, we will go through some historical reminders in order to allow the reader to see the importance of the parallels that can be established between historical periods and the relevance of our modelling approach. Granted, it might seem hard from here to foresee how a model could be extracted from so few examples: two occurrences (Ancient Greece and Europe, Ancient Rome and America, Ancient Judaic Civilization and Islam, Assyrian and Persian Empires and Turkish Empires) corresponding to each civilizational cycle (A, B, C and D). However, it will become obvious that the numerous similitudes between the first occurrence and the second one compensate, in each case, for this methodological limit. Furthermore, we will show, at least partially, that there is evidence for further parallels into a third, more ancient, occurrence. Given the partial nature of the available evidence for these ancient times, the historical reminders and analyses of facts for this period will be more detailed.

I. THE AB CYCLIC COUPLE: SYMMETRY BETWEEN GRECO-ROMAN AND EURO-AMERICAN HISTORIES

The two first cycles to which we will pay attention function as a two-person team. This is why it is convenient to present them together.

1. Cycle A: Symmetry between Ancient Greece and European Civilization

A) HISTORICAL REMINDERS

Greece

During the VITH century B.C., at least half of known shores were under Greek influence or control. At the margins of this colonial empire, Rome was born under a Greek influence[1] which was both direct and indirect. The direct influence came from the proximity of Greece. The indirect influence came from the teachings of the Etruscans, who had themselves undergone this influence.

The origins of Ancient Greece go back to the Mycenaean Empire, which was progressively invaded by a barbarian people, the Dorians, and fell slightly later (around 1100 B.C.). It is on the ruins of the Mycenaean Civilization that Ancient Greece was born.

In fighting the oriental world dominated by the Persian Empire, Greeks successfully put a stop to their progression during the Greco-Persian Wars, notably with the maritime victory of the Battle of Salamis.

The Greek world, despite being endowed with a strong cultural unity, was constructed by city-states that were independent from one another, and these city-states had distinct cultural identities. With time, at the two poles of Ancient Greece, two enemy factions rose: the maritime, commercial and democratic power of Athens, and the continental, totalitarian and autarkic power of Sparta. A progressive worsening of the interactions between these two poles brought the Peloponnesian War, which by its ferocity broke the more sacred and ancient conceptions of war. Sparta crushed Athens, imposing the Thirty Tyrants regime and securing its hegemony for a brief period.

The conflict had exhausted Greek power, which saw its empire crumble, in particular under the attacks of the new power of Ancient Carthage, which had taken over Sicily. Among other things, Greece lost its independence to Macedonia. Later, this Macedonian hegemony would be broken off by the rise of Rome turning Greece into a province of its empire.

Europe

European civilization had an unmatched influence over the rest of the world. On the brink of World War I, the entirety of America, Africa, India and Oceania had encountered or were still undergoing the suzerainty of European colonialism. The influence of the European Empire extended into Turkey, which was colonized after the conflict with Mustapha Kemal. We could also add to these zones of influence Russia, above the Ural, since these lands, up to Siberia, were the colonies of a nation that had itself been partially influenced by the occident.

After the fall of the Roman Empire, Occidental Europe found itself the heir of Roman, Celto-Germanic as well as "barbarian" elements. Despite geopolitical rivalries, Europe found a novel common identity. This new identity, founded first on religion and then on culture, was Christianity. This common identity did not keep the continent from developing into independent nations, each with its cultural, institutional, political and religious specificities.

In turn, Europe had to combat the progression of the oriental word, which it successfully stopped with the maritime victory in the Battle of Lepanto in 1571. It is in the same period that the movement for colonization began, which over three centuries led Europe to become the master of the World. On the brink of the two World Wars, while Africa and Asia were still firmly under European influence, the greater part of America had escaped the Old World and was in turn dividing into national identities. Internally, after centuries of wars more or less codified by a Christian or humanist spirit, a radical antagonism developed between two groups of European nations: continental nations (central empires) and heavily colonial nations (France, England). This antagonism would result in the conflicts of two World Wars, which, in reality, in their deep underlying mechanisms, form a single one. During the Second World War, the antagonism came to worsen even more between the maritime, liberal and democratic powers of France and England and the continental, totalitarian and autarkic powers of fascistic regimes, in particular Nazi Germany. The two World Wars led to the abandonment of the ancient codes that had guided previous wars to the favor of all-out conflict. Civilians became military targets when not massacred purely for ideological reasons. The conflict, at the European level, was concluded at the European level by the defeat of democracies and the imposition of a fascistic regime in France as well as a short period of hegemony for Nazi Germany.

Europe, following these horrible wars, was exhausted. While it was strong enough to reconstruct itself, it wasn't able to maintain control over its colonial empire, and lost it within a few decades. Russia penetrated up to the heart of Europe. Finally, Russia was pushed back in its attempt to impose hegemony by the American power, which extended its protection over all of Europe, for instance through NATO.

Having stated these historical reminders, we can now attempt to establish a historical model for "Cycle A," which will apply to Ancient Greece as well as to European Civilization.

B) PRESENTATION OF CYCLE A

For clarity, and in order to highlight the relevance of the historical scheme, we will present each "stage" of the cycle as well as its Greek and European occurrence. We will proceed in the same manner for the next cycles.

In bold: stage of Cycle A
In upright: corresponding Greek historical fact
In italics: corresponding European historical fact

1) Invasion of the territories of the future civilization by a more civilized foreign empire.

Greece is invaded by the Achaeans, founders of the Mycenaean Empire.

Occidental Europe is invaded by the Romans.

2) New invasion by barbarian populations revert the political order imposed by the first invaders.

Greece is invaded by the Dorians and the Sea Peoples. The Mycenaean Empire collapses.

Europe is invaded by Germanic barbarians. The Roman Empire collapses.

3) Period of disappearance of the ancient culture and gestation of a new order.

Greece undergoes its "dark ages." The exchanges that were operating in the old Mycenaean Empire cease, Mycenaean culture disappears, and a new culture emerges with the contribution from the new invaders.

Europe undergoes its "dark ages." The Roman order has disappeared. Communication and trade paths are perilous. Medieval European Culture partially forgets Greco-Roman heritage and creates novel cultural standards.

4) Progressive appearance of political entities unifying into a common civilization.

Greek cities form, while maintaining their identity as part of the Greek Nation. Religion and common ceremonies such as the Olympic Games and the Sanctuary of Delphi maintain a sense of common identity.

European Kingdoms draw their borders while maintaining a common identity through Christianity. Each of the Kingdoms share the same religion and acknowledge the authority of the Pope.

5) Progressive cultural differentiation and competition between political entities for hegemony.

Greek cities construct an identity of their own, acquiring specific deities and special cults. They fight in order to retain their sovereignty or to gain control of others.

The European States construct a national identity beginning with the differentiation of religion by state: Gallican Church for France, Anglican Church for England, Catholic Church for Spain, Protestant Principalities in Germany... These subdivisions fight with one another for supremacy (Spanish domination in the XVIth-XVIIth centuries, French domination in the XVIIth-XVIIIth...).

6) Creation of a colonial empire stimulated by internal crises and technical progress.

Internal crises in Greek cities (*Stasis*) favor sociopolitical changes as well as technical progresses. This allows the creation of a Greek colonial space on the coasts of the Mediterranean Sea.

Religious wars and the progresses of navigation push Europeans toward a colonization of the coasts of the entire world.

7) Confrontation with the threat of a foreign civilizational superpower. War of resistance by Civilization A.

Confrontation to the advances of the Persian Achaemenid Empire. Greco-Persian Wars, the outcome of which is a stop of the progression to the advances of the Persian Empire on Earth and Sea (Salamis, Plataea...)

Confrontation to the advances of the Turkish Ottoman Empire. Wars, the outcome of which is a stop of the progression to the advances of the Turkish Empire on Earth and Sea (Lepanto, Vienna...)

8) An antagonism appears within the civilization: a democratic, cosmopolitan and maritime bloc opposes a totalitarian, militaristic, autarkic and continental bloc.

Athens, an open and democratic society, opposes Sparta and its allies, a society that is totalitarian, militaristic, autarkic and continental.

France and England, open democracies as well as colonial and maritime powers, oppose Nazi Germany, a totalitarian, militaristic and autarkic regime with ambitions of continental domination.

9) All-out war internal to the civilization, relentlessness from both sides, disappearance of conventional prohibitions.

Peloponnesian war, Corinthian war.

First and Second World Wars. All-out wars, massacres of civilians.

10) All-out internal war results in a weakened civilization, leading to the crumbling of its colonial empire and the loss of its global hegemony. The Empire is taken over by an emerging power of a superior size.

Greece is weakened after the Peloponnesian and Corinthian wars and the defeat of Sparta in Leuctra. It is incapable of defending its colonies and loses Sicily to Carthage. It is also threatened both by the neighboring Macedonian Power and by the rise of Rome, which expose Greece to even further risks.

Europe is exhausted by its "European civil war[2]." It loses its colonial empire and the Russian power threatens its independence.

11) All of the states forming Civilization A are taken under tutelage by the superpower of Civilization B[3].

Greece is completely dominated by Romans who triumph against Macedonian power.

Europe becomes a protectorate of Americans who triumph against Soviet power.

2. Cycle B: symmetry between Ancient Rome and American Civilization

A) HISTORICAL REMINDERS

Rome

At its apogee, the Roman Empire included the greater part of what used to be the Greek world, as well as Western lands that had been influenced by Greeks.

A couple of reminders are in order as to how Rome succeeded at reaching this degree of power. The City of Rome was dominated by Etruscan Kings[4], who were banished by its High Aristocracy, under the direction of Lucius Junius Brutus according to the legend. An aristocratic regime was established, directed by the Senate and composed of Patricians.

Thereafter, Rome progressively established its domination over neighboring cities and conquered the entirety of the Italian territory. Internally, after a series of *Secessio plebis* during the "Conflict of the Orders," the plebeians were successful at obtaining a democratization of the regime, specifically with the appointment of their own representatives, tribunes and the guarantee of rights to citizens by the Law of the Twelve Tables.

During its rise, the Roman power ended up encountering the Carthaginian power. The antagonism led to the Punic Wars, a conflict for supremacy over the Mediterranean Sea. Rome came out victorious and won important territories in North Africa and Spain.

At the East, the Republic extended its empire by intervening under the justification that it was defending Greek cities against Macedonian aggression.

In the Ist century B.C., the Republic faced grave internal troubles. First, from 91 to 89 B.C., the Social War, during which the allies of Rome seceded and created a confederation with a new capital and a new senate, because Rome refused to give them equal status. The allies eventually obtained Roman citizenship.

Then came the bloody conflicts between Marius and Sylla, between the people and the old Nobility. This was the beginning of the Civil war. Then, from 73 to 71 B.C., Rome had to suppress the slave uprisings led by Spartacus. Finally, the troubles attained new heights with the conflict between Caesar and Pompey, and then Mark Antony and Octavian. Rome got out of these conflicts not only stabilized but its Empire extended into the territories of Gauls, Brittany and Egypt.

The Empire remained stable for two centuries and a half, and then encountered a period of military anarchy before being reformed by Diocletian and Constantine. However, the great migrations, and impoverishing of the historical centres that Rome and Italy were, being deprived of economical dynamism, as well as the ambitions of local chiefs and the carelessness of the Oriental Empire, of very Greek cultural inclinations, in front of a more recent Occidental civilization, led to the progressive dismembering of the Empire.

The United States of America

Nowadays, the American Empire extends over a good share of the Globe. If one limits to the most obvious presence of the power, the empire in its military form, including the implantation of bases, alliances or strong partnerships, then we can consider part of the American Empire all of the NATO countries, Australia, the Philippines, South Korea, Japan, Egypt, Israel, Saudi Arabia, Somalia as well as the north-eastern part of South America: Colombia, Equator and Peru.

Two events appear to be foundational for the American Nation: the founding of Jamestown in 1607, a first permanent British colony as well as the establishment of the Pilgrim Fathers of Mayflower, in 1620. During the following century and a half, other colonies were born and developed under British suzerainty. This heavy-handed suzerainty was eventually contested and the royal authority was rejected by those who had most interests in independence: the aristocracy and large land owners, under the leadership of one of them, George Washington. For a certain time, property remained a condition for having the right to vote. Other conditions also limited this right: sex, religion, skin color… but the long fight for civil rights extended the right to vote to an increasing share of the population. The heart of the American Civilization remained the North-East, with its sizable and dynamic population.

Meanwhile, the young American Nation was expanding toward the West, through war against the Native tribes that were already populating these regions and also through treaties allowing either the purchase of lands (Louisiana) or the integration of already-existing entities as states (for instance, California).

The integration of new states and the cohabitation between the first states of the Union were not without tensions. The multiple differences between the North and the South (lifespan, social structures, economy…) culminated into a conflict around the issue of slavery, the American Civil War. The states of the South seceded and unified into a confederation with a new constitution. The North triumphed after a bloody war and imposed its model by abolishing slavery and by forcing the South to remain in the union.

The end of the XIXth century was an occasion for America to extend its influence by developing a small colonial empire in the Caribbean, while refusing, in accordance with the Monroe Doctrine, to intervene in European affairs. Thus, the United States were protecting their independence by acquiring a sufficiently dissuasive power, including maritime forces.

At the brink of the World Wars, the United States had become the first worldwide industrial power and its coal and iron productions were surpassing that of the three greatest European powers combined.

In comparison, at the beginning of World War II, the American military was ridiculously weak. It is during the conflict itself, as it recruited its industrial power to the service of the military, that it became a superpower.

The fall of Europe created a void, which the Soviet giant was willing to exploit. This made it impossible for the United States to stick to the Monroe doctrine and let Europe handle its own affairs: the USSR would have become too powerful and too dangerous. In order to protect against this threat, America engaged in an arms race: The Containment, during the Cold War. For half a century, America led this fight for global supremacy, which was also a fight for survival. Having triumphed over Russian power, America was henceforth engaged in the entire world, equipped with important tools of power (such as NATO) and rid of its only rival at the global level. It had to maintain order over the entire planet, a situation that was taxing and costly but advantageous because it was fully guaranteeing the independence and safety of the American Nation, a worry of any and all American policies since its founding.

B) PRESENTATION OF CYCLE B

In bold: stage of Cycle B
In upright: corresponding Roman historical fact
In italics: corresponding American historical fact

1) A human community is founded by a pre-existing civilization, under the influence of Civilization A.

Rome is founded under Etruscan domination and has undergone Greek influence (through the Etruscans on the one hand, and through the proximity of Greece on the other).

The colonies at the origin of the United States are founded by England (and other European contributions), and placed under its domination.

2) Rejection of the suzerainty by the mother-civilization under the leadership of the aristocracy.

Romans led by the aristocracy of Lucius Junius Brutus expel the last Etruscan Kings.

The colonies proclaim their independence under the leadership of George Washington, a large land owner, and successfully repel British domination.

3) Establishment of the Republic with limited democratic mechanisms, conflicts over political rights.

Establishment of the Roman Republic, a highly aristocratic regime, followed by the Conflict of orders between Plebeians and Patricians.

Establishment of the American Democracy with voting rights limited to white men landowners (along with other restrictions specific to states, notably religious ones). Long process in the fight for civil rights (Chinese, Natives, Blacks, Women, non-protestants…).

4) Conquest of the natural territory by the historical center of the civilization.

Conquest of Italy by Rome against Greeks and natives: Latin Wars, Samnite Wars, Pyrrhic War.

Conquest of the West by the historical center of the American power (the North-East): American Indian Wars, Mexican-American War, purchase of Louisiana and Florida from Europeans.

We now reach the stages of the cycle where the chronology is uncertain because the steps seem to have occurred in a different order in the Roman and American cases. The problematic step is that of the Roman Social War and the American Civil War, both having been foundational events for the nation. These two events, respectively, gave rise to the unification of Roman Italy (citizen rights for all of Italy) and to the United States as we know them today. However, for the United States, this step came in early, before it became a superpower and dominated Europe. For Rome, the Social War occurred at the beginning of the I^{st} century B.C., while the Roman Empire had already been largely established. We will thus designate this step as "x."

x) Civil war: the nucleus of the civilization faces a desire of separation from its allies due to inequalities. The allies secede and form a confederation imitating the institutions of the nucleus, but in opposition to it. This secession concludes with the victory of the nucleus of the civilization and the imposition of its model to the other parties as well as the unification of the nation.

Social War: Rome faces the uprising of its allies who secede and unify into a confederation with a new capital and a new senate. At the outset of a brutal war, Roman citizenship is extended to all free men of Italy. Italy is henceforth under the domination of Rome.

American Civil War: the historical nucleus of the American Power, the North-East, is confronted to separatism in the Southern States. These states form a confederation with a new constitution. A brutal and traumatizing war ensues, but results in the definitive unification of the American Nation, which henceforth extends from the Atlantic Ocean to the Pacific Ocean.

5) Confrontation to a powerful conquering nation. A fight for survival and supremacy leaves Civilization B without rival and able to dominate the world.

Opposition of Rome to Carthage during the Punic Wars, fight to death for supremacy over the Mediterranean. The fall of Carthage leaves Rome as the sole master of the occidental Mediterranean and sufficiently powerful to impose itself in Orient.

Opposition of the United States to the USSR during the Cold War. Fight to death for global supremacy. The fall of the USSR raises the United States to the rank of superpower without rivals and leaves it in charge of global governance. America becomes able to interfere practically everywhere.

6) The states of A become dominated by B.

Greece is conquered by Rome and becomes a province of the Empire.

Europe remains an American protectorate with the continuation of NATO despite its initial raison d'être having been disposed of: The Soviet threat.

The United States are currently in this stage. The following stages, which are found in the history of Rome, have not yet occurred for the American case. Thus we do not know what will be the degree of similarity between future events and these Roman events. We will thus retain, temporarily and without certainty regarding their relevance, three stages which appear to be important:

7) Absolute hegemony over the known world, absence of rivals (it is at this step that Stage 1 of the next Cycle A occurs).

Rome controls everything around the Mediterranean and reaches the maximal extent of its domination (invasion and Romanization of Gaul, Spain and Brittany).

?

8) The Empire, a militaristic and autocratic regime, succeeds to the Republic.

Establishment of the Empire by Augustus, end of the Roman Republic.

?

9) Decline and dismemberment of Empire B (corresponds to Stage 2 of the next Cycle A).

Fall of the Roman Empire (invasion of Western Europe by Germanic barbarians).

?

3. Notes on the A-B couple: Before Greece and Rome, before Europe and America, Crete and Mycenae?

We have noted, through our description of cycles A and B, the symmetry between Greco-Roman antiquity and Euro-American history. In order to confirm the patterns we have identified, we can look a little further into the past, into the very origins of Ancient

Greece, which was itself born unto the ruins of the Mycenaean Empire just as Europe was born unto the ruins of the Roman Empire.

Considered as absolutely mythical a century and a half ago, the history of Minoan Cretans and of Mycenaeans[5] dates back to more than a thousand years before Greek Civilization. While the writing system of Mycenaean Civilization, Linear B, has been decrypted, that of Minoan Civilization, Linear A, remains a mystery. One can only begin to fathom everything that we could learn from these cultures if their documents became, one day, understandable.

Nevertheless, we know enough to quickly retrace the course of development of these two civilizations and their interactions, allowing us to compare what we know about these civilizations —with more or less certainty— against our patterns identified for Greece and Europe as well as Rome and America.

A) HISTORICAL REMINDERS

Crete and Minoan Civilization, c. 2700-1350 B.C.

The island of Crete was the place of birth for the first great European Civilization, Minoan Civilization. This civilization was baptized by its discoverer, a British man named Evans, in reference to the legendary King Minos.

Around the XXVIIIth century B.C., populations would have arrived from Anatolia and would have mixed with populations who had been inhabiting the island since the Neolithic (who were already present, for instance, in Knossos), carrying new cults and mores. The civilization developed and reached its apogee around a thousand years after these arrivals.

Minoan civilization was truly brilliant. The very ancient Cretans knew about writing and mastered a number of advanced architectural technologies, including the construction of canals in order to provide water to inhabitants and evacuate sewers, as well as the paving of roads. The territory of the island was divided in a small number of political units organized around urban centers.

Crete ruled for centuries over the archipelagos of the Aegean Sea, notably the Cyclades, as a powerful and wealthy thalassocracy. It is probable that the Cretans have colonized several of these islands, and the influence of the brilliant maritime civilization must have attained the Peloponnese, even if this territory does not seem to have been under control by the Minoans. On that point, one can wonder about the meaning of an origins myth such as that of Theseus, which invokes the payment of a tribute by Athens to Crete, controlled by King Minos. In fact, it is believed that Crete had numerous contacts with the rising power on the peninsula which we have called Mycenaean Civilization, and an initial subordination of the continentals toward the insulars is probable.

The Cretan Decline began in the XVth century B.C.. The causes of the decline are being debated. We have found traces of sudden destruction on the island. Various theories were proposed regarding these destructions: earthquakes, floods related to the eruption of the Santorini Volcano, external invasions or civil war between the various political entities for control of the island. The later hypothesis invokes a reaction from the secondary centers of Crete against the domination by the main center, Knossos, and seems the most probable[6].

At the outset of this decline, Crete became prey to Mycenaean Civilization which had borrowed much from it and was integrated to its larger Aegean Empire.

The Mycenaean Empire, c. 1550-1100 B.C.

As is the case with the history of Crete, the history of Mycenaean Civilization is mostly constructed from conjectures based on archaeological data that leaves place to contradictory hypotheses. Nevertheless, we have at our disposal sources of written material that is more eloquent, not only internally thanks to our understanding of Linear B but also thanks to testimonies left by the Hittites, a neighboring empire which dominated Anatolia. Historians sometimes resort to using the Iliad of Homer, which mentions the Achaean in conflict with the city of Troy, in order to interpret archaeological discoveries. It seems unfortunate that they are less inclined at using the great sagas of Greek heroes: Perseus, Theseus, Jason, Heracles, which taken together seem to offer nothing less than the history of the rise and fall of Mycenaean Civilization. This information is very useful given that the Mycenaean documents discovered by archaeology appear to be administrative documents, mostly useful in picturing an economic and hierarchical understanding of the Mycenaean political structures. These administrative documents are less useful in establishing the sequence of events, contrarily to those provided by the Hittites. This is where heroic mythology can become useful, if not by providing real information, at least by providing interesting accounts, for instance a tale establishing links between pieces of information. In order to uncover the most complete and plausible synthesis of this history, we will thus use all of these sources combined.

Mycenaean civilization was born on the continent and produced, notably, the famous city of Mycenae, whose name is associated to the Trojan War. Homer describes it as a crucial center that was "rich in gold." Archaeological research demonstrated the power of the city but do not allow to determine whether it was the exclusive center of power for Achaeans. Other important centers for Mycenaean Civilization include Argos, Tiryns, Thebes and Pylos (to which we can add Knossos, but only after its conquest by Achaeans, and as such it cannot inform us on the origins of Mycenaean Civilization).

The entirety of the Greek legendary tradition considers Mycenae, and more broadly the Argolis, a region of continental Greece in the North-East of the Peloponnese, the main location for Achaean Civilization. The cities of Argos and Tiryns have been the subject of extensive archaeological research and are located in the same province. From a tentative reading of the heroic myths, it seems that Argos was linked to Mycenae, perhaps as a subordinate. At the beginning of the Trojan War, Agamemnon confiscates Argos from its rightful King, Diomedes, and returns it only in exchange for his participation to an expedition (which resembles the feudal mechanism of the Right of Commission, in which a vassal sees his fief be confiscated due to having failed at fulfilling his obligations). Later, Orestes, son of Agamemnon, seeks refuge in Argos after having been expelled from Mycenae. According to the legend, Perseus, the founder and King of Mycenae, was the grandchild of the King of Argos. Similarly, for the city of Tiryns, its King, Alcaeus, son of Perseus and brother of Electryon, King of Mycenae, and for whom subordination is indicated by the obedience of Heracles, grandchild of Alcaeus, to Eurystheus, King of Mycenae. At the origin of Mycenaean Civilization, we thus find three great cities of the Argolis region: Argos, Tiryns and Mycenae.

The other important Mycenaean center, outside of Argolis, is Thebes. It is also the only city to have been founded by a hero as legendary and ancient as Perseus, that is, Cadmus, in no way linked to Argos, nor Tiryns, nor Mycenae. From archaeological research, the site appears in the Bronze Age, which corresponds to the era given by Herodotus for its mythical foundation, at the junction between the IIIrd and IInd millennia B.C. [7]. During the first part of its history, until the death of its most famous King, Oedipus, Thebes is rigorously independent from the triad of Argolis. This changed with the rivalry between the sons of Oedipus, Eteocles and Polynices. The latter, rival with his brother for the throne of Thebes, goes to Argolis[8] in order to raise an army and attack Thebes. The war of the Seven Against Thebes, led by Adrastus and Amphiaraus, Kings of Argos, was a failure, but the city was taken a few years later by the Epigoni, the sons of the Seven Chiefs, still under the leadership of Adrastus, who gave the throne to Thersander, son of Polynices. These legendary events suggest a historical conflict opposing the Argolis triad to Thebes, resulting in the subordination of Thebes and its integration to the Mycenaean Empire.

A similar fate awaited the last important Mycenaean center, Pylos. According to the legend, Heracles, sieged the city and killed its king, Neleus, and his eleven sons, who had attempted to steal the cattle of Geryon, which he had acquired during the tenth of his twelve labours. This made of the only surviving son, Nestor, the king of Pylos and of Messenia, the surrounding region. The legendary episode is interesting because Heracles was himself acting under the orders of Eurystheus, king of Mycenae, who had imposed the twelve labours. Thus, at the heart of this myth, we find that the Mycenaean had imposed a subordination of another Achaean city.

Despite the paucity of archeological evidence allowing to conclude that a Mycenaean center had subordinated the other centers, the entirety of the Greek heroic tradition, not only Homer's Iliad, seems to point toward a domination of the Argolis over the Mycenaean world, and in turn of Mycenae over the Argolis. The latter seems to have been initially accepted and permanent, while the former seems to have been acquired progressively through conflicts. Again based on heroic tradition, this hegemony of Mycenae over continental Greece is fully formed one or two generations later.

Heracles[9], with the rule of Agamemnon who had married Clytemnestra, daughter of Tyndareus, King of Sparta, and who had his half-sister Helen, who would become Helen of Troy, marry his younger brother Menelaus, making him the heir of Sparta. Thus, Sparta passed under Mycenaean influence. As part of this marriage, the Achaean Kings took the "Oath of Tyndareus," by which they committed to protecting whoever of them would be attacked, this precaution being taken to avoid Helen's choice potentially provoking a war among the Greeks. This legendary element might be the trace of an ancient unification of the Achaeans under Mycenaean hegemony, through an agreement applying to relationships within the federation of cities which forbids conflicts. The nature of the Oath of Tyndareus also implies a social contract guaranteeing rights to citizens, or at least to individuals considered as free, such as citizens (or barons, who are the citizens in the kind of feudal order that seems to have been in effect at the time). If that were the case, we could see the Oath or a putative document at the source of the legend as equivalent to the Law of the Twelve Tables in Rome and the Bill of Rights in America. These guarantees of liberty would all have, in their own way, formed the foundation for social cohesion and for the dynamism of these societies.

Half a century before, the legend of Theseus features an Achaean movement for independence from Cretan hegemony. In fact, Mycenaean Civilization owed a lot to Minoan Civilization which dominated Aegean Sea during the first few centuries of its own establishment. Archeology tends to show a strong influence of Crete over the development of the new continental civilization. The legend of Theseus describes an Achaean rebellion against Cretan suzerainty, a fight for independence, as well as the first Mycenaean interventions on Cretan soil. These Mycenaean expeditions in Crete are also described in the seventh labour of Heracles, who takes the bull from King Minos. Archeological research shows that when Crete was weakening, the Mycenaeans filled the void by invading the island and establishing hegemony over the Aegean Sea. We thus observe a notable unification, a relative weakening of local specificities to the advantage of Mycenaean culture, and the establishment of a cultural and artistic unit that Minoan civilization had never succeeded at imposing over the Aegean Sea.

In this period contemporaneous to Theseus, when Achaeans had claimed their independence from Crete and inverted the relationship of subordination, the heroic accomplishments of Greek mythology describe Mycenaean expansionism, with the Trip of Argonauts to Colchis, and more importantly the adventures of Heracles.

Heracles was operating under the orders Eurystheus, king of Mycenae, who imposed on him the famous Twelve Labours. This comical duo of an invincible hero and of his coward master seems to be the satirical exaggeration between a Mycenaean ruler scared of war for himself but who had a family member (Heracles is the cousin of Eurystheus) who could become a powerful general and, in the end, would have been more worthy of the title of King. Thus, according to the legend, Heracles cleaned Greece of its ferocious beasts and brigands under the orders of Eurystheus, before going to Troy, where he led a first victorious war, two generations before that of Achilles, Agamemnon and Menelaus. This legend deserves to be taken seriously in its general form because the Hittite archives, for the period given by Herodotus for the accomplishments of Heracles, c. 1400 B.C., describe an armed conflict in which a man named Attarsiya expels a man named Madduwatta from Wilusa, under Hittite control. For archeologists, it has become more and more likely that the Kingdom of Ahhiyawa from Hittite texts is the Achaean Nation (sometimes known as Akhaia, in Homer), and that Wilusa is the Hittite equivalent to the Archaic Greek term Wilios, which became Ilios in Ancient Greek, that is, Ilion, the city of Troy. For archeologists and students of heroic mythology, the Hittite name Attarsiya reminds of Atreus, successor of Eurystheus for the throne of Mycenae, of which Heracles was an agent. Thus, as early as the beginning of the XIVth century, both the Greek mythological tradition and archeological research describe a form of Mycenaean expansionism toward Troy, through which the Achaeans challenge the powerful Hittite Empire, the greatest empire of its time along with the Egyptians. The confrontation turns out in the favor of the rising Mycenaean power, which probably saw in Troy a dangerous point of access to the Aegean Sea. The city was thus integrated, according to Hittite records, to the Mycenaean Empire under the rule of Tudhaliya I[st] (who died c. 1430 B.C.)[10].

This first conflict, just like the more important Trojan War, which, according to Herodotus, happens a century after Heracles, appears to be part of a secular rivalry between the Achaeans and the Hittites, which culminated in the complete eradication of the Hittites. It is plausible that the Homeric tale, which describes an epic duration of ten years for the conflict, actually compresses a series of facts and wars occurring over numerous decades. A diplomatic document found in the Hittite capital, the great city of Hattusa, describes a confrontation c. 1280 B.C., that is about one century after the attack of Attarsiya. This happens to correspond to the same duration that was given by Herodotus and the mythological tradition. Furthermore, a treaty between the Hittite Empire and Alaksandu, King of Wilusa, was found and is believed to correspond to the Alexander of Troy from Homer (Paris, son of Priam, King of Troy). This correspondence would support the idea of a military support being provided to Troy by the Hittites in a recent conflict.

Another Hittite document, the "Tawagalawa letter," dates from c. 1250 B.C., and is written by a Hittite sovereign, which is believed to be Hattusili III, and is sent to the "Great King of Ahhiyawa." The name of this king does not appear on the Hittite tablet, but the title "Great King" implies that the Hittite sovereign recognizes his interlocutor as having a status equal to his own, and thus to be the leader of Ahhiyawa. In this letter, Hattusili mentions a recent conflict between the Achaeans and the Hittites over Wilusa and requests the extradition of a character, Piyama-Radu, considered as a bandit and troublemaker. This name bears resemblance to that of Priam, King of Troy[11], but after consideration of the correspondence between Alaksandu and Alexander, this does not correspond to the chronological order in the Homer mythology. Nevertheless, while the mythological tradition may have mixed up the names and give them a new order, the deep sequence of events, that is, the geopolitical confrontation between Achaeans and Hittites, was described one more time.

In the current state of archeological research, we do not encounter mentions of Ahhiyawa in the Hittite archives after c. 1250 B.C.. However, it must be noted that the Hittite Empire disappears completely c. 1200 B.C., the cause of this disappearance being described in Egyptian sources as the enigmatic "Sea Peoples."

The described Sea Peoples are invaders belonging to diverse ethnicities and having attacked Egypt twice: once c. 1200 B.C. under the rule of Pharaoh Merneptah and a second time in 1177 B.C. under the rule of Ramesses III. The first time, they came through Lybia, having formed an alliance with the Libyan King Meryey. The second time, they came through Syria, after having destroyed the Hittite Empire.

The first wave, according to Egyptian sources and the interpretation of archeology, was formed by Ekwesh (Achaeans), Teresh (either Etruscans from Lydia, or men from Tarsus, in any case, Anatolians), Lukka (from Lycia, in the Anatolian peninsula), Sherden (either from Sardinia or Anatolians from Sardis, in Lydia) and Shekelesh (either from Sicilia or Anatolians from Sagalassos). In brief, the invaders were Achaeans and Anatolians, which were former subordinates of the Hittite Empire.

The second wave included Peleset (originating from Crete or natives from Greece, before the arrival of Achaeans), Tjeker (probably Thracians), Weshesh (originating from Wilusa/Troy or Issus, in both cases Anatolians), Denyen or Danouna (which could designate Danaans, which is another term used by Homer to describe Greeks, thus they would be Achaeans)[12], and again Shekelesh.

The only consensus that seems to emerge from historians concerning the Sea Peoples is that they were largely Achaeans. Their role in the upheavals of the end of the recent Bronze Age is being debated. Historians are wondering if they were responsible for the disappearance of the Mycenaean Empire, whether they really destroyed the Hittite Empire, or they simply profited from its internal fall.

The hypothesis that seems the most probable in our view, which is given very little attention in these debates, is that the Sea Peoples were not merely invading migrants, but that they were coalitions formed by Mycenaeans for the purpose of conquest. It would not be surprising for a new and powerful hegemony to recruit outside forces to continue its expansion. About two thousand years later, the Persian campaign of Roman Emperor Julianus Apostata, formed a roman legion with Gauls, as well as Syrians and Anatolians, allied with the Armenians of King Arsaces, in order to confront the Persians. The hypothesis that the Sea Peoples were sent with a *modus operandi* by Mycenaeans should therefore not be excluded, and indeed some elements seem to favor it.

First, at the archeological level, we have seen that for each attack, the Egyptian sources describe the presence of Greeks. Most certainly with the term Ekwesh in the first wave, and perhaps more tentatively with the term Denyen in the second one. In the counts of enemy casualties from the Egyptian records for the first invasion, we find 6 359 Libyans, 222 Shekelesh, 742 Teresh, 2 201 Ekwesh, as well as 200 Lukka and Sherden[13]. Taking for granted that these losses would be proportional to the headcount in the overall invading army, then it would have been mostly Libyans, but for the Sea Peoples, more than two thirds of them were Achaeans. The fact that the Achaeans formed, at least initially, the majority of the headcount of the Sea Peoples in this invasion makes it doubtful that these very people would also be held responsible for the disappearance of the Mycenaean Empire. It would be equally doubtful that the disappearance of Mycenaean Civilization would have led to these population movements, given that the Achaeans were obviously numerous enough to raise an army and organize an expedition to Egypt. We can scarcely imagine what, in these conditions, would have been enough to expel them from their own lands. Furthermore, the fact that beside Achaeans, the other part of the Sea Peoples was constituted by Anatolians, which were formerly under Hittite subordination, and that the very Empire disappeared following a conflict with the Mycenaean Nation, suggests that these people may have simply passed from suzerainty under the Hittites to suzerainty under the Mycenaeans. This hypothesis remains valid whether the crumbling came as a result of Mycenaean conquest or was simply the result of internal causes to which the Achaean pressure was added. We have evidence of similar joining of forces in other circumstances, for instance in ancient traces of alliances between Achaeans and Hittite subordinates against the Hittites themselves, in the expedition of Attarsiya to Cyprus with the help of Madduwatta (who he had vanquished and who was referenced above) and of the Lukka, who happen to be part of the Sea Peoples from the first wave[14].

Another important element is the fact that the Egyptian record suggests concerted plans rather than the chaotic invasion of barbarians put into motion by some systemic crumbling occurring simultaneously over the entire Orient. This is obvious for the first coalition assembled along with Meryey of Libya, but even more in the testimony of Ramesses III written on the walls of the Medinet Habu Temple, in Egypt: *"The foreign countries plotted on their islands and the people were scattered by battle all at one time and no land could stand before their weapons [the Sea Peoples], from Hatti, Karkemish, Arzawa and Alashiya. They established their camp in a single location, the Country of Amurru. [...] The ensemble [of these peoples] included the Peleset, the Tjeker, the Shekelesh, the Denyen and the Weshesh. All of these countries were united in wanting to gain control of all the countries up to the circle of Earth. Their hearts were confident and assured that their plans would succeed."*[15]. These writings clearly describe an organized coalition, launched from a gigantic empire ruling over a large area, circling Egypt. Thus, if the Mycenaean Empire had briefly extended over Hittite territories, it included Greece, Crete and the Aegean Sea, Anatolia, Cyprus, the Syrian coast and Lebanon, totaling to an area more than three times larger than the Egyptian Empire, and the entirety of the world known to Egyptians outside of Libya. Never had Egypt been confronted to an adversary of this size, and putting aside the potential motivation of Ramesses III in overrepresenting the strength of his enemy, in order to highlight his own glory, we can imagine that the danger that was hovering above the old Empire was great and unmatched by any previous event. After its total victory over the Hittites, the Mycenaean Empire was a superpower, just like Rome after the fall of Carthage and the United States after the fall of the USSR.

The main objection that could be raised against the thesis presented above is that, according to archeological evidence, simultaneously to the destruction of the Hittite Empire and the invasions of the Sea Peoples, we observe a wave of destruction in continental Greece, located at the heart of Mycenaean power. This raises a question as to why Mycenaeans would have organized ambitious expeditions so far from their lands if their own lands were under assault, or at least were undergoing great destruction. There are numerous problems with archeological data. First, the dates are too imprecise to determine the exact order of events. Greeks may have left and an invasion may have occurred in their absence, all of it within a few months. The other problem is in interpreting the destructions. These could very well have been caused by a "domestic conflict," a sort of civil war between Achaeans, a hypothesis that I prefer and on which we shall come back. Finally, one must note that destructions on the Achaean territory does not mean a sudden death of the civilization and an incapacity to launch expeditions. For instance, archeological and document analysis of Gauls in the IVth century show massive destructions, both the result of Germanic invaders and Bagaudae, groups of natives turned bandits and rebellious against the Roman Empire, and this did not keep Julian from launching his Persian Expedition, for which he regrouped a massive army of around 90 000 men. A domestic conflict, whether it has internal or external origins, is thus not sufficient to definitely exclude expeditions being launched by the Sea Peoples as being orchestrated and led by the Achaeans.

Furthermore, mythological tradition gives us one more story that helps in interpreting archeological data. In the myth of Herodotus, we find a strong clue that the Sea Peoples were a coalition formed around Achaeans. The Greek Historian reports having questioned Egyptian priests on the reality of the Trojan War. What these priests knew about, they had gotten it from Menelaus, King of Sparta and brother of Agamemnon, who would have gone to Egypt to find Helen at the end of the war and who would have pillaged the country, before fleeing to Libya. The Odyssey in Books II and IV, as well as Apollodorus of Athens[16] provide other information about the expedition of Menelaus, who leaves Troy after the victory while Agamemnon stays there with half of the Achaean army. Menelaus' adventures not only reach Egypt and Libya but also the lands of the Erembes (probably Arabs) and in Ethiopia. With the exception of Ethiopia, which is close to Egypt, the steps of Menelaus as described by Homer correspond to the zones targeted by the Sea Peoples: Cyprus, Syria, Lebanon, Canaan. The time period, however, does not exactly correspond, because according to the chronology of Herodotus, the Trojan War occurs c. 1250 B.C., which seems to be confirmed by Hittite sources, while the two waves of attacks by the Sea Peoples in Egypt are dated between half a century and three quarters of a century later. Here again, the legend may have compressed facts that were in reality occurring over long periods, but it is unclear why the chronology of Herodotus, based on the mythological tradition, seems to perfectly correspond to the data extracted from the Hittite archives for a more ancient period. This would explain why Eratosthenes, who generally provides correct dates in light of archeology, dates the fall of Troy to 1183 B.C., barely six years before the massive attack on the Egypt of Ramesses III. Perhaps the date he provided is not for the fall of Troy, but the fall of Hattusa, destroyed by the Mycenaeans who had allied with the former subordinates of Hittites after having been victorious in Troy. Thus Herodotus would have correctly provided the date for the beginning of the secular conflict between Achaeans and Hittites, and Eratosthenes would have the correct date for the end of this long conflict.

The adventures of Menelaus are not the only trace of Mycenaean military expeditions into Egypt. We also find in the story delivered by Odysseus in the fourteenth song of the Odyssey: "*There, for nine years, we, the sons of Achaeans, made war. In the tenth year, after having destroyed the city of Priam, we boarded our ships in order to return home. [...] My heart then led me to navigate into Egyptos, after having carefully equipped my ships with the help of divine companions. I armed by nine ships and crowds of seamen promptly joined. [...] We reached it in five days! Egyptos was a beautiful watercourse, and I dipped my boats in this river, our ships alternating between one coast and the other. Arrived there, I ordered my loyal companions to stay close to their ships and to protect them, and I sent observers on high grounds. My people, then conceding to their violent instincts, and guided by envy, started destroying the pleasant lands of this people of Egypt, bringing with them women and children, and massacring men. The scream of combat attained the city. The Egyptians, hearing these clamors, arrived at dawn. The entire plain was filled with infantry, chariots and the shine of bronze. Zeus thrower-of-bolts unleashed on our people a disastrous panic. No one dared to hold the line because from all directions hardship was coming. Thus the Egyptians killed many of us with sharpened bronze, and took those who survived to work for them. [...] Immediately, I removed my helmet from my head, abandoned the shield that was attached to my shoulders, and my hand threw my spear far from me. Advancing slowly toward the horses of the King, I took his knees and kissed them. He protected me and took me in pity. Then, having seated me in his chariot, he brought me to his palace, while my face was covered in tears. Meanwhile, numerous of his subjects were charging in my direction with their ash tree spears, ardently desiring to kill me, as their furor had reached its maximum.*"[17] This testimony is probably the result of the integration into mythological tradition of stories that have survived the expedition against the Egypt of Ramesses III, who would have captured and imprisoned the protagonist for a moment. As is the case in the expedition of Menelaus, a violent incursion into Egypt is concluded by failure.

Taken together, the Mycenaean historical progression seems to go as follows: slightly before 1200 B.C., at the outset of a series of conflicts against Hittites having begun around Troy and extending over close to a century, the Achaeans triumph over the Hittite Empire, which falls and sees its lands and its subordinate territories occupied by the Achaeans. The Achaeans, having obtained new allies, having gotten rid of a very powerful enemy and probably motivated by a historical victory that could be talked of for a thousand years, prepare new expeditions in order to dominate over Egypt as they did over the Hittites. For their first expedition, they ally with the king of Libya, but are pushed back by the troops of

Merneptah. One generation later, the Achaeans assemble their subordinates and leave from Anatolia toward Egypt by passing through Syria. They take over Cyprus (Alashiya, for the Egyptians). One more time, the invasion fails and Egypt pushes them back, but the Achaeans and their allies succeed at conquering Canaan, where the colonizers known as Pelasgians decide to stay, becoming the Philistines of the Bible, along with Anatolians (Sherden) and Thracians.

Nevertheless, this dual defeat of an important coalition is hard to take for the Mycenaean Empire, which not only made its Asian domination ephemeral, but also deprived it of an important part of its soldiers and exposed it, in turn, to aggression. This potential weakness would correlate well with the archeological data showing that the Mycenaean world had undergone massive destruction: *"at the end of the Late Helladic IIIB [c. 1200 B.C.], we see an important modification of the economic and political organization of the society, but this modification does not seem to bring major cultural changes*[18].*"* What could be this important modification of the economic and political organization occurring in a cultural continuity? The description reminds of a revolution or a regime change, but archeology has not yet answered this question, and we are therefore left to conjectures. We can try understanding this event by looking at mythology: when returning from the Trojan War, Agamemnon is assassinated by the lover of his wife, Clytemnestra, who then usurped his throne before he, in turn, gets killed by Orestes, son of Agamemnon. At the very least, this part of the legend describes a struggle for power at the height of the Mycenaean Empire, in which Agamemnon is presented as the suzerain of all Achaean Kings. However, much of Homer's mythology shows that a great portion of the Kings who left for expeditions never came back, while the tales provide little details to what happens to their city after they left. Thus we can conjecture that a weakening of the aristocracy after a bloody war with the Hittites and the Egyptian expedition may have occurred. A reinforced centralization of the Mycenaean government could have brought civil troubles in Greece similar to the civil wars of Rome after its victory against the Carthaginian enemy, leading to the fall of the Empire. Similarly, in medieval France, the important losses by the Nobles during the Hundred Years' War favored the growth of Royal power. Such a conjecture could explain the destruction of numerous Mycenaean Palaces, local centers of powers that would have been opposed to an increased control by Mycenae. The centralization would have represented a violation of the spirit of equality between the Achaean cities, embodied in the Oath of Tyndareus, previously held by Agamemnon.

One thing is certain: at the end of the XIIth century B.C., Mycenaean Civilization disappears: *"Around the end of Late Helladic III C [c. 1050 B.C.], we see the almost complete disappearance of certain practices, such as collective burials in chambers, and the multiplication of alternative practices: individual burials in wells and cremation of cadavers*[19].*"* Mycenae itself is definitively destroyed in the second half of the XIIth century B.C.. Then again, archeology provides no information on the precise conditions and causes for this fall. Climatic changes have been proposed (it's quite fashionable for the last few decades) or an overly rigid administration, which would correspond to the consequences, after a century, of a brutal movement for centralization.

The mythical tradition seems to have retained a trace of the terminal evolution: after the assassination of the usurper of Clytemnestra, Orestes flees and goes to Athens, where he is absolved for his crime by the assembly of citizens, before returning to Mycenae, according to Apollodorus[20]. This event might constitute a mythical reading of an effort by Orestes to legitimize his political rise to the throne after a period of civil war in Greece, a sort of foundation of a new regime after the abolition of the order established by the Oath of Tyndareus, similar to the imperial transformation operated by Augustus a thousand years later.

After Orestes, his son Tisamenus rose to the throne, but lost power during the Return of the Heraclidae, interpreted in archeology as the migration of the Dorians from Illyria toward the Peloponnese. This event could have had a role in the fall of the Mycenaean Empire akin to that of the great barbarian migrations in the fall of Rome, in that it would have contributed to the fall of an Empire already fragilized by administrative and economic rigidities. The dating of this migration corresponds to the extinction of the Mycenaean civilization and the cultural changes described above. This period corresponds to, in the mythical tradition, the end of the Time of Heroes, since the generation of Tisamenus is the last one[21].

Interestingly, despite the differences in the chronology of Herodotus and that obtained from Egyptian archeological data concerning the invasions of the Sea Peoples, if we take as an approximation for the return of Agamemnon the period between the fall of the Hittite Empire (c. 1200 B.C.) and the victory of Ramesses III over the invaders (c. 1180 B.C.), the rule of Tisamenus begins around a generation later, in the second half of the XIIth century B.C.. This means that in total, the count of generations is in accordance between the mythology and their corresponding events in the archeological data concerning Heracles and the Trojan War and its conclusion up to the fall of Mycenaean Civilization. However, the tale of Homer of the Trojan War occurring over ten years is too short by half a century, or the mythical tradition has forgotten one or two generations, perhaps those of the expedition toward Egypt, the failures having been a poor subject for glorious tales. Thus these failures would only be recorded in the tale of Menelaus, returning from Troy. I tend to accept the hypothesis that the tale incorrectly compressed the Trojan War within one generation, because the mythical tradition seems to be inclined in that direction. Archaic and ancient Greek authors offer a dozen different dates for the Trojan War, but most estimate it as occurring between the middle of the XIIIth and the middle of the XIIth centuries, a broad range which could be the result of a conflict much longer than the Homeric decade.

As a reminder, it is on the ruins of the Mycenaean Empire that the brilliant Greek Civilization would be born after dark ages during which the knowledge of writing was lost. Archeologists have noted that, in the Mycenaean administrative hierarchy, local representatives of power that are of lower status are noted in Linear B tablets as *qa-si-re-u*, which is interpreted as a primitive form of the title *basileus* used in Archaic Greece and Ancient Greece to designate a king, and which would later be used to designate the

Byzantine Emperor. At the time of Mycenae, the sovereign is not the *qa-si-re-u*, but the *wa-na-ka*, believed to be the *anax* in Homer, a title wore by few characters, most importantly Agamemnon, often referred to as the *anax anthropon*, the "High King of Men."

In the Homeric tradition, the *basileis* are not monarchs but rather seem to exert power in a collective manner, through peer counsels[22]. During the Trojan War, they are assembled around Agamemnon, *wanax*, like the counsel of barons surrounded the King in the feudal era. The evolution of the term *qa- si-re-u* toward *basileus*, that is, from a specific function, perhaps partially inherited from a tradition of the Mycenaean Empire, toward a monarch status in Archaic and Ancient Greece, seems analogous to the evolution of the Roman term *comes* toward the feudal Count. Originally, a *comes* was, under the Republic, an informal counselor accompanying a Roman Magistrate in their movements. The term only became official under Augustus, who created the *comes Augusti*, and the title became, in the imperial government of the Late Roman period, a sort of ministry. There was the *comes* of treasury, the *comes* of military affairs... The function attributed with the title evolved again under the Merovingians and the Carolingians, first representing a non-hereditary governmental attribution of a territory in the name of the monarch, then transforming in a hereditary attribution and property by the titular, a title of high nobility. The title of Duke has a similar history: military grade in the Late Empire, it becomes a sort of super-Count obtaining overarching powers over broader territories, and like the counties, it becomes hereditary at the end of the reign of the Carolingians. Numerous Counts and Dukes, in the middle age, were so powerful that they were virtually independent, quasi-sovereign on their lands. This was the situation for the Count of Toulouse, the Duke of Brittany. Others, more numerous, were peers of their Kingdom, i.e. influential counselors to their King. Similarly, it seems that with the disappearance of the *wa-na-ka*, the *qa-si-re-we* have developed over the ruins of the Mycenaean administration as a strong local power, forming the basis for the political organization of cities of Archaic Greece.

B) TESTING THE CYCLES

The quickest way to highlight the new correspondences is to try to fit the known elements of Minoan and Mycenaean history to Cycles A and B which we have already identified.

Cycle A and Minoan history

In **bold**: stage of Cycle A
In upright: corresponding Minoan historical fact

1) Invasion of the territories of the future civilization by a more civilized foreign empire.

In the Neolithic, the people living in Crete forms initial cities: Knossos, Phaistos, Hagia Triada...

2) New invasion by barbarian populations revert the political order imposed by the first invaders.

Invasion by new peoples coming from Anatolia, mixing with more ancient populations.

3) Period of disappearance of the ancient culture and gestation of a new order.

(No information)

4) Progressive appearance of political entities unifying into a common civilization.

Apparition of a few political centers sharing the island of Crete.

5) Progressive cultural differentiation and competition between political entities for hegemony.

Probable opposition between the Cretan political entities for political hegemony.

6) Creation of a colonial empire stimulated by internal crises and technical progress.

Cretan thalassocracy and colonies in the Aegean Sea.

7) Confrontation with the threat of a foreign civilizational superpower. War of resistance by Civilization A.

(No information)

8) An antagonism appears within the civilization: a democratic, cosmopolitan and maritime bloc opposes a totalitarian, militaristic, autarkic and continental bloc.

Known elements: opposition between the hegemonic thalassocracy of Knossos to secondary centers of the island of Crete.

9) All-out war internal to the civilization, relentlessness from both sides, disappearance of conventional prohibitions.

Known elements: very probable war between Knossos and other Cretan centers, destruction of Knossos.

10) All-out internal war results in a weakened civilization, leading to the crumbling of its colonial empire and the loss of its global hegemony. The Empire is taken over by an emerging power of a superior size.

Loss of the hegemony on the Aegean Sea, weakening benefits Mycenaeans (and Troy?).

11) All of the states forming Civilization A are taken under tutelage by the superpower of Civilization B.

Crete is invaded by the Mycenaeans and is subjugated to their empire.
Cycle B and Mycenaean history

In **bold**: stage of Cycle B
In upright: archeological data from Mycenaean history
In *italics:* Greek mythology

1) A human community is founded by a pre-existing civilization, under the influence of Civilization A.

Arrival of the Achaeans in continental Greece. The Achaeans are an Indo-European people originating in the Balkans. Development of urban centers: Mycenae, Tiryns, Argos, Thebes, Pylos. Cretan influence.

Foundation of the cities by heroes: Cadmus establishes Thebes. Perseus of Argos establishes Mycenae.

2) Rejection of the suzerainty by the mother-civilization under the leadership of the aristocracy.

(No information)

Rejection of a form of Cretan suzerainty. Legend of the Minotaur: annual tribute required by the King of Crete, Minos. Rebellion of Theseus.

3) Establishment of the Republic with limited democratic mechanisms, conflicts over political rights.

(No information)

Federation of the Achaean cities and establishment of an institutional political order by the Oath of Tyndareus, guaranteeing peace and mutual support.

4) Conquest of the natural territory by the historical center of the civilization.

(No information)

Mycenae, which holds suzerain power over Argos and Tiryns in Argolis, extends its influence over Pylos through Heracles, under the orders of Eurystheus, King of Mycenae, over Thebes through the war of Seven and through the Epigoni, as well as over Sparta through the double-marriage of Agamemnon with Clytemnestra and Menelaus with Helen.

x)   Civil war: the nucleus of the civilization faces a desire of separation from its allies due to inequalities. The allies secede and form a confederation imitating the institutions of the nucleus, but in opposition to it. This secession concludes with the victory of the nucleus of the civilization and the imposition of its model to the other parties as well as the unification of the nation.

(No information)

Possible repeated interpretation of the elements presented in 4), in particular the long Thebes conflict.

5)   Confrontation to a powerful conquering nation. A fight for survival and supremacy leaves Civilization B without rival and able to dominate the world.

Trojan War and confrontation with the Hittite Empire.

Expedition of Heracles against Troy and the Trojan War.

6) The states of A become dominated by B.

The Mycenaeans invade Crete.

Interventions of the Achaean heroes in Crete: Heracles steals the bull from King Minos, Theseus kills the Minotaur.

7) Absolute hegemony over the known world, absence of rivals (it is at this step that Stage 1 of the next Cycle A occurs).

Mycenaean hegemony over the Aegean Sea. Subordination of all of Greece and the coasts of Anatolia by the Achaeans/Mycenaeans. Participation to the expeditions of the Sea Peoples, vanquished by Egypt.

Victory of the Greeks unified in the Trojan War. Expedition of Menelaus to Cyprus, Phoenicia and Egypt (where he is expelled), as well as Libya. Tale of Odysseus about the Egyptian expedition.

8) The Empire, a militaristic and autocratic regime, succeeds to the Republic.

Apparition of a supreme Mycenaean power, the Great King of Ahhiyawa according to Hittite archives[23]. Destruction of numerous Mycenaean Palaces in continental Greece. Probable signs of a centralization of authority after a destruction of local authorities.

Assassination of Agamemnon and rule of the usurper, Aegisthus. Conflict with Orestes, who is then recognized by the assembly of the people, establishing a new order that goes beyond the Oath of Tyndareus.

9) Decline and dismemberment of Empire B (corresponds to Stage 2 of the next Cycle A).

Definitive destruction of Mycenae in the XIIth century B.C.. The Dorians invade the Mycenaean Empire, on which will be built Greek Civilization: institutional inheritance in the Achaean *qa-si-re-u* transformed into the Greek *basileus*.

Return of the Heracleidae, who overthrow and kill Tisamenus, last king of Mycenae.

Thus we observe in the current state of knowledge that Cretan and Mycenaean history largely fit the patterns of unfolding of cycles A and B.

II: TWO AUTONOMOUS CYCLES: C AND D

Let us now take a look at two other cycles, which operate independently.

1. Cycle C: symmetry between Ancient Judaistic Civilization and Arab-Muslim Civilization

Whoever consulted the book *Guerre des Juifs* by Flavius Josephus or merely got interested to the Zealots who resisted the Roman army until their suicide in the fortress of Masada will have, no doubt, noted the parallel with what would be today described as Islamic terrorism. Importantly, both groups have a similar relationship with the civilization to which they reacted: Rome for the Jews, and the United States of America for the Muslims.

On the basis of this dual clue, let us thus expand, as we have done previously, our intuition through research, in order to determine whether or not the comparison can be pushed and established into a recurring pattern.

A) HISTORICAL REMINDERS

The Ancient Judaism of Moses and the Jewish People

The history of Judaism is more ancient and therefore understood with less certainty than the history of Islam[24]. We have three main sources of information on Judaism: archeology, the writings of ancient historians and the tales of the Bible. These sources, particularly the first and the last, can sometimes be incompatible and often contradict each other. We hope to stick the closest possible to the truth by adopting the method we have applied to Mycenaean history: by relying on the most commonly accepted theses, and in the case of a lack of information from archeology and ancient historians, we shall rely on the biblical text alone.

The history of the Jewish People as a Civilization only begins with Moses, and the biblical episode of The Exodus. Previously, all the information we have regarding the origins of the Jewish People lies with the Patriarchs: Abraham and his descendants.

The historical veracity of The Exodus from Egypt and of the military conquest of the Promised Land by Joshua is largely put into question by archeology. However, these tales can provide very interesting information. According to the text, the lands of Canaan would have, between the Early Bronze Age and the Iron Age, undergone cycles of colonization by native nomads or migrants from the close-by desert, establishing themselves there sedentarily. A first wave would have occurred between 3500 and 2200 B.C., a second one between 2000 and 1550 B.C., and a third one between 1150 and 900 B.C.[25]. Between these periods, we observe a crisis and a depopulation, which seems to correspond to a return to the nomadic lifestyle. During the third wave, that of the XIIth century B.C., and during the whole period of the Monarchies of Israel, we observe that, contrarily to all surrounding peoples, the inhabitants of Canaan and surrounding lands stop consuming pork[26]. We thus observe two things: the lands of the first Israelites have undergone a wave of population increase between the XXth and the XVIth centuries B.C., which is the era supposed to be that of the biblical patriarchs Abraham, Isaac and Jacob. Between 1550 and 1150 B.C., we observe a crisis relating to habitation, which implies a return to nomadism. Then, the historical "First Israelites" become sedentary "definitively" starting c. 1150 B.C.. However, the Bible describes an absence of the Hebrew from Canaan for four centuries[27]. The biblical text places the Hebrews in Egypt during this period, but the archeology seems to invalidate The Exodus.

Nevertheless, Joseph Davidovits seems to have demonstrated quite convincingly the historicity, or at least the historical origin, of the biblical character of Joseph, son of Jacob, sold in slavery by his brothers and who ends up becoming Vizier of Egypt, thanks to his extraordinary talents. He would be the Vizier of the Pharaoh Amenhotep III (ruling between 1390 and 1350 B.C.). The Vizier would be renamed Amenhotep, son of Hapu, and was the architect of the first pyramids. He would strand alongside Imhotep (XXVIIth century B.C.), as one of the greatest scribes and savants of Ancient Egypt. In the temple dedicated to him in Thebes, a supreme honor never seen for a scribe, French archeologists have discovered an inscription which Davidovits noted was recopied in the Bible, and applied to Joseph: "zaf-e'-nath-pa-ne'-a," a Hebrew transliteration of Amenhotep, son of Hapu (1430-1450 B.C.)[28]. This identification of Joseph as the Vizier of Amenhotep III in the XIVth century, precisely at a time where a crisis of habitation is observed in Canaan (1550-1150 B.C.) is in agreement (in the chronological dimension, at least), with the biblical episode of the exile to Egypt of Jacob and his sons. According to Jospeh Davidovits, the absence of archeological traces of the Hebrews in Egypt in this period results from the fact that the Hebrews, originally, were Egyptian workers. He conjectures that The Exodus could be linked to the workers strike of Deir el-Medina of 1157 B.C.. The camp of these workers was located just in front of the funeral temple of Amenhotep, son of Hapu, historical basis of the biblical Joseph. The episode of this strike, as witnessed in archeology, was concluded by, it seems, the pillaging of the Tombs of the Pharaoh by the workers themselves: "*Year 16, day 22 of the third month of flooding [...] Interrogation of the men found violating the tombs of Thebes; accusations formulated by the mayor of Thebes and the Chief of Police at the great and noble tomb of millions of years of the Pharaoh [...] It is possible that, given the general situation not improving for generations of workers, under the successors of Ramesses III, the workers decide to pillage the tombs, and no one would be better than them at doing so, since they built them.*" [29] The historical origin of The Exodus could be the overthrowing of a power by its workers, constrained to pillaging in reaction to an economic and administrative crisis, who would then have fled toward Canaan. According to Davidovits, they would have chosen this destination in order to join the first wave of migrants, who were loyal to the Heresy of Akhenaten. This location would be the Israel mentioned in the Merneptah Stele (before the arrival of the second wave c. 1157 B.C.). "iisii-r-iar," Israël, originally means "those exiled in haste because of their faults," the disciples of Akhenaten exiled by the priests of Amun. Davidovits believes he has thus resolved the problematic question of the existence of an Israelite people as early as 1200 B.C. from the records of populations and the Merneptah Stele while The Exodus would have only occurred half a century later. We must note that the dates for Amenhotep, son of Hapu (deceased in 1350 B.C.) and for the strike of Deir El-Medina (1157 B.C.) are only separated by two centuries, which does not fit the biblical duration for the presence of Hebrews in Egypt, stated to be of four centuries. However, Flavius Josephus states that there was, between the death of Joseph and the time of Moses, approximately 170 years, which corresponds better to the events identified by Davidovits[30].

The debates around these contradictory names and dates may be hard to digest. We note, in any case, that the Bible has preserved the memory of a return to the nomadic lifestyle within a relatively precise period according to archeology (400 years). It seems to also have preserved the memory of a return to sedentary lifestyle in the XIIth century B.C., since it is in this period that the biblical text dates the conquest of Canaan. Thus, even if the biblical details are not fully confirmed by archeology, the periodic nature of the presence and absence of the Hebrews in the biblical text appears to correspond to the cyclical phenomenon of the adoption of nomadism and sedentary life in the lands of Canaan. Among other things, the coincidence of the return to the sedentary lifestyle in the XIIth century with the forbidding of pork, both confirmed by archeology, show that a political-spiritual change occurred in this period. It is not unreasonable to think that a real character becoming a preacher of the desert could have been at the origin of the story of Moses, who brought with him new religious doctrines. Interestingly, Moses was integrated to an ancient civilization (Egypt) and following a revelation in the desert, his people rose and left the desert in order to conquer fertile lands. We should also note that pork was forbidden for Egyptian priests, according to Herodotus[31]. The forbidding of pork in the first population zones of the Israelites c. 1200-1150 B.C. constitutes another clue supporting the thesis of Davidovits of an Egyptian origin for the Hebrews. Davidovits thus conjectures that Moses would have been the director of the funeral Temple of Joseph/Amenhotep, son of Hapu[32]. Without concluding the historicity of The Exodus as described in the Bible (the exiled would have been a few hundreds instead of six hundred thousands), the historical elements that have inspired the biblical tale are far from inexistent: the disappearance, witnessed by archeology, of the sedentary lifestyle around Canaan precedes by little the rise of Joseph/Amenhotep as Vizier (without necessitating the Canaan origin of the historical character; the Hebrews could have appropriated a purely Egyptian character by inventing his origin). This depopulation period corresponds to the duration provided by the Bible for the expedition of Hebrews in Egypt, a complete sedentary establishment being revealed by archeology in the XIIth century B.C.. This correlates with the banning of pork, and supports an external contribution coming from Egypt.

The idea that neither Moses, nor the few individuals who, fleeing Egypt, would be the basis of The Exodus while not being Hebrew is not at all shocking in my view. Contrarily, their will to claim themselves as descendants of Abraham while having no ethnic links to him would echo the appropriation of the tradition of Abraham and Moses by the Arabs, who were living side by side with Jewish communities in Arabia. This recuperation could, in addition, explain the incoherence between the law of Moses and observable behaviors in the history of the Patriarchs. We should also add that the Egyptian origin of Hebrews was proposed by numerous authors of the Antiquity: Flavius Josephus cites, with the idea of refuting them, the writings of Manetho, Chaeremon of Alexandria and Lysimachus concerning Moses and the Jews. Josephus is right to point to the multiple contradictions in these texts, but these three authors were agreeing on one point: Moses and those who followed him were Egyptians, eventually joined by others who were already on their way[33].

We note that the opinion of Josèphe himself, which prevailed for a long time, identified the Hebrews with the Hyksos invaders, who dominated Lower and Middle Egypt during the XVIIth and XVIth centuries B.C.. However, when it comes to correspondances between the biblical text and archeological data, it is often not relevant to seek to reason in terms of "true" or "false." The Bible having been written later on the basis of oral tradition, it is possible that the successive episodes were mixed, and the writers in the time of Josiah could have confounded or passed on a tradition that confounded the episodes of the (partially) semitic Hyksos and their massive expulsion with the tale of the historical Moses. We can imagine that, in Canaan, an oral tradition was perpetuated recording the Hyksos exodus, and that this tradition intermingled with Moses' exodus, of a much smaller size. With time, the carriers of the tale, who had an approximate idea of the dates, could have attribute an epic dimension to the exodus of Moses, in terms of the number of refugees, borrowed from the Hyksos exodus. The epic dimension would have been more convenient for the tale of a prophet.

In contrast, the theory according to which the cult of Yahweh as a unique God would have appeared progressively seems unrealistic: the doctrine of Moses is too close, in its substance, to that of Islam for us to conceive of a progressive birth, when we know how Islam was structured immediately after the death of Muhammad. Furthermore, the fact that the forbidding of pork is archeologically observed as early as the beginning of Israelite history in Canaan (XIIth century B.C.) constitutes another supporting element. This forbidding is central, in that it separates communities of Israelite believers and their neighbors. We have difficulty imagining how such a distinctive religious obligation could accommodate a non-exclusivity of cult among its followers. Thus, strict monotheism is likely present as early as the XIIth century, in the time of Moses. Obviously, the Israelite community must have interacted, in the lands of Canaan, with polytheistic cults, without necessarily imposing itself to them. However, this does not put in question the belief in the uniqueness of the divinity of Yahweh. Even in the times of David and Solomon, it is very probable that a part of the subjects of these Kings would have retained previous beliefs instead of adhering to Moses' doctrine, in the same way that Muslim conquerors do not immediately require the conversion of all residents of a conquered territory. There were even influences in the opposite direction, the Bible accusing Solomon to have succumbed to polytheism at the end of his life.

The text of origins has thus probably been re-worked and embellished, as stated by Israël Finkelstein, under King Josiah, in the VIth century B.C., for the purpose of political-religious propaganda, in order to turn it into an epic tale, but the historical bases of the text remain manifest. It is not a pure invention for what concerns our purpose, because we want to show the deep parallel between the biblical history of Israel, from Moses to David, and that of the first centuries of Islam. This parallel would be of no interest if it is not established between similar historical facts, but rather would rely on the comparison of historical facts to an invented tale. It does not matter whether there are miracles or not, whether the Hebrews have truly descended from Abraham from Canaan, or whether a few Egyptian workers were joined on the road by Canaan nomads, whether they were half a million or half a thousand, whether they crossed the Sinai in forty years or four days. These details are unimportant for our question, and thus the debate between maximalists and minimalists is foreign to our view. What matters is the general series of events.

It should also be noted that the existence of a population is well documented in this period, and this remains true whether Davidovits is right in linking The Exodus to the strike of the workers of Deir el-Medina, or if this migration stemmed from migrant populations in the XIIIth rather than the XIIth century B.C., or even if there were no such thing as an exodus from Egypt to Canaan and that the reappearance of the Israelites in the XIIIth and XIIth centuries are due to a return to the sedentary lifestyle of populations of more or less native nomads (although this seems disproved by the adoption of an Egyptian Vizier as a Hebrew figure, Amenhotep, son of Hapu, and the presence in the biblical text of a fragment copied from a fresco from his funeral temple[34]).

Concerning the military conquest of Canaan, the archeology is in strong contradiction with the biblical tale: there would have been no conquest of Canaan, because the dates of observed destructions do not coincide with the description of an existing Israel c. 1200 B.C. by the Merneptah Stele (which is confirmed by the archeological traces of population increases). Let us remind what we have said concerning the Sea Peoples. The Philistines, famous enemies of Israel in the Bible, were likely Cretans and Pelasgians, subordinates and allies to Mycenaeans who would have established themselves in Canaan during the second expedition of the Sea Peoples. There, these invaders became the ruling elite of native Canaan populations, just like, for instance, the Franks became the ruling elite of the Gallo-Romans in Northern France in the VIth century.

It is plausible that the Hebrews would have simply established themselves in lands already ravaged by war and largely abandoned, and that they partially came from Egypt, in the hypothesis of the historicity of the Exodus, or that they merely left, as natives, the high deserted lands of Canaan in order to establish themselves on lower altitude, more fertile lands. Thus they would have merely filled the void left by the fall of the local regime at the end of the Bronze Age. The episode of the blowing of trumpets breaking the walls of the city of Jericho for Joshua could then be interpreted as a mythical metaphor for the fact that Hebrew populations having migrated there found an abandoned city, deprived of a fortified surrounding, and thus offering no resistance.

Let us note that there is a strong historical analogy characterizing the intersection between the different cycles. This absence of real resistance to the Hebrew expansion toward the lower altitude, more fertile lands of Canaan, results from a systemic crumbling which we have interpreted not to be a mysterious phenomenon affecting simultaneously numerous civilizations (Hittites, Mycenaeans, Canaan), but rather as the sole effect of the formidable Mycenaean expansion and the crumbling of this civilization, leaving its old empire in ruins and subject to disorder, just like the Roman world after the fall of Rome. The fact that the Hebrews could have profited from this fall in order to extend their population into Canaan shares a strong similarity with the Arab conquest of Egypt and Orient during the weakening of the Roman Empire.

Later in time, the archeological data are in agreement with the biblical text more than they were for the earlier history as described above, as long as one takes the biblical tale for its major elements only, while ignoring the importance that it attributes to specific men and events. While the biblical text seems to exaggerate the greatness of Israel and its kings, it seems to be standing on a solid historical basis.

Archeology seems to have demonstrated the historicity of King David and his lineage (from the Tel Dan stele). Concerning the period of unity of the Kingdom of Israel under David and Solomon, the archeological data provide a smaller view of the extant of the power of this Kingdom, showing that Jerusalem was not a great city in this era, and that the region of Judas, which the Bible describes as a vast empire, was in reality poorer than the future Israel, in the north. The United Monarchy of David and Solomon would thus have been more of a period of control of the North by the South, the Great Kings being, in reality, lords of war extorting the cities around Canaan[35].

Following what the Bible presents nevertheless as a golden age of unity under a single King and of independence of the Hebrew people, the Kingdom appears to be divided in two, Israel and Judah. The Bible presents this event as an uprising of the North against Rehoboam, son of Solomon. In the hypothesis of extortionist kings, this could correspond to a vigorous reaction of the cities against a lord of war who was too gluttonous.

Then, the kingdom of the North, Israel, fell under the domination of the Assyrian Empire, and the Kingdom of Judah benefited from its weakening, by developing economically and by welcoming, from Israel it seems, numerous migrants.

After the fall of the Assyrian Empire at the end of the VIIth century B.C., Palestine is stuck in a power struggle between Egypt and the Babylonian Empire. The latter takes over Jerusalem, destroys the Temple and expels the Jews on the lands of Babylon.

The conquest of Babylon by Cyrus the Persian frees the Jews from Babylonian servitude, and Judah, being repopulated by returning Jews, becomes a province of the Persian Achaemenid Empire.

The Jewish country remains subordinated to the Persian Empire until its fall against Alexander the Great, who becomes the new master, followed by the Greek sovereigns, Lagidae and Seleucid. The weakening of the latter and their exactions lead to the Maccabean Revolt, establishing a new period of independence for Judah under the Hasmonean dynasty, starting in 140 B.C..

The Hasmonean state expands through the conquest of Samaria, Transjordan and then of Galilee. The Hasmonean sovereigns rule over a state where Jews are not a majority, and the kingdom itself is highly influenced by Greeks, with an army of mercenaries and a Royal Court. This creates tensions with pious Jews, the Pharisees, who were originally supporting the Hasmoneans in their revolt but then begin fomenting a revolt against them, because they deem them not sufficiently faithful to the Jewish religion. This leads to a violent repression in which King Alexander Jannaeus crucifies Jewish rebels and suppresses them using Pagan Greek mercenaries.

After the death of Alexander Jannaeus in 76 B.C., his sons Hyrcanus and Aristobulus have a dispute for power, leading to the Roman intervention by Pompey, who takes over Jerusalem and turns Judea into a Roman protectorate.

Following a Parthian invasion of Judea initiated by the son of Aristobulus, nephew of King Hyrcanus, the Romans take back the province along with Herod, who is made King of Jews.

Herod extends the Hasmonean policy of support for Pagan Greeks and Samaritans, which triggers a similar hostility from the religious Jews, the Pharisees.

When Herod dies, in 4 B.C., the Kingdom is shared between his sons. Herod Archelaus being unable to properly govern his Kingdom of Judea, formed by Samaria and Idumea, he is removed by Rome, leading to the creation of the Province of Judea province, placed under the control of a prefect. Roman presence thus increases, since the region switches from a client state of Rome to that of a land dominated by the Empire.

This Roman presence is annoying to religious Jews who dislike this new subordination to a pagan power. Among other things, the Pharisees inherited from a secular tradition of opposition, and even revolt, against the policies of the Hasmoneans and of Herod the Great.

Let us turn our attention for a moment on the situation of Judaism outside of Judea. We note that in Antiquity, Jews were proselytes, and worked hard to spread their faith on the coasts of the Mediterranean Sea. Judaism had claims of hegemony, and many Jews believed it would become the one religion of all men. When, nowadays, we think of the idea of the "chosen people," we see a community closed on itself, defending its identity amidst persecutions and interbreeding. This perception is certainly reinforced by the creation of the State of Israel, in reaction to centuries of exclusions, pogroms, and the modern German attempt to exterminate the Jews. And it seems certain that for modern Jews themselves, proselytism is no more on the table, or when it happens it is from religious Jews to atheist Jews. Non-Jews are no more a target. For the Jews of antiquity, being the "chosen people" meant being the first, but not the only ones to receive the divine message. The divine "choice" as it was experienced by Jews in the Greek and Roman periods was much more similar to that experienced in modern Muslim tradition than it is to that of modern Jews. It was a mission, not an heritage.

Thus in those times Jewish proselytism was very efficient, and hundreds of thousands of individuals converted to Judaism on the coasts of the Mediterranean Sea, the population of Jews summing up to four million souls, corresponding to between 5 and 7% of the Roman Empire[36]. But while Judaism could exert seduction, it also incited mistrust and repulsion. Bernard Lazare, in his erudite history of anti-Semitism, described the hostilities encountered by Judaism just before the birth of Christianity, during the Greek and Roman periods[37]. He notes, among other things: "*Despite having left Palestine, they wanted first and foremost to remain Jewish and their homeland to be Jerusalem, the only town where God could be adored and where sacrifices could be made in the temple. They were forming, everywhere, sort of Republics, linked to Judea and Jerusalem [...] they separated from other inhabitants through their rituals and customs; they considered as impure the soil of foreign lands and attempted to constitute, in each city, a kind of sacred territory. They lived secluded, in special quarters, imprisoning themselves, living in isolation, managing themselves in virtue of privileges that made others jealous [...] The same causes that had operated in Alexandria operated in Rome. There also, the excessive Jewish privileges, the wealth of some of them, their unmatched luxury and ostentation, provoked the hate of the people.*" Martin Goodman also observes the cultural misunderstandings between Jews and Greco-Romans. For the latter, jokes relating to sexuality or human excrements were considered impolite and vulgar by the most sophisticated, but appreciated by the people. For Jews, such statements were not only seen as impolite, which is a matter of decency, but as impure, a matter of religion and the sacred. One does not get into a fight for decency, but misunderstandings hurting the sacred can quickly degenerate into a brawl, which happened, as it seems, regularly. Furthermore, Lazare notes the success encountered by Jewish proselytism in the Roman Empire: "*the ancient people, in their decline, was deeply seduced by Judaism, by its dogma of divine unity and its moral. Many, among the poor people, were attracted by the privileges given to Jews.*" This worried many Romans, including Cicero: "*Cicero, who had learned from Apollonius Molon, had inherited his prejudices. He found Jews on his path. They were part of the People's Party against the senate, to which he belonged.*" The People's Party was, in Roman politics, the "left," while the senate was the "right." Cicero was greatly worried about the rise of Judaism: "*one day, he exclaims: 'we must combat barbarian superstitions,' accusing them of being a nation with a tendency for suspiciousness and calumny,*" and he adds that they "*display disdain for the Roman power.*" They were to be feared, according to him, as men who, having detached from Rome, were turning toward the distant city of Jerusalem, and were supporting it with the money taken from the Republic. Among other things, he accused them of converting citizens to the Shabbat rituals.*" The Latin author was himself the heir of a Greek view of Judaism: "*Appion repeated, in his treatise against the Jews, the fables of Manetho, which had already been restated by Chaeremon of Alexandria and Lysimachus. He was adding to it what had been said by Posidonius and Apollonius Molon. According to him, Moses was 'merely a seducer and sorcerer,' and his laws were carrying 'nothing less than evil and danger.'*" Flavius Josephus noted with chagrin, while trying to find an honorable reason for it, the opinion of Greco-Romans concerning the inability of the Jews at inventing anything, paralyzed by their religious legalism: "*It is also a critique that is thrown at us, of having produced no inventors in the arts or thought. Indeed, other peoples find it honorable to be loyal to no customs of their own fathers. They reward those who violate it with more audaciousness with a certificate of deep wisdom. We, to the contrary, believe that the only wisdom and virtue is to take absolutely no action, to have no thought that is contrary to the laws originally established*[38]." On their side, the Jews had no doubts about their coming triumph: Bernard Lazare notes that the Jewish author

Philon of Alexandria *"recommends to his religious community not to irritate them [the Roman sophists], in order to avoid riots, and to patiently wait for their chastising, which will occur when the Jewish Empire, that of salvation, will be globally established."* Importantly, Jewish authors were very annoying to Greek philosophers because of their practice of concordism, a position that affirms the superiority of one's religion by pointing to its correctness, often declared in premonition: *"The Jews even pretended to bring back to themselves Greek philosophy and literature. In a comment on the Pentateuch, preserved by Eusebius of Caesarea, Aristobule tried to demonstrate that Plato and Aristotle had found their ethical and metaphysical ideas in an old Greek translation of the Pentateuch."* Philon, triumphant, declared: *"Our customs win and convert by themselves the barbarians and the Greeks, the continent and the islands, the Orient and the Occident, Europe and Asia, the entire Earth from one side to the other."*

These attitudes and mutual accusations caused several issues, made worse by the fact that Judaism was birthing an increasingly radical fringe, inclined toward terroristic violence. Suetonius notes in *The Life of Claudius* that in 41, the emperor expelled the Jews from Rome (a statement corroborated by the *Acts of the Apostles 18, 2*) due to troubles they were causing, at the request of "Chrestus." One should not necessarily assume that they were Christians, to the contrary indeed: Romans had a tendency to designate as Christians all messianic Jews. In Greek, the word for Messiah is Christos, and most revolted Jews from the Greek Orient (thus speaking Greek) designated their chief as the Messiah (this was the case, among others, for Judas of Galilee, founder of the sect of Zealots, and also for Simon of Cyrene and Simon bar Kokhba). This habit of revolted Jews to acknowledge the messiah, or Christos, in so many places according to any local uprising, keeps us from concluding that they were truly Christians, disciples of Jesus. This would be an anachronism, committed *a posteriori*: until the fall of bar Kokhba in 135 A.D., any uprising of Jews is Christian simply because it recognizes its chief as Christ (thus, the Messiah), without him being related to the character and teachings of Jesus Christ. After this, Judaistic messianism was disappearing at the same time as the hopes of the Jews for a land, and there were no more Christians, other than the followers of Jesus Christ. But until then, that is in 135 A.D., it is hard to designate as Christians in the modern sense all of those that the Romans were referring to as such. Who were these agitated Jews who caused the reaction of Claudius? We have difficulty imagining how, only ten years after the affliction of Jesus, there would have been enough of his followers in Rome to cause such troubles that the Emperor would decide to expel all of the Jewish community. Thus they were most probably not the disciples of Jesus Christ, since at this date Paul had never went to Rome, Peter probably neither, and the predication of apostles was still limited to the Greek Orient.

The Jews who were partisans of "Chrestus" were thus probably radical messianic Jews annoyed by Rome's establishment of Herod Agrippa as allied King of Judea since he was from Idumaea, and not from the home of David, and thus not the Messiah, the Christos (and thus, in their eyes, illegitimate). Even more troubling, Nero accused, during the Great Fire of Rome, the Jews of the city for starting the fire—for Tacitus, the "Christians," but in these ancient times the two movements were very much linked through their origins and customs and certainly very hard to differentiate for the Romans. The hostility of the authors of the time, in particular Suetonius, would describe this accusation as being intended to divert the people from the very real guilt of the Emperor. This occurred in 64 A.D., two years before The Great Revolt of 66, at the time when the fanaticism of the Zealots was already very active. Historiography was never able to determine who was responsible for the incident, having no proof that it was even criminal, despite the certainty of the ancient authors because of its speed and mode of propagation. Thus we can propose the idea that it was indeed fanatic Jews that originated it. Some historians have defended the hypothesis of a Christian origin, who would have been motivated by apocalyptic prophecies. However, attacks based on eschatological texts were, in this time, a practice more common under Judaism than Christianity (in the sense of the disciples of Jesus), as demonstrated by the Zealots' movement and the sect of Sicarii, a hypothesis made even more plausible given that these groups, a few years before the Great Fire in 60-61 A.D., had been exalted in their hate against the Romans by the arbitrage of Nero favoring the Syrians during the sedition of Caesarea, arbitrage which put an end to the equality of political rights between Jews and Syrians. It is thus tempting to see in the attribution of the Great Fire to Christians (disciples of Jesus) a confusion with Christian-Jews (fanatical messianic Jews). The thesis of a fire provoked by Jewish Zealots of Rome would sadly echo the attacks of September 11th 2001, perpetrated by Islamists in Manhattan, heart of the American power (and also to conspiracy theories concerning this attack: the declaration of guilt of the imperial power echoing the conspiracy theories describing the attacks on the World Trade Center as an *inside job*). The hypothesis is unfortunately unverifiable but plausible, due to the series of clues offered by the troubles under Claudius, the crescendo of Jewish agitation with the sedition of Caesarea, and then the uprising of Judea in 66, and the quasi-universal uprising of Jews of the Empire in 115-117.

Indeed, it is in 66 A.D. that begins the great revolt initiating the First Jewish-Roman War. After half a century of provocations and anti-Roman acts, included in Rome itself, the situation degenerates between the Roman procurator Gessius Florus and the Jews in Jerusalem. The governor of Syria, Cestius Gallus, comes to the rescue, but as he withdraws from Jerusalem, he loses an important part of his legion to an ambush by the Jews. This is the true trigger of the Roman furor, who end up attacking the rebels with three and then four legions. The Zealots, more fanatical than the religious Jews, took power in Jerusalem and killed noteworthy characters of the Roman regime. They were in agreement with the Pharisees on the doctrine, but were fierce sovereigntists and did not hesitate to commit murders and even massacres. They were convinced that their war would result in the coming of the Messiah, who would lead to their triumph and domination over all of Earth.

Things unfolded differently in reality: Jerusalem was taken by the Romans and destroyed. The Sanhedrin, the assembly of Jews, was dissolved, and hundreds of thousands of Jewish prisoners were massacred. The Temple that had been rebuilt by Herod was destroyed.

The Pharisees regrouped around Jaffa and elaborated a new doctrine around the Torah, Rabbinic Judaism, which would become the new norm for the Jewish religion and still remains as of today.

A second uprising, less famous because it was very much ignored in Jewish sources, but remains interesting due to its geographical extent, happened from 115 to 117 A.D.. This conflict was named the Kitos War, or the rebellion of the diaspora. This conflict not only affected Judea, but also the entirety of the diaspora of Jewish populations living in the East of the Mediterranean Sea: Cyrene, Cyprus, Alexandria and all of Egypt. The causes of this uprising are quite unclear, but it seems to begin with the contact between Jews of Persia with the Romans during Trajan's Parthian campaign. Refusing to have as their masters the destroyers of the Temple of Jerusalem, an insurrection against the invaders ensued, and the revolt was repressed with extreme brutality by Lusius Quietus, general of Trajan, who gave his name to this episode (Kitos). It may be the news of this uprising and its repression which motivated the Jews of the Empire to revolt in turn. There again, the repression was fierce. Local populations responded vigorously to riots in which the insurgent Jews attacked their properties and religious symbols (they were destroying the temples and public buildings) as well as individuals (they committed massacres of Greeks, notably in Cyprus). In Egypt, the prefect of the Praetorian Guard, Marcius Turbo, exterminated a large part of the three hundred thousand Jews who lived there. This conflict, proportionally to the Jewish population at the time, made as many deaths as the Shoah, and in absolute numbers as much as the murderous conquest of Gaul by Caesar: around one million victims, with the difference that the latter conflict extended over a period four times longer and involved a larger population.

Finally, a new uprising occurred in the first third of the IInd century under the leadership of bar Kokhba, whose bloody crushing by Hadrian's legion spelled the end of the political-religious Jewish dream of Antiquity. From this time on, the proselytism outburst of Judaism disappeared, supplanted by that of Christians who had stayed out of the Jewish wars in that they advocated, as the Apostles did, a submissiveness toward the masters, not seeking to build an Empire or attain liberty in this world, but in the other instead, contrarily to revolted Jews, who hoped to establish a worldwide Empire. Rabbinic Judaism diverged from the original doctrines of Moses, became a minority religion, spiritualized, no more pretending to seek hegemony, but preserving its specificity and identity, which it succeeded at doing for two millennia, until today. Going forward, we will refer to the past version of Judaism that followed the doctrine of Moses as Ancient Judaism, as opposed to the modern form, Rabbinic Judaism.

Islam and the Arab Muslims

The history of Islam and of the Arab Muslim world is more recent, and therefore known with better precision and certainty than that of the Hebrews and the Ancient Jewish State.

Muhammad is born at the Mecca in 570. As an adult, he undertook a career as a tradesman in the commercial city. He started teaching the Muslim faith in 610, after having, according to the tradition, received divine revelations in a cave, in a mountain located in the desert lands of Arabia. Disliked in the Mecca, he fled to Medina during the Hegira, which marks the beginning of the Muslim calendar, and represents a sort of Exodus for Islam. Through teachings and force, he became a military leader in addition to a prophet and succeeded at imposing his religion to the Arabic Peoples. At the moment of his death, the united Arabic Peoples were ready to undertake the conquest of the surrounding lands and were living under a political-religious law.

Through its recuperation of the biblical character of Ishmael, first son of Abraham who the Patriarch had with his servant Hagar, Islam affirms its affiliation with the Abrahamic religion and legitimizes its capture of Moses' heritage. In its form and its spirit, Islam does not bring much novelty as was the case with Christianity adding to Judaism: it is not an overtaking but a new beginning, in terms of the teachings of Moses. The teachings of Muhammad, while they mention Jesus of Nazareth ('Isa), deny any divine nature to him as well as to his death and resurrection. Importantly, the novelties brought by Jesus with respect to the traditional doctrine of Ancient Judaism are completely ignored. Five centuries after the appearance of Rabbinic Judaism modifying the spirit of Ancient Judaism and spiritualizing its laws, Islam is a return to the primitive fundamentals, with a strict religious law bringing precise prescriptions, diet interdictions, identification of the community of believers, an absence of separation between the temporal and the spiritual as well as a strong messianic hope. Islam is, in essence, a new doctrine of Moses, and Muhammad has recuperated, in his own way, the great lines of Ancient Judaism, just like the historical Moses seems to have taken a pre-existing tradition which the Bible retained as that of Abraham, affirming its affiliation with it (an affiliation which is impossible to verify historically).

The first four caliphates, chiefs that are both political and religious and perceived as heirs of Muhammad, led the Islamic conquest up to the Maghreb and western Spain, and down to Persian and Eastern India. It is the golden age of Islam, a time for successes and unity. Islam is structured itself into a brilliant civilization, which became dynastic and culminated with the century of the Umayyad Caliphate, from 661 to 750.

In 750, it is the end of unity: The Abbasid family takes over the Caliphate, and the Umayyad flee to create a new state in Spain. The conflict marks the beginning of the decline of the Arab-Muslim civilization. In the Xth century, new divisions weaken the Abbasid Caliphate, which ends up falling under the Seljuk Turks who, coming from the East, have built an Empire encompassing the eastern half of the Muslim world, from India to Egypt.

The Western half, meanwhile, remained independent, in particular under the Egyptian dynasties of the Fatimid Caliphate, and for Maghreb and Spain, the Akmoravid dynasty and then the Almohad dynasty. The fall of the Seljuk Turkish Empire at the end of the XIIth century left half of the Muslim world to domination by local sovereigns until the rise, from the XIVth to the XVIIth centuries, of the Ottoman Empire which turned into vassals most of the Arab-Muslim world, from Egypt to Maghreb and in Arabia.

The Arab-Muslim world remained subordinated to the Ottoman Turks until the XIXth century, during which Europe progressively took control of North Africa. At the beginning of the XXth century, at the end of the First World War, what was left of the Arab-Muslim world under Turkish control also passed under European control, as colonized lands or protectorates.

After the Second World War, the Arab-Muslim world benefited from the weakening of their occidental masters in order to recover their independence, after centuries of Turkish and European domination. It was the era of Pan-Arabism. Nationalist authoritarian regimes were established which, while they fiercely defending their independence, adopted numerous occidental behaviors and concepts, including socialism and secular government. This led them to repress, often with violence, the partisans of Islamic Law.

The rise of Islamic movements was favored by the interventions of the American and Soviet powers, which replaced the former European domination, as well as by the presence of Israel, perceived as an occidental colony. Iran, not being part of the Arab world but having been Islamicized for just as long, reacted to these American interventions with the Islamic Revolution, which overthrew the authoritarian and secular regime of the Shah in 1979, a regime which had been imposed and supported by the Americans. The same year, the Great Mosque of Mecca was overtaken by a few hundred Islamist fundamentalists who were opposed to the alliance between the Saudi princes and occidentals.

The Arab-Muslim Islamists were influenced by Wahhabism, which originated from two centuries earlier. The most extremist Islamists, who desired the establishment of Islamic States and got involved in terrorism, believe in a prophecy announcing the invasion of the sacred land of Arabia (which they consider to have occurred through the arrival of the USA in 1991), and a great war against the infidel nations from which Islam will come out triumphant, thanks to the help of God, who would send the Mahdi, a religious and military chief capable of guiding Islam toward total victory and establishing its global domination[39]. The terrorists who took the Mecca in November 1979 presented one of their own as the Mahdi, Mohammed Abdullah al Qahtani. Simultaneously, the taking in hostage in Teheran of the staff of the American Embassy occurred, and the American Embassies of Islamabad and Tripoli were attacked by angry crowds. In response, the Americans supported the Iraq of Saddam Hussein during the lengthy and bloody Iran-Iraq War (1980-1988), and strongly hit the naval Iranian forces during Operation Praying Mantis in 1988.

Thereafter, in numerous places and repeatedly, Islamists used force of all scales, up to overthrowing of states. In Afghanistan, the Talibans took power. Elsewhere, similar attempts to establish an Islamic regime were repressed through blood by the authoritarian or secular Arab nationalists.

In 1991, the Gulf War further engulfed the Americans in the Arab world, and created a shock for Muslims by having a massive penetration of occidental forces on the sacred lands of Arabia. The decade that followed was marked by a strong rise of Islamic terrorism, targeting both occidentals and Muslims judged to be insufficiently religious.

These violent acts culminated in 2001 with the September 11th attacks of the World Trade Center, and the simultaneous attack of the Pentagon. Up until this point, the Occident in general and the USA in particular were attempting to contain Islamists by moderate actions at the intelligence level and through anti-terror actions. The importance of the attacks resulted in a brutal reaction: the invasion of Afghanistan, then of Iraq, and the expansion of global anti-terror operations. In Iraq, the Shi'ite resistance to the American invasion, following their religious leader Muqtada al-Sadr, are referred to as the army of the Mahdi, which places them within the Millenarist Muslim movement.

These wars exhausted the terrorist networks, which were crushed and dissolved progressively. As of today, Al-Qaeda seems to be militarily defeated.

In 2011, a turning point seems to have occurred: The Arab-Muslim peoples rose against the old authoritarian regimes. The protests were not led in the fashion of the last centuries, but rather by the youth which seemed to reject the heritage of Pan-Arabism as well as the Islamist political ideology. Thus, to the military defeat of Islamists, a moral and political defeat was added, and numerous signals tend to indicate that the revolted youth of these Arab-Muslim societies desired a continuation of the secularisation of authoritarian regimes and a better opening toward the world, allowing a "modernization" of Islam.

However, in 2012, this enthusiasm seems to have been moderated by the recuperation of the revolutionary movement by Islamists and their electoral victories, leading many to fear that the "Arab spring" would be followed by an "Islamic winter." In 2014, the brutal rise of the Islamic State testified of the intact vigor of Millenarist Jihadism, which attained a new apogee with the proclamation of a new caliphate. The leave of numerous Muslims who, residing in Occident, sought to join the war, demonstrated that radical Islamist ideas could penetrate Muslim communities implanted outside of the Muslim world, which increased the tensions between communities and the general distrust toward Muslim populations. This distrust was made worse by the multiplication of small scale attacks: knife attacks, car attacks and desecrations of cemeteries. Often, delinquency and religious fanaticism tend to mix, the latter pretending to give moral respectability to the first. This was the case for Khaled Kelkal, responsible for the 1995 bombings in France. He was a criminal turned terrorist. It was also the case for the Kouachi brothers, responsible for the Charlie Hebdo shooting, and it was also the case for numerous fanatics leaving to Syria and Iraq, hoping to profit and commit rapes in full impunity.

Just like the Jews of Antiquity, the Muslims living in Occident are often perceived, especially by the popular layers who are more confronted to their lifestyle, in the suburbs of great cities, as privileged individuals benefiting from social welfare and tolerance by the authorities. Such privileges allow them, for instance, to establish themselves in no-go zones ruled by traffickers, who gain a lot by maintaining the cultural specificities of immigrants and of the children of Muslim immigrants. The frequent submissiveness of local authorities to the desiderata of Muslim populations as it relates to food preferences in cafeterias as well as the occupation of the public space for prayers also contribute to the perception by a share of the European populations of a sense of inequality of rights advantaging Muslim populations. This inequality is explicitly captured by the concept of dhimmitude in the works of Bat Ye'or[40]. The luxurious lifestyle of the Arab princes of oil, especially the Qataris in France, reinforces this perception, European governments showing themselves complacent in order to ensure their provisioning in hydrocarbon. Muslim proselytism, which expresses itself strongly in the majority Muslim suburbs, where a social pressure can be exerted on non-Muslims, or on insufficiently religious Muslims, exacerbates even further the feeling of an Islamic threat weighting on occidental civilization, often expressed in the same terms used by Cicero to describe Ancient Judaism.

B) PRESENTATION OF CYCLE C

After Cycle A, accounting for the common evolution of Greece and Europe, and Cycle B for Rome and the USA, the numerous similarities that we see between these two rapid reviews of the history of the Arab-Muslim world and Islam on the one hand, and Ancient Judaism and the Jewish State on the other, allows us to establish a pattern summarizing these political-religious movements.

In **bold**: stage of cycle C
In upright: corresponding Jewish historical fact
In *italics*: corresponding Muslim historical fact

1) Civilisation C is born in a nomadic community: a prophet, leaving his place of origin, delivers a politico-religious law to his people based on a more ancient tradition and guides them toward the appropriation of a territory.[41]

After The Exodus leading them (or a part of them) outside of Egypt, the first Israelites become sedentary on the high lands of Canaan while adopting specific interdictions (pork), probably under the influence of a prophetic figure at the origin of Moses. Moses' tradition integrates and borrows from the legend of Abraham.

Muhammad flees Mecca with his disciples toward Medina during the Hegira. He gives the Quran to the Arabs, in the desert of Arabia, and leads them into a conquest of the world, being both their prophet and their chief. The Quran integrates and borrows from the tradition of the great Judaistic figures.

2) C establishes into fertile lands outside of the desert, by benefiting from the weakening of the Civilization B of the previous cycle.

The first Israelites become sedentary in the high lands of Canaan, and take advantage of the disorder resulting from the fall of the Mycenaean Empire to extend their control over the lower lands.

The Arabs conquer and establish themselves throughout North Africa and Spain starting from Arabia, taking advantage of the disorder resulting from the fall of the Roman Empire in Occident and the weakening of the Oriental Empire for its eastward expansion in Persia.

3) Civilisation C undergoes a golden age of political and religious unity. Appearance of a single power.

Biblical golden age, the Times of the Judges and then of King David and Solomon. Religion and state unified under a single power.

Period of the triumphant Arab Islam: Islamic Rashidun caliphates. Religious state unified under the dynasty of the Umayyad caliphate.

4) Divisions weaken C.

Division between Israel and the Kingdom of Judea: political division and religious schism.

Political division of the Ummah, religious schisms (sunniism, shi'ism…) and political schisms (Umayyad, Abbasid…).

5) After centuries of decline, C is dominated by the powers of a foreign civilization, which come under different successive identities. The first identity of this foreign civilization does not dominate the historical center of C, but the second one attains it.

The Jews are dominated by the Assyrian and then the Achaemenid Empires. The Assyrian Empire only dominates Israel and not Judea. The Persian Achaemenid Empire turns Judea into a vassal.

The Arab-Muslims are dominated by the Turks, Seljuk and then by the Ottomans. The Seljuk do not take over the Mecca and Arabia, which remain possessions of the Fatimid Caliphate. The Ottoman Empire dominates the entirety of Arabia.

6) After the fall of the foreign civilization, C is dominated by powers of Civilization A

The Jews are dominated by Greek powers after the victory against the Persian Achaemenid Empire.

The Arab lands are colonized by the powers of Europe after the victory against the Ottoman Empire.

7) Nationalist uprising. The structures of the new independent State are inspired by those of the states of Civilization A, secularized and hostile to the partisans of a political application of religion.

Maccabean Revolt and establishment of the Hasmonean State. The state is structured like a Hellenistic kingdom, and the powers repress, with mercenaries, the revolts of the Pharisees.

Pan-Arabism, Arab socialism and Nasserism. Creation of the Arab League in 1945. The Arab Regimes are independent but have inherited from occidental conceptions of the State and politics, including secularism. Strong repression of Islamist parties.

8) Interventions of Civilization B. Its power is increasingly present.

Intervention of Pompey in the succession of Alexander Jannaeus, and establishment of Herod on the thrown. After his death, deposition of his heir in Judea, which becomes a Roman province, led by a Roman Prefect rather than a Jewish king.

Creation of the State of Israel, closely linked to the USA, 1948 Arab-Israeli War, Six-Day War (1967), Yom Kippur War (1973). Submission of Egypt to the American power in 1978. American intervention through the coup in Iran in 1953 as well as during the Gulf War in 1991 with the deployment of troops in Saudi Arabia. American presence in the world becomes more important and visible.

9) Radicalization of the defenders of a political-religious view of the State, birth of violent groups and rise in power with respect to the presence of Civilization B.

Radicalization of the Pharisees (religious Jews), emergence of the Zealots, refusing submission of Jewish lands to the Roman power.

The supporters of political Islam radicalize themselves: Islamic Revolution of Iran, development of Islamic terror networks and organizations. Islamic fanaticism rejects the submission of Islamic lands to American or Occidental "infidels."

10) A limited attempt at policing the problem fails: the movement gains in strength and size and becomes more of a threat, with increasing potential for violence. The diaspora of Civilization C in the lands of A and B raises the mistrust and hostility of local populations in relation to its distinct way of life, its refusal to integrate and its vindictive spirit.

Limited Roman reprisals do not provide any results. The Zealots become stronger and win partisans. In Rome and in Greece, the Jewish way of life, their privileges as well as the progression of their proselytism exasperate local populations.

Rise of the terrorist networks (Armed Islamic Group of Algeria, Al-Qaeda, Hezbollah…), rise of Salafism and Jihadism in Arab-Muslim countries despite the Occidental interventions seeking to repress authoritarian secular regimes. In Europe, native populations are increasingly mistrusting of Muslim populations and of Islam as a religion, doubting its capacity and willingness to integrate to the Occidental way of life. European peoples start questioning the tolerance of their governments toward the establishment of ways of life that are perceived as incompatible with their civilization.

11) The fanatics of Civilization C aggravate the situation through terrorism, in order to cause a war thought of as eschatological within a religious logic.

Terrorist acts of the Zealots in order to realize the eschatological prophecy of Ezekiel: a war to be won *in extremis* by a small group of chosen ones against the entire world thanks to divine intervention, to be followed by the establishment of the reign of the Messiah.

Terrorist acts of Islamists in order to realize prophecies: a war won in extremis by a small number of chosen ones against the entire world thanks to divine intervention and the appearance of the Mahdi. Multiple attacks against Americans: World Trade Center in 1993, American embassies in Africa.

12) In the face of the rising provocations, which reach an intolerable degree, Civilization B, infuriated, opts for the military solution and crushes the fanatics in bloody wars, repeatedly.

Revolt of Jerusalem and massacre of the legion of Cestius Gallus, governor of Syria. Jewish-Roman Wars: Rome crushes the Zealots and the religious party and destroys the temple. Kitos War in 115-117 and massacre of the Jews in Egypt and Persia. Crushing of the revolt of Simon bar Kokhba in 135.

Events of 1979, attacks in Europe, September 11th attacks. Afghanistan and Iraq wars, the War against Terrorism and the worldwide fight against Al-Qaeda. Military victory against Islamist terror organizations, resurgence of the Islamic State.

13) Confirmation of the dominance of the model of Civilization B. Civilization C is eradicated as a political power.

Jewish diaspora, disappearance of the Zealots, killed in the Siege of Masada. Surviving Pharisees create Rabbinical Judaism.

Secularization of the societies of Arab countries, hope for the establishment of a democratic model after the great revolutions of 2011, progressive disappearance of the remaining radical Islamic organizations, death of Osama bin Laden.

Step 13), for Islam, shows some signs of realization, but the awakening of the Islamic State and its vigor shows that it may not have been completed.

C) A CYCLE ZERO FOR C TOO?

It may seem like we have a problem: for cycles A and B, we have a "Cycle Zero," the Cretan-Mycenaean cycle, which does not present all of the features of their respective cycles but share enough similarities with them to be related, and to constitute the appearance of the phenomenon, which truly takes its full form with Greece and Rome. With the Judaism of Moses and the Islam of Muhammad, we only have two steps.

Thus one can ask if we could find a "Cycle Zero," where the patterns could have begun to appear.

As we have stated before, the ancient origins of Judaism are hard to discern with a high degree of certainty due to the absence of archeological data. The Bible seems to contain exaggerations with respect to what could be confirmed by archeology, and the figure of Moses as he is described is not supported by historical data outside of what is found in the Bible. As a consequence, any work on eras that preceded this one will, at the scientific level, be limited by high uncertainty.

However, we have also noted above that we could surmise that some of the facts stated in the Bible may have a historical foundation, and that the tale, even if considered embellished, could give general indications on ancient events. In addition to the identification of the Patriarch Joseph, who became Vizier of Egypt, with the historical person, the Vizier of Amenhotep III, named Amenhotep, son of Hapu, we can invoke the probable historicity of Abraham. Indeed, a fact that remains poorly known by the broad public is that he seems to appear in an Egyptian execration text, a sort of voodoo Egyptian practice in which misfortune was brought toward an enemy. This text dates from the XIIth dynasty, thus between the XXth and the XVIIIth centuries B.C., and it mentions a certain Abourahan (*'Ibwrhni*), prince of "*Snw'nw*" which could be Samhuna, in the northern half of Canaan, or could correspond to the territory attributed in the Bible to the Tribe of Simeon, in the southern half[42]. In any case, the date and localization correspond to what is generally attributed to Abraham. Furthermore, in the biblical tale, Abraham is expelled from Egypt by the Pharaoh after the Pharaoh had undergone multiple misfortunes for having slept with the wife of Abraham, who the Patriarch had presented as his sister. This pharaonic hostility in the Bible seems to correspond to the desire of a malediction in the execration text mentioning this Abourahan. Here we already have numerous elements justifying a correspondence, even if not demonstrated further by archeology. Thomas Römer, from the Collège de France, seems to believe that the fact that the Bible places Abraham close to Hebron suffices to disqualify this correspondence, since the Egyptian text places Abourahan more to the north. But in the Bible, Abraham travels a lot, and even establishes himself in Haran, which is further north[43]. This reticence seems even more questionable given that the archeology and Egyptology communities have quickly agreed on the fact that the *Israr* of the Merneptah Stele proves the existence of the Israelites in Canaan around 1200 B.C. and that the House of David of the Tel Dan Stele is considered by most a confirmation of the historicity of King David. This Egyptian execration text, which shows four points of correspondence with the biblical tradition (era, location, name and nature of the text) should thus be commonly admitted as proof of the historicity of Abraham (without prejudice on the question of the historical reality of his prophetic mission).

Abraham and Joseph can thus be considered as two points of historicity in the biblical tale, although nothing, at the archeological level, allows us to link Abourahan with Amenhotep, son of Hapu, as the Bible does by presenting Joseph as the descendant of Abraham through Isaac and Jacob, two generations that would be insufficient to fill the five centuries or so that separate the two historical traces. However, as we have seen with Greek mythology, colorful characters are a good way to write History: for oral traditions, it is impossible to treat and preserve information as is done in the *Annales* school, by applying a modern academic treatment of the scientific knowledge of the past, by invoking social movements, economical problems or by producing statistical tables. History is thus often told as that of individuals and lineages, of which the adventures include contextual elements: wars, famines, migrations and alliances, in order to preserve a summary memory of such events.

This traditional process of construction of the historical tale can easily lead one to confound different characters, by attributing to a dominant figure the great realizations of various minor characters, who disappear by the same process. Such process can also merge multiple parallel or successive conflicts into a single one. Furthermore, it tends to erase periods of peace and tranquility, for which there is little place in this type of tale, because of the lack of notable events. The same forgetfulness could apply to what we could call routine agitation periods. As an illustration, we note that the common man in today's time has difficulty telling how much time separates the great historical figures learned in school: how much time separates Clovis from Charles Martel, Charlemagne from Saint Louis, Saint Louis from Francis I, and Francis I from Henri IV. Those are figures that teachers have found useful to use as historical landmarks. They are important enough to summarize a period, or a breaking point, just as it would have been done in an oral tradition, but in the latter case, Clovis would have probably been perceived as the father or grandfather of Charles Martel, Charlemagne the father or grandfather of Saint Louis, Saint Louis that of Francis I and Francis I that of Henri IV. At best, about ten generations total would be taken to represent a thousand years of history; something that would complicate the life of historians trying to find correspondence between oral tradition with the real historical chronology.

One must not neglect the aspect of the intensity of the tale, necessary to its transmission and success. Here the same dramatic mechanism operates as it operates in cinematographic adaptations. Often, the main defect, for purists, of how movies represent history is that the script-writers significantly compress the chronology of the events in order to increase the intensity of the drama.

In practice, this explains why there are always missing generations in the mythological chronology with respect to the historical reality and why we should not expect to find exact correspondence between myths and archeology. We had already noted this for Mycenaean history and the Trojan war. The tales formulated in oral tradition allow the preservation of traces from the past, and for its recipient to have an idea of its cultural roots as well as be able to transmit it without hampering themselves with considerations of secondary importance. Thus, in historiography, to not understand History as first and foremost the acts of a few successive historical characters is a very recent attitude. The academic disdain for events originated in the second half of the XXth century. What seems today to be the primary focus of historical science, the history of societies, has been, up to the XIXth century, very neglected, with the exception of a rare few precursors, such as Ibn Khaldun and Montesquieu. In ancient myths and legends, it is thus the main elements of the tale that can be informative, instead of the details of the adventures or the exactitude of the genealogies.

We will limit ourselves, here, at considering whether the biblical tale anterior to Moses, in its great lines, presents a pattern sufficiently resembling that which we have established for Judaism and Islam.

As it turns out, we can observe a part of the pattern previously established in the history of Abraham that precedes the fleeing from Egypt:

- Abraham is a prophet but also some kind of a warrior (he fights in Genesis, leading a group). He is a nomad who lives in the desert but originally comes from a city belonging to the great Chaldean Civilization (Ur), which he left with his group to go to Haran (in Syria). He brings the promise of plentiful descent, which corresponds to **stage 1**.

- Abraham takes the road of Canaan, where his son Isaac will live all of his life, which corresponds to **stage 2**.

- Then come the times of Isaac and Jacob, the united descent of Abraham, **stage 3**.

- Then come the times of Joseph and his brothers, sons of Jacob. The divisions between the brothers and Joseph (**stage 4**) end up leading all of the family in Egypt, under the reign of the Pharaohs (thus a foreign civilization, but neither of type A or B: Crete and Mycenae are contemporary, but distantly located), **stage 5/6**.

- In the time of The Exodus, the domination of Egypt became important. The Hebrews are reduced to slavery (or at least perceive themselves as such; there was no slavery in pre-Hellenistic Egypt), although we know that slavery can be subjective. Many workers, in Europe, in the XXth century, perceived themselves as slaves of capital, without truly being slaves. Tensions and conflicts with pharaonic power, with a promise for divine support, **stage 11**.

- The Jews are finally expelled from Egypt (Exodus 12, 39) and are exiled as nomads in the desert, **stage 13**.

Thus we find the main pattern: prophet, time of unity, development, time of division, time of foreign domination, time of fighting and time of dispersal.

The period between Abraham (the prophet) and The Exodus (the final dispersion) thus seems to indicate that the Bible does contains the trace of a first iteration of Cycle C. As was the case with the Crete-Mycenae cycle, not all of the steps can be discerned, but the fundamental sequence seems to be present.

2. Cycle D: symmetry of the ancient Assyro-Persian Civilization with the Seljuk and Ottoman Turkish Civilization.

By describing an instance of Cycle C, which establishes the similarities between the political-religious phenomena that are Ancient Judaism and Islam, we have identified these two stages among many others:

5) After centuries of decline, C is dominated by the powers of a foreign civilization, which come under different successive identities.

The Jews are dominated by the Assyrian Empire and then by the Persian Achaemenid Empire.

Arab-Muslims are dominated by the Seljuk Turks and then the Ottoman Turks.

6) After the fall of the foreign civilization, C is dominated by the powers of Civilization A.

The Jews are dominated by Greek powers, who are victorious over the Achaemenid Empire.

Arab lands are colonized by Europe, victorious against the Ottoman Empire.

In these two stages, we observe that the Ancient Judaistic and Arab-Muslim Civilizations have entertained an identical relationship with an external power that is neither of type A or B. We note that these foreign powers, that is, the Assyrian and Persian Empires, and the Seljuk and Ottoman Empires, are vanquished by Civilization A during Stage 6, respectively by Greece and Occidental Europe.

We have already mentioned, in our description of Cycle A, the similar danger that was faced by Greece and Occidental Europe at some point of their history: the progression of the oriental foreign enemy. For Greece, this enemy is the Persian Achaemenid Empire, whose attacks were repelled during the Greco-Persian Wars. For Occidental Europe, it is the Ottoman Empire which was threatening for a long time before being repelled during the Battle of Vienna in the XVIIth century. Thus we observe, at first glance, the existence of multiple similarities between the Assyrian and Persian Empires and the Seljuk and Ottoman Empires. Let us see if we can find more, and if these similarities can form a systematic cycle as was the case with A, B and C.

A) HISTORICAL REMINDERS

The Assyrian and Achaemenid Empires

The Assyrian Empire. The history of the Assyrian Empire started with the rise of the city of Assur, in Mesopotamia. The empire began relatively weak and subordinated to foreign kingdoms, such as that of Mitanni, in the XVth century B.C.. Beginning in the XIVth century B.C., the King of Assur took the title of Great King, which established the empire as a sovereign entity in the region. Assur appropriated important swaths of territories which had belonged to the Mitanni Empire, and became the dominant power of the North of Mesopotamia, limited at its western border by the Hittite Empire and at its southern border by the Babylonians. In the XIIIth century, Assyria grew even more by vanquishing the Hittite Army and temporarily taking over Babylon.

During the three following centuries, Assyria became weaker, but the greater difficulties faced by its neighbors (notably the fall of the Hittite Empire, likely under the assault of the Mycenaeans) allowed it to maintain itself, retracted to its most important centers: Assur and Nineveh.

At the end of the Xth century B.C., a new period of expansion began, interrupted by difficulties during the first half of the VIIIth century B.C., but the expansion restarted during the second half. Reforms allowed the empire to come out victorious against new rivals, in particular against Urartu, allowing the Assyrians to retake Babylon. Palestine was conquered as well as a part of Syria.

The Sargonid Dynasty, from the end of the VIIIth to the end of the VIIth century, marks the apogee of the Assyrian power, which had become a true dominant Empire exerting control over neighboring nations. Egypt to the West, Elam to the East, if not conquered, were at least successfully invaded for a time.

Due to internal dissent and the defection of the Babylonian ally to the Medes, the Empire fell at the end of the VIIth century, shortly after having attained its apogee.

For the following half century, Babylon and the Kingdom of Medes likely shared the old possessions of High Mesopotamia, and the Babylonians took over the Kingdom of Jerusalem, whose population was deported.

The Persian Achaemenid Empire. The Persians were a people living on the margins of the Assyrian Empire during their apogee, just behind Elam, at the Eastern border. Subordinated to the Medes, they rose against their masters in the middle of the VIth century B.C., under the leadership of their king, Cyrus II. Victorious, he established the Persian Achaemenid Empire by taking over the administrative structures of the Medes and by assimilating the neighboring Elamites, after a military victory against them. He also conquered all of Anatolia against the Lydians and all of Mesopotamia, Syria, and Palestine against the Babylonians. At its western border, he extended his empire up to the Indus Valley.

The incredible expansion of the Achaemenid Empire led it to become a threat, on its western front, to Greek cities. Minor Asia and Thrace were subordinated to the Persian power.

At the beginning of the Vth century B.C., the Greco-Persian Wars opposed the Greeks, in particular Athens and Sparta, to the Empire. The war lasted for half a century and concluded with a Greek victory, both on the sea (notably with the Battle of Salamis), and on the land (notably with the Battle of Plataea). The Persian progression toward the West was then stopped, and Greek independence was ensured.

After a century of global stability of the Persian Empire and border wars with the Greek world, the Empire was finally invaded and fell under the attacks of the Greeks led by Alexander the Great of Macedon. It was the end of the Ancient Orient and the beginning of the Hellenistic Orient.

The Turkish Seljuk and Ottoman Empires

The Turkish Seljuk Empire. The Seljuk People get their name from Seljuk, the founder of the Dynasty which reigned over these tribes. They were nomads coming from the steppes located to the north of the Aral Sea, and were related to a broader ethnic group, the Oghuz Turks, over whom they reigned since the end of the Xth century. At this time, the neighboring Ghaznavid Empire, a power that was dominating over Persia and which had profited from the divisions of the Abbasid Caliphate to expand, attempted to subordinate the Seljuks. The sons of Seljuk defied the Ghaznavids, took over Khorasan, and pushed back the Ghaznavids to Afghanistan.

Starting from the Khorasan, which was used as the new base for their power, the Seljuk Turks launched a conquest of all of the occidental possessions of the Ghaznavids, and then conquered the kingdoms that were heirs of the Abbasid Caliphate up to Syria. They also conquered Anatolia against the Byzantine Empire. The reign of Malik-Shah I (1072-1092) marks the apogee of the great Seljuk Empire, which at that time covered almost half of the Muslim world.

At the death of Malik-Shah I, internal divisions caused the fragmentation of the Empire. The Seljuk Dynasty survived in Anatolia, in the Sultanate of Rum, until the beginning of the XIVth century, whereas the remaining regions which had been under control in the times of Malik-Shah I became kingdoms and rival principalities with changing borders.

The Osmanli or Ottoman Turkish Empire. The Ottoman Turks originated in the Oghuz Turkish Tribes having invaded Anatolia under the leadership of the Seljuks. The family rose to power under the reign of Osman (1258-1326, who gave his name to the empire) in the Seljuk Sultanate of Rum, which was in decline at the end of the XIIIth and beginning of the XIVth century. Osman conquered the strong locations of his neighbors,

Byzantine and Turk, and established a powerful army. It was the beginning of an expansion that would last more than three centuries.

The Ottomans first took over most of Anatolia and Greece, and took Constantinople in 1453. The Empire progressed both in the Muslim world and in Christian Europe, for which it constituted a considerable threat.

At the end of the XVIth century, the Turkish Ottoman Empire had reached its apogee: it had subordinated almost all of the Arab-Muslim world, and penetrated Europe up to Vienna, without being able to take it. In 1571, the maritime defeat of Lepanto marked the end of Turkish expansionism toward Europe, confirmed one century later by the terrestrial defeat of Vienna in 1683, which marked the beginning of Ottoman recoil.

The two following centuries are characterized by stagnation and decline: local uprisings and European attacks led the Ottoman Empire to lose the Balkans, Greece, the Maghreb and Egypt. Its participation to the losing side in 1918 led to its loss of Syria, Lebanon, Palestine, Iraq and Arabia, leaving only Turkey, where the Empire died by the hand of Mustafa Kemal Atatürk in 1922.

a) *Presentation of Cycle D*

Let us try to find a common pattern in these two histories.

In **bold**: stage of Cycle D
In upright: corresponding Assyrian and then Persian historical fact
In *italics*: corresponding Seljuk and then Ottoman historical fact

1) A nation begins to develop at the margins of neighboring, stronger powers.

The city of Assur develops at the border between the Mitanni and Babylon.

The Seljuk Turks arrive from the oriental steppe in Khorasan (east of Iran) in the Ghaznavid Empire, where they become stronger.

2) The nation takes over a part of the territories of the Empire to which it belonged until then, and enters an expansionist dynamic.

The city of Assur takes over half of the territories of the Mitanni and faces the Hittites and Babylonians.

The Seljuk Turks become masters of the Khorasan and of the whole western part of the Ghaznavid Empire.

3) The nation establishes an empire which integrates a part of the lands of Civilization C, sparing its historical center.

The Assyrian Empire dominates the Kingdom of Israel, Northern Kingdom of the Jews. Judea remains independent.

The Seljuk Empire takes over the Eastern half of the Arab-Muslim lands (old Abbasid Empire). The Mecca remains under Arab Fatimid control.

4) The nation begins a phase of decline and decomposes, leaving a fragmented political space.

The Assyrian Empire decomposes to the benefit of the Babylonian and Medes kingdoms.

Decomposition of the Seljuk Empire to the benefit of the shahs of Khwarazm and then the Ilkhanate, and the Ayyubid Dynasty of Egypt.

5) A population at the margins of the old empire rises to power.

Rise of the Persians at the margins of the empire (Achaemenids, formerly tributary of the Assyrians).

Rise of the Turkish tribes arrived to Anatolia under the leadership of the Seljuk, with Osman.

6) The new population establishes an empire which takes several elements from the former one, and takes over all of its lands, including the historical center of Civilization C.

The Achaemenid Empire. This new empire covers the old Assyrian territory and extends its domination over Jewish lands, Israel as well as Judea.

The Ottoman Empire. Covers the entire western part of the Seljuk Empire and conquers virtually all Arab lands, including the Mecca.

7) The progression of the empire threatens Civilization A, and absorbs a part of its territories.

The progression of the Achaemenid Empire at its western front threatens Greece. Subordination of the cities of Asia Minor.

The progression of the Ottoman Empire threatens Europe. Conquest of the Balkans and progression up to Austria.

8) Defeats on land and on sea against A. End of the progression.

Defeats against Greece (notably the Battle of Salamis and the Battle of Plataea). End of the western progression.

Defeats against Europe in the Battle of Lepanto and the Battle of Vienna. End of the western progression. Beginning of a stagnation.

9) Recoil of the empire, weakening of the central power and important losses of territories.

Achaemenid recoil: Egypt becomes independent (404 B.C.). Great Satraps' Revolt (370 B.C.).

Ottoman recoil: weakening of the central power. In the XIXth century: loss of Crimea, Maghreb, Balkans and Egypt, colonized by Europe.

10) Complete crumbling against A, the Empire is conquered by Civilization A.

Alexander the Great: fall of the Achaemenid Empire, Greek colonization.

Complete fall with the First World War, most of the Empire is conquered by Europe.

C) A CYCLE ZERO FOR D?

For A and B, we have found a very plausible Cycle Zero in Minoan and Mycenaean history, which is relatively well-known. For Cycle C, we have only found indices in the biblical writings relating to the origins of the Hebrew people, backed by archaeological data that remains very sparse.

If a Cycle Zero occurred for D, it could be in the Mesopotamian period of the Archaic dynasties, and in the Third Dynasty of Ur, since those were the only considerably-sized empires in these regions in these ancient times. The Assyrian Empire would have then inherited of the Sumerian culture by the Babylonian intermediary, just like the Seljuk Turks inherited from Persians by conquering the Ghaznavid Empire.

This hypothesis is tempting since it would show a continuity of the movements in the western direction, a movement which we have already found in Crete, and then in Greek cities and Occidental Europe, from Mycenae to Rome, to America, and then in the Abrahamic Hebrew nucleus, Ancient Judaism, and then the Arab-Muslim world. In the same way, we would have the Mesopotamian Empires, the Assyrian Empire and Persia up to Anatolia and Egypt, and then the Seljuk Empires, and in particular the Ottoman Empire, up to the heart of Europe and Maghreb.

Furthermore, we would have, at this Zero stage, a primitive occurrence of the cycles in a completely separate manner, without contact between A-B, C and D.

Everything we have reviewed up to now seems to confirm our working hypothesis according to which there is indeed a civilizational system: the only limits that we have encountered are due to lacking information in historical data, keeping us from pushing the comparison toward what we have called Cycle Zero.

Nevertheless, we can deepen these first results by looking at other aspects or by analyzing the great lines of the phenomena in order to understand its fundamental mechanisms. This quest toward understanding is necessary before we can claim to be able to use the results of our observations in order to guess what the future has in store for us.

1. Strabon even goes to state that Rome was founded by Greeks, *Géographie, V, 3, 3*, and that the Etruscan King of Rome, Tarquin, would have been, through his father, originating from Corinth, according to Livy, *History of Rome*, I, XXXIV.
2. In order to take back the original title of the work of Ernst Nolte, *La Guerre civile européenne (1917-1945) : nationalsocialisme et bolchevisme*, Paris, 2000.
3. Cf. *infra* our description of Cycle B.
4. Tarquin, the first King of Rome of Etruscan origins, was himself the son of an immigrant from Corinth, and thus a member of the Greek Aristocracy through his father, Demaratus. This constitutes an enlightening element on the precocious influence of Greece on Rome. See Jean-Pierre Martin, Alain Chauvot and Mireille Cébeillac-Gervasoni, *Histoire romaine*, Paris, Armand Colin, 2010, p. 16.
5. We will be relying for most of our information about Minoan and Mycenaean civilizations on René Treuil, Pascal Darcque, Jean-Claude Poursat and Gilles Touchais, *Les civilisations égéennes du Néolithique et de l'Âge du Bronze*, Paris, 2008.
6. René Treuil, Pascal Darcque, Jean-Claude Poursat and Gilles Touchais, *Les civilisations égéennes du Néolithique et de l'Âge du Bronze...*, *op. cit.*, p. 464.
7. Book II, CXLV.
8. In Argos, according to Appolodorus (III, 5-6) and Mycenae, according to Homer's Iliad (IV, 376-381).
9. According to the indications provided by Herodotus, the great realizations of Heracles would be dated to the middle of the XIVth century B.C., and the Trojan War would be dated to the middle of the XIIIth century. Hyginus, in his tenth fable, states that Nestor received from Apollo the grace of living three generations (Hyginus writes *tria saecula*, which are not to be understood as centuries but

as ancient generations, thus 33 years and 4 months, that is, a third of a century). Nestor was thus gratified by a life of a hundred years, which separates its young age in the time of Heracles and his old age at the time of the Trojan War. This probably constitutes the basis for the calculation of Herodotus.

10. In these Hittite documents, the sovereign states that he has conquered twenty-two countries including Taruisa and Wilusa, where we find the two names of Troy and Ilion.

11. S.P. Morris, "A Tale of Two Cities", *American Journal of Archaeology*, 93, 1989, p. 532.

12. For the reusing of the term *Danaoi* by the Egyptians, some have also evoked the term *Tanaju*, appearing in the annals of Thutmose III, in the XVth century B.C., and in the mortuary of Amenhotep III, in the XIVth century B.C..

13. Robert Drews, *The End of the Bronze Age: Changes in Warfare and the Catastrophe Ca. 1200 B. C*, Princeton, 1996, p. 49 where he gives as a count of enemy casualties: 6359 Libyans, 222 Shekelesh, 742 Tursha, 2201 Ekwesh, 200 Lukka and Shardana.

14. Trevor Bryce, *The Kingdom of the Hittites*, Oxford, 1999, p. 147.

15. I have reused the translation proposed here (French version): http://www.archeostudio.net/44.html

16. *Épitomé*, VI, 29-30.

17. Translation by Mario Meunier, 1943, http://iliadeodyssee.texte.free.fr/aatexte/meunier/odysmeunier/odysmeunier14/odyssmeunier14.htm

18. René Treuil, Pascal Darcque, Jean-Claude Poursat and Gilles Touchais, *Les civilisations égéennes du Néolithique et de l'Âge du Bronze...*, *op. cit.*, p. 382.

19. *Ibid.*, p. 383.

20. *Épitomé*, VI, 23-24.

21. Cf. Giovanni Tosetti, « La dernière génération héroïque, un parcours historico-religieux et sémio-narratif, d'Hésiode au ps.-Apollodore », *Actes du Xe colloque du CIERGA, Kernos*, 19, 2006. http://kernos.revues.org/440#tocto2n5

22. See Pierre Carlier, « *Qa-si- re-u* et *qa-si -re-wi-ja* », *Aegeum*, Liège, n° 12, 1995, p. 355. We find a beautiful synthesis of current knowledge on positions in the hierarchy and the meaning of the terms *wa -na-ka* and *qa-si- r-u* in Jan Paul Crieelard's, "The '*Wanax* to *Basileus* model' reconsidered: authority and ideology after the collapse of the Mycenaean palaces" and "*The 'Dark Ages' revisited, acts of an international symposium in memory of William D. E. Coulson," University of Thessaly, Volos, 14-17 June 2007, Vol. 1*, p. 83-111.

23. The identification of the kingdom of Ahhiyawa as belonging to the Mycenaean Empire ruling over the Aegean Sea is the thesis that makes the most sense within our theory of cycles. See *Les civilisations égéennes*, p. 368.

24. For this brief review of the history of the Jewish people and of Ancient Israel, we will mostly use the Hebrew Bible and the synthesis of Israël Finkelstein and Neil Asher Silberman, *The Bible Unearthed, Archaeology's New Vision of Ancient Israel and the Origin of Its Sacred Texts*. Touchstone, 2002, as well as Martin Goodman's, *Rome and Jerusalem: The Clash of Ancient Civilizations*, 2008.

25. Israël Finkelstein, *The Bible Unearthed*, p. 180.

26. *Ibid.*, pp. 188-189.

27. Gn 15, 13.

28. Cf. Joseph Davidovits, *La Bible avait raison, tome 1, L'archéologie révèle l'existence des Hébreux en Égypte*, Paris, 2005, as well as *La Bible avait raison, tome 2, Sur les traces de Moïse et de l'Exode*, Paris, 2006 and *De cette fresque naquit la bible*, Paris, 2009.

29. http://www.egyptos.net/egyptos/histoire/la-premiere-greve-connue-de-l-histoire.php

30. *Contre Appion, I, XXIII*

31. II, 47.

32. Davidovits believes that the origin of the Levites, a Jewish tribe dedicated to serving the Temple in the times of the Kingdom of Israel, a tribe to which Moses belonged, according to the Bible, is supported by the fact that the brother of Amenhotep son of Hapu, named Heby (a name which is close to Levi, brother of Joseph, father of the tribe of the Levites) would have been tasked, with his descendants, to maintain the funeral temple of Amenhotep, son of Hapu. This would explain, notably, why the Hebrew tradition states that, contrarily to other Hebrews, the Levites were always exempt of work in Egypt. This would be the memory of the Exodus uniting two very different castes: the servants of the funeral temple of Amenhotep, son of Hapu, and a more important group of workers, perhaps those of Deir el-Medina.

33. *Contre Appion, I*.

34. The fact that a part of the biblical text concerning Joseph has originated from an Egyptian text could echo, if it is founded, the thesis of Christoph Luxenberg according to which the Quran would be largely recopied from syro-aramaic Christian lecturers. Christoph Luxenberg, *The Syro-Aramaic reading of the Koran: a contribution to the decoding of the language of the Koran*, 2007. Moses, like Muhammad, would have thus founded a new religion by reusing not only beliefs but also texts that were more ancient.

35. Israël Finkelstein, *The Bible Unearthed*, p. 212.

36. Eduard Lohse, *Le Milieu du Nouveau Testament*, Paris, Seuil, 1953, p. 152. The authors estimate the number to be 4.5 million. *L'Histoire Universelle des Juifs* published under the direction of Elie Barnavi and Denis Charbit (Hachette, 2002) gives a similar estimate.

37. Bernard Lazare, *L'Antisémitisme, son histoire et ses causes*, Paris, 1894. Available in full on Wikisource: http://fr.wikisource.org/wiki/L'Antisémitisme

38. *Contre Appion*, II, XX. Translation of René Harmand, Revised and annotated by Théodore Reinach, 1911. This translation is available at http://remacle.org/bloodwolf/historiens/Flajose/Apion2.htm

39. This eschatological belief and its correspondence to Jewish messianism in the Antiquity formed the basis of my thoughts on the general parallel between the history of Judaism and Islam. It was brought to my attention by my theologian friend Arnaud Dumouch and his brother Rodolphe, whom I thank.

40. Notably *Eurabia: L'axe Euro-Arabe*. Jean-Cyrille Godefroy, 2006.

41. Curiously, the biblical text taken literally, with the revelation of Moses in the desert and the military conquest of Canaan by Josuah, delivers a history that is even more similar to the beginnings of Islam than that which could be recovered by archeological research.

42. René Dussaud, « Nouveaux textes égyptiens d'exécration contre les peuples syriens », *Syria*, Tome 21, fascicule 2, 1940, p. 177-177, http://www.persee.fr/web/revues/home/prescript/article/syria_0039-7946_1940_num_21_2_4188

43. http://annuaire-cdf.revues.org/182#tocto2n1

Chapter II

General remarks on the phenomenon

Our description of the cycles raises many questions. While our analysis may have identified a phenomenon, we still know very little about it other than its existence. In this second chapter, we want to focus on studying the mechanisms at play, by exploring the gears behind the observations, and hopefully developing a mechanistic understanding of the cycles.

In the absence of a pre-existing method, we will start by making certain observations on the cycles that are already established, in order to isolate notable characteristics. How can, from one cycle to the other, the location and geographic scale change, while the A, B, C and D cycles seem to entertain similar relationships producing a global system that we could call a "supercycle." From these observations, we will draw a first definition and a first conclusion on the nature of these cycles.

We will then see that it is possible to deepen our understanding of these cycles by considering the history of the identified civilizations relating to other aspects: economics, religion, scientific developments, military… or by focusing on a specific part of that civilization, in order to identify what could be called "sub-cycles."

Finally, we will attempt, on the basis of these remarks, to reach conclusions about the value of these phenomena for a theory of History.

I: OBSERVATIONS ON THE CYCLICAL PHENOMENON

Showing the existence of the cycles is one thing, but understanding their origin and function is another. Before we can attempt to explain the phenomenon, we must improve our understanding of the civilizations concerned by the phenomenon. For this, let us review the elements already obtained as an ensemble and try to extract the constants that could point to the underlying rules.

1. The change of entity (peoples, locations)

The first observation we can make on the previously-described cycles is that the entity affected by a given stage changes from one cycle to the other. First, we had the Greek cities, Rome, the Jewish People and the Assyrian and Persian empires, and in the following cycle, we had Occidental Europe, the USA, the Arab-Muslim world and the Turkish empires.

The phenomenon is thus not purely cyclical from this point of view, since the cycle does not apply to the same entities: locations and people do change.

2. The change of scale

In addition to the change in which entity the cycle applies to, we also observe a change of scale: each new cycle leads to a gain in geographic and political scale for the affected civilization.

Thus, if we observe the AB couple since Cycle Zero, it goes from Crete-Mycenae to Europe-America, and we can see in each step the growth of the concerned entities: from the Cretan and Mycenaean palaces to Greek Cities and Rome, and then from the cities of the countries of Europe to the United States of America. The case of America and its rivals (Russia, China) leaves us to think that we are headed for super-countries, covering almost entire continents. The gain in scale is such that, in comparison, the population of only the city of New York (without its suburban area) is superior to the whole population of Roman Italy.

The same can be said of Cycle C: we pass from a Jewish domination of Palestine to the Arab-Muslim domination of all of North Africa and the Middle-East.

For Cycle D, the observation is more mitigated. While the area concerned has changed, the surface area covered by the Ottoman Empire at its apogee is not very different from that of the Persian Achaemenid Empire, although a displacement is observed.

The continuity of our historical model independent of this change of scale seems to evoke the mathematical concept of homothety (which perhaps constitutes a better mathematical equivalent for our concept than that of symmetry, which we have used previously). We could say, for instance, that Europe is the projection of Ancient Greece, in a homothetic transformation of which the center and the ratio remain to be determined[1].

3. The links from one cycle to the next

We note that there are two types of links between cycles: on the one hand, the vertical links between the cycles of the same type, and on the other hand, the horizontal links formed by interactions between the cycles of different types, that is, A, B, C and D.

A) VERTICAL LINKS: CONTINUITY BETWEEN THE CYCLES OF A SAME TYPE

The cycles of a same type systematically present links of succession which leads to a genuine continuity despite the differences in the concerned entities. This is not an observable process at specific moments of History, but rather a continuous process, which goes on without interruption. The way in which the link presents themselves differs for each cycle.

The case of the AB Couple

We have seen that the A and B cycles are particularly linked to each other. They function as a dynamic binomial. Arnold Toynbee was not wrong when he spoke of an Aegean Civilization, a Hellenistic one and an Occidental one. We have simply evoked a similar progression between a Creto-Mycenaean, a Greco-Roman and a Euro-American cycle. Nevertheless, this great historian had not described the full depth of the parallels between these societies and the important distinction between what we have called Model A and Model B. Their particular configuration makes it such that a given Cycle A is not directly linked to the next Cycle A, but linked only indirectly through the intermediary of B. Similarly, a given Cycle B is not directly linked to the next Cycle B, but goes through the intermediary of A.

Let us remind ourselves that Cycle A is absorbed by Cycle B in the stages that we have separately described before but that form, in reality, a single stage:

- from Cycle A **11) All of the states forming Civilization A are taken under tutelage by the superpower of Civilization B.**
- from Cycle B **6) The States of A become dominated by B.**

Cycle A thus concludes into Cycle B, which in turn concludes with, notably, the two following steps:

7) Absolute hegemony over the known world, absence of rivals (it is at this step that Stage 1 of the next Cycle A occurs).

9) Decline and dismemberment of Empire B (corresponds to Stage 2 of the next Cycle A).

where we can see that the two first stages of Cycle A occur during the domination of B.

Inversely, B reappears under the influence of A, as noted in Stage 1:

1) A human community is founded by a pre-existing civilization, under the influence of Civilization A.

And since A is born under the domination of B, we can affirm that there is indeed a continuity between a given Cycle B and the next, as well as between a given Cycle A and the next.

The case of C

Islam is greatly inspired from Judaism, and its precepts have inherited the Laws of Moses. There is an obvious filiation between Islam and Judaism: Abrahamic heritage, the reuse of the biblical character of Ishmael… Judaism, having been dispersed after the Jewish-Roman wars, can thus be seen as having carried the seeds for a rebirth under another form. The desert of Arabia was home to a Jewish population which has no doubt influenced the doctrine of Muhammad.

There is thus a link between the last stage of the Judaistic Cycle C (the victory of Rome (B), which expelled the Jews from Judea), and the first step of the Arab-Muslim Cycle C (the birth of Arab Islam in the desert of Arabia).

C truly follows C.

The case of D

For Cycle D, the link seems to exist as well. The Turkish Seljuk Empire built itself by conquering the old regions of the Persian Empire, and reached its apogee under the reign of Malik-Shah I who had, as a vizier, Nizam al-Mulk, an Iranian who imprinted the Seljuk state with the Persian Imperial heritage in terms of administration. The Turks, nomadic warriors coming from the steppes, reused a great share of the Persian Imperial tradition by becoming sedentary in the Middle-East and by solidifying their domination over it.

B) HORIZONTAL LINKS: THE RELATIONSHIPS BETWEEN A, B, C AND D

Examples of links

We note that between two cycles, the relationships are constant.

For instance, a Type A Civilization always entertains the same relationship with a Type B Civilization, that is:

- A influences B (Crete influenced Mycenae; Greece influenced Rome through the Etruscans and Greater Greece; Europe influenced the USA through founding and trade).

- B subordinates A (Mycenae conquers Crete, Rome conquers Greece, the USA turns Europe into a vassal).

Other example: Type C Civilization always has the same relationship with A and B:

- A subordinates C (Hellenistic conquest of Palestine, European colonization of the Arab-Muslim world).

- C emancipates from A while preserving certain cultural and political contributions (Jewish Hasmonean Kingdom, Arab nationalist regimes).

- B intervenes in the affairs of C (establishment of Herod the Great by Rome and creation of the province of Judea, establishment by the US of the Shah of Iran and deal concluded with the Egyptian and Saudi regimes, intervention in Iraq in 1991).

- C faces a rise of the political-religious fanaticism and goes into a war with B (Jewish-Roman wars, American war against terrorism, Iraq, Afghanistan…).

These interactions are often absent from Cycle Zero due to the distance separating the starting points for different types of civilizations: the coasts of the Aegean Sea for AB, the surroundings of Palestine for C, Mesopotamia for D. Nevertheless, we note that A and B, in contact since Cycle Zero, have indeed maintained the relationships described above.

Notes on the intervals

While the interactions appear constant across the cycles, we can still observe intervals between the relationship and the internal unfolding of a cycle.

For instance, a Type A civilization always has the same relationship with D:

- A is threatened by D (Greece threatened by the Persian Empire; Europe threatened by the Ottoman Empire).

- A stops the advances of D on land and sea (Greece victories on land and sea during the Greco-Persian Wars, end of the Persian progression in Greece; victories of the Battle of Lepanto and of the Battle of Vienna over the Ottoman empire, end of the Turkish progression in Europe).

- A conquers and colonizes the Empire of D (conquest of the Persian Empire by the Greeks with Alexander the Great; conquest of the former territories of the Ottoman Empire by the European powers).

However, these steps do not occur at the same place in the internal unfolding of Cycle A: for Greece, the victory of the Greco-Persian Wars occurred after the transformation of Athens into a democracy. For Europe, the victory over the Ottoman Empire occurred before the transformation into a democracy. Similarly, for Greece, the conquest of the Persian Empire occurred after the Peloponnesian War. For Europe, the conquest of the territories of the Ottoman Empire occurred before the Second World War, a total war sealing its destiny as a dominating power.

We still observe a consistency despite the variation of intervals: the two events, relative to the internal unfolding of Cycle A, occur earlier in the European iteration than in the Greek iteration. We note that A remains similarly constant in its internal unfolding as it relates to its relationship with D. Since the relationships between A and D remain the same despite the different timings, we can deduce that the interval is relative to the point of contact between the two cycles. The Greek Cycle A has encountered the Persian Cycle D later than the European Cycle A has encountered the Ottoman Cycle D.

In summary, we can conclude that the four cycles A, B, C and D form a system of cycles articulated between one another, a historical "supercycle" combining simpler cycles interacting through relationships that are also cyclical.

Nevertheless, we can ask whether this system of cycles is stable. Indeed, if it was formed by the contact between cycles which previously were independent (see the case of Cycle Zero), nothing guarantees that the way they are ordered with respect to one another is meant to last. Let us reconsider the example of the conflict between Greek cities and the Persian Empire, which occurred later when compared with the conflict between European nations and the Ottoman Empire. If a new cycle succeeds to the current cycle (Europe, America, Islam…) and that the interval diminishes further, then the next Civilization A will be confronted even sooner to an opposition of the next Civilization D with respect to its internal unfolding. Such an earlier confrontation could be fatal, if this civilization has not sufficiently developed in order to overcome the threat. The succession of Cycles A (and therefore of B, which is heavily linked to it) would then conclude, and perish with the system of cycles that we have observed.

4. The entities outside of the cycles: notes on the distribution of roles

The Peloponnesian War and its European equivalent, the two World Wars, have considerably weakened these two civilizations and have caused the loss of their colonial empire to emerging powers. Greece, just like Europe, passed under the tutelage of Rome/America after their request for help against an enemy. Among the first beneficiaries of the weakening of Greece after the Peloponnesian War was Carthage, which took over Sicilia and extended its influence at the expense of Greece. Macedonia also benefited from this weakening, by establishing its hegemony over Greece. This is mirrored by the USSR benefiting from the weakening of Western Europe, in particular of the disappearance of the German power, in order to take over Eastern and Central Europe. On the other hand, it was against Macedonia that Greek cities requested help from Rome, two hundred years after the Peloponnesian War, while Europe entered the American Empire by requesting its help against the German threat during the Second World War, and, in the process, protected itself against the Russian Giant.

We note that the same country can play one or many roles in the cycle, as the USSR played the role of both Carthage and Macedonia relative to Rome and Greek Cities (let us note, however, that against Rome, Carthage and Macedonia were allied: there is thus a repetition in the interaction between Carthage-Macedonia/Rome and USSR/USA). We also note that a given event can play one or many roles in a given cycle. For instance, while the wars between European nations were the initial cause of the American intervention in Europe, the wars between Greek cities was not the cause of the Roman intervention in Greece, which only came two hundred years later due to other events.

5. Cycles and linearity: the "qualitative leap" of each iteration

We have already noted the continuity which exists in the link between one cycle and the next. Let us also observe that each iteration seems to repeat a "qualitative leap" in that we see on each iteration a significant increase of the potential of concerned societies. Thus the "Greek miracle" of Ancient Greece has an echo in the Age of Enlightenment and in the industrial revolution that marked the history of Europe.

It may be the case that these qualitative leaps are possible due to the combination between the cyclical evolution with the conservation of the inheritance from the previous cycle, allowing amplification by recurrence[2] of human capacities in the domains of sciences, arts, etc.

6. Conclusions about the nature of cycles

What are these cycles made of? We note that many of the mechanisms observed appear relatively mundane and not unique to the cycles described[3]. For instance, the fact that Civilization B is born from the influence of Civilization A before surpassing it in power and dominating it, such as was the case with Rome/Greece and USA/Europe, does not appear to be a phenomenon specific to these civilizations. We find the same relationship in the history of oriental peoples with the Persian people, which takes the Assyrian heritage and succeeds to this empire, or with the Seljuk Turks who, after having been the auxiliaries of the last representatives of a Persian Empire, become their masters while conserving many elements of the Persian Empire, particularly their administrative structure.

Similarly, the fact that an empire falls under the invasion of a less civilized people, and that a mix occurs between the ruins of the empire and the culture of the occupants, leading to the rise of a new nation, is a common historical phenomenon. We certainly observe this phenomenon in the invasion of the Mycenaean Empire by the Dorians, which results in the apparition of Greek Civilization. We also see it in the invasion of the Roman Empire by the barbarians and the apparition of Christian Occident. However, we see the same type of unfolding with the invasion of the Sasanian Empire by the Arabs, and in the invasion of the Chinese Empire by the Mongols of Genghis Khan.

The cycles are thus not unique because of the content of each step they go through, which can be individually found elsewhere, but rather because of the order of these steps. It is not single events that are to be compared between Ancient Greece and Modern Europe, but the evolution of these civilizations, which adopt a similar trajectory in all domains (artistic, sociopolitical, geopolitical). The cycles we have observed can thus be viewed as *complex combinations of mechanisms* (social, political, etc.) that are not necessarily unique to the civilizations studied.

The combinations, however, do constitute differentiated cycles, because Cycle A in its full precision does not apply to civilizations of type B, C, or D (and reciprocally), nor to any other civilizations to my knowledge.

Thus, if we must define them, then the models or cycles that we have described behave as *stable and periodical historical structures*, and are in some way *self-replicative*, having appeared spontaneously on the basis of the universal rules of human psychology. We can thus say that humanity, throughout History, has taken the shape of multiple civilizations and cultures, but behaves in the way of what is referred to in mathematics as cellular automata, a sort of model which, from simple rules of behaviors that may seem unstable at the individual level, produces stable complex structures at the macroscopic level[4].

These structures, as we have noted above, are *stable and periodical*. The structure of the ABCD supercycle repeats, and is currently in its second occurrence. The structures A, B, C and D, we have noted, were also emerging before in Cycle Zero, where they were also individually stable, and were maintained after they were first observed, despite the appearance of novel points of frictions that did not exist in Cycle Zero.

This mechanism is analogous to what is known to occur to living organisms in biology. While the two mechanisms operate at a different scale, they share many similarities. From this standpoint, this ABCD supercycle could be considered a "historical ecosystem".

These structures are also, in some way, self-replicative. A, B, C and D do not appear from anywhere, but rather entertain a relationship with the civilizations of the previous cycle (with a particular case for the AB couple).

Pursuing the biological analogy, self-replication in biology implies the transmission of information, which in our case is DNA. For the observed civilizations, the information appears to be contained in the culture that survives the institutions and allows them to be reborn. For instance, Greek Philosophy became Roman Law, and biblical religious precepts became the precepts of other religions.

Thus the intuition of authors like Oswald Spengler, a century ago, according to which civilizations encounter cycles like living organisms, is correct, but not because civilizations reproduce what living organisms do. Rather, it is because civilizations, like living organisms, are the product of mathematical rules, which result in the spontaneous emergence of stable and/or periodical complex structures from simple rules.

II: A DEEPER UNDERSTANDING OF THE CYCLES

The cycles we have presented in the first chapter must not be understood as a finished work. We do not claim to have exhausted every possible similarity and the cycles could be subject to the addition of new stages or made more precise in their description. Here, I will show three examples of how these cycles can be studied more precisely. Firstly, we will show that comparative research allows to identify patterns in the evolution of the very character of civilizations: politics, institutions, arts, etc. Secondly, we will show that the cycles described can also be subjected to a "zooming effect." For this we will adopt a comparative approach on a specific subject: the nature and the role of secret societies in scientific and political history in Ancient Greece and Modern Europe. Finally, we will provide an example of a "sub-cycle" completing the main one and explain some of its stages.

1. A similar evolution of all the aspects of society

We will describe the similarity of the evolution of society in all its aspects for Cycle A and B. This two-cycle approach will allow not only to reinforce the hypothesis of the existence of cycles, by showing their concrete character, but also deepen our understanding of their specificity in order to show that they do not constitute an arbitrary intellectual construct.

A) RETURN TO CYCLE A

We will show that a Type A Civilization encounters a particular evolution in the institutional, political, social, cultural, artistic, religious and scientific domains. In order to demonstrate the similarity of this evolution between Ancient Greece and European Civilization, we will employ the previously-employed comparative method.

As is the case for any progression throughout History, it is difficult to develop an incontestable and absolute cut-out of the events. In the absence of real edges to historical phenomena, we propose a pattern formed by five periods in order to show the similarity between the evolution of Ancient Greece and Europe on the subjects we have identified, and we title these periods according to the state structure of that time, which generally reflects the structure of the entirety of society. Because each period can last many centuries, the description of each of them will remain broad and underscore only the major events and changes of the time, while presenting the parallels for both civilizations.

Thus, again:

In bold: designation of the period
In upright: corresponding Greek historical fact
In italics: corresponding European historical fact

1) Primary gestational period—Absence of State
(Greek Dark Ages, *Middle Age of the VIth-XIth centuries*)

Political institutions: Aristocratic order based on the ownership of land and war. Fragmented powers.

Absence of Greek Cities. Lords and Warrior-Kings are ruling and adopting a Noble lifestyle: Hunting, games…

Golden Age of Feudalism: absence of a central power, governance by Lords, appearance of the Knights.

Society/Law: Caste system, primitive modes of justice. Rural society, peasantry and communal populations.

Populations formed by free or semi-free individuals, as well as slaves, controlled by Lords.

Society is divided in three orders: clerks, warriors and peasants. Absence of urban centers, small rural communities centered around agriculture. Trade is limited.

Arts/Culture: Art is almost exclusively religious. Theater, representational art, and architecture are limited to religion. Exception for literature, which celebrates the ancient heroes in line with the values of the ruling aristocracy.

Monumental constructions are religious. Theater is a Dionysian cult. Poetry, notably with Homer's Iliad and Odyssey, celebrates historical facts and characters in an embellished manner, with an epic tone.

Art is only present in religious sanctuaries. Wealthy lords construct their fortresses instead of luxurious palaces. Theater is limited to Christian mysteries and religious representations. Culture of minstrels and troubadours, with heroic recitals pleasing the Lords, cult of the Knights' accomplishments, gestural songs about Charlemagne and his companions (The Song of Roland), then Matter of Britain.

Religion: Common religion for the whole of the nebulous Civilization (not yet structured with nation states). Religion is a factor of cultural unity for lands deprived of a central power. Superstition is dominant.

The Greek people shares a common form of polytheism. Later, the Olympic Games and the Sanctuary of Delphi will remain common markers of Greek religion.

Catholicism is the sole expression of Christianity in Occidental Europe. The lack of education is important, even among the clergy.

Sciences: Science is virtually confounded with religion. Nature is explained with myths and beliefs.

Greek mythology is the only source of explanations for nature.

Almost complete absence of the rational process and of any understanding of nature.

Relations with the external world: Period of isolation and resistance to foreign threats. Civilization, economy and technologies are characterized by a clearly lower level of development compared to more evolved contemporaneous civilizations.

Absence of any form of expansionism. Very limited civilizational developments in comparison to Egypt and Oriental Empires.

Resistance to Muslim pressure in the Mediterranean Sea and to Nordic invasions. Clear inferiority in comparison to the Arab and Byzantine civilizations.

Methods of warfare: War is mostly an affair for aristocrats, armies are few and used for private wars.

War is limited to lords, combatting on chariots.

Feudal wars. Impossibility of amassing great masses of men for long periods.

2) Secondary gestational period—Normalization and reappearance of a central power.

(Xth-VIIth centuries B.C., *Middle Age of the XIth-XVth centuries*)

Political institutions: Appearance, from among the aristocracy, of a structural central power.

The first Cities are born, Athenian Synoecism.

Kingdoms that would eventually become prosperous are appearing gradually: France, England, Germanic world, Spain, with the seed of a central power for each entity.

Society/Law: Development of a bourgeoisie which stimulates trade, development of urban centers which are more secure for trade.

Development of Ionian commerce, currency minting, development of a merchant class.

Rebirth of commerce, development of cities and fairs. Rebirth of Roman Law, increasing judicial security.

Arts/Culture: Art begins to detach from religion. The enrichment of a bourgeois class and the establishment of a developing central power funds new forms of art, sometimes on profane themes.

Development of luxurious furniture: ceramic vases, decorated jars… Introduction of naturalistic elements coming from Orient.

Development of profane pictorial representations (ex: Bayeux Tapestry, The Lady and the Unicorn, the Arnolfini Portrait of Van Eyck, luxurious furniture…)

Religion: Religion remains an important aspect of society, but the supernatural loses its status as the only source of explanation for the world.

Decline of traditional mythical explanations with the appearance of natural philosophy.

Conciliation between faith and reason with Thomas d'Aquin and scholasticism.

Sciences: Beginning of the search for causes beyond mere observation. Birth of reason. First explanations of the world that do not directly appeal to the supernatural.

Development of natural philosophy with Miletus. Search for first causes and first principles.

Scholasticism, rediscovery of Greek philosophers. Rediscovery of Roman Law, creation of Procedural Law, withdrawal from superstitious practices such as trial by ordeal.

Relations with the external world: Affirmation of sovereignty and first offensive against foreign powers, first movement for colonization. The economical and technological gap with respect to other great civilizations diminishes.

First colonies in the Black Sea and the south of Italy.

Crusades and foundation of the colonial entity of the Crusader states, reconquest of Spain.

Methods of warfare: Development of more massive armies, assembled under a senior command functioning under a traditional aristocratic system.

Transition toward the Hoplite army for cities.

Accruing of royal powers allows the unification of major armed forces. Philip II of France enrolls the royal militias in the Battle of Bouvines, creation of permanent armies in England and France, abandonment of the feudal Hueste.

3) Renaissance Period—Consolidation of the State
(VIIth-VIth century B.C., *XVIth-XVIIth century*)

Political Institutions: At the outset of a period of gestation, the State is established as a political entity that concentrates public legislative, executive and judiciary powers.

The State has completed its normalization, reforms of Draco, Solon, Peisistratids, Lycurgus.

Renaissance. Establishment of Royal absolutism.

Society/Law: Thanks to the safety guaranteed by a concentrated and efficient public power, trade increases, the bourgeois class grows and extends its social influence (appearance of large bourgeois fortunes). This class takes a great political weight and tends to replace the old warrior aristocracy whose protective role was taken over by the state. Beginnings of the rational organization of justice. Growth of cities.

The reforms of Draco and Solon rationalize the management of the State.

Royal justice becomes rational and supplants ecclesiastic jurisdictions. Royal officers are often enriched commoners.

Arts/Culture: Art becomes profane. Theater turns away from religion, loses its cultural aspects and becomes political, philosophical and bourgeois. Rediscovery of the classics from the previous Type A Civilization.

Greek theater becomes philosophical and political, straying from the Dionysian tradition.

Rediscovery of Greco-Roman Art, development of sumptuous palaces, development of profane theater (Shakespeare, Molière...).

Religion: Tensions between the emancipation movement and traditional beliefs. Progressive withdrawal of religion to the benefit of sciences and philosophy. Differentiation of beliefs between different states.

Development of the cult of the founding hero, and specific cults for each city.

Reduction in the prestige of theological studies to the benefit of Law studies. Growth of the Nobles of the Robe. Reforms and appearance of national religions (Peace of Augsburg and Cuius region, eius religio, i.e. "whose realm, their religion").

Sciences: Rise of philosophy. Reason divorces from religious beliefs and becomes inquiring. Birth of schools of thought. Development of astronomy, medicine, mathematics. Decline of mythical and traditional explanations.

Development of philosophy, rational approach to understanding nature. Pythagoreanism, sophists. Tensions with traditional religion: Anaxagoras is accused of impiety and atheism, similarly to Protagoras.

Philosophy develops and spreads thanks to printing. Conflicts between science and religion: executions of Giordano Bruno, Étienne Dolet...

Relations with the external world: Decisive victory over foreign threats. The technological and economical gap is no more. Exploration movements are initiated, based on new navigational techniques, establishment of first colonies.

Greco-Persian Wars, victories against the Persian Achaemenid Empire. The colonization movement of Greece extends toward western Mediterranean territories and the Black Sea.

Defeats of the Ottoman Empire and end of its progression in Europe, thanks to the creation of new boats equipped with more advanced rudders and navigational instruments (compass...). Discovery of America, creation of colonies.

Methods of warfare: Disappearance of private wars, development of permanent and professional armies. Caste system is abolished.

Appearance of the Hoplite citizen-soldiers. The fighting style changes toward a more collective enterprise instead of the aristocratic duel.

Wars occur between kingdoms, permanent army becomes the norm, the preponderance of the aristocracy is limited to higher command and does not constitute the main driving force of war as was the case during the time of knighthood.

4) Classical Period—The Nation state
(VIth-IVth centuries B.C., *XVIIth-XXth centuries*)

Political institutions: Establishment of democracy. Progressive extension of the concept of rights to the citizenry. Development of an identity around States, supported by historical glorification and celebration of benefactor heroes from the community. Virulent and violent competition between States.

Reform of Cleisthenes, Athenian democracy, isonomia, rise of the antagonism between Sparta and Athens.

English and French revolutions. Citizenship is extended progressively: central suffrage, and then universal male suffrage... Appearance of nationalism, cult of the nation, founder-heroes...

Society/Law: Almost complete disappearance of the aristocracy. Movement for the equality of rights between citizens, priority of the law, softening of the customs (notably of legal punishment). The great urban centers reach record sizes.

Democracy transfers the power of the Eupatrids to the citizens of Athens. Reform of Cleisthenes, appearance of the death penalty by poisoning, suppression of torture for free men.

The noble titles inherited from the Middle age lose any meaning and privilege. Government operates by law. Softening of legal penalties (end of corporal punishment, quick death penalty). Strong urbanization.

Arts/culture: Development of entertainment. Art loses virtually any religious significance.

Theater becomes a popular form of entertainment.

Theater, opera and importantly cinema become entertainment spectacles, often with little philosophical or political meaning.

Religion: Religion is excluded from the public sphere through rationalization of the political domain. Anti-religious reactions. Intellectuals are attempting to find a rational origin for traditional beliefs.

End of magical-religious monarchies. Euhemerism (theory attributing to the cult of divinities an origin in ancient kings, heroes or historical characters who, with time, because they were highly admired, became perceived as divine).

End of the alliance between the throne and the clergy. Political emancipation from the religious. Mystical theses (Jesus Christ would not have existed; the Gospels would be literary constructions taking mythological elements from the Orient in order to construct an archetypal figure).

Sciences: Development of general education and organized teaching systems. Knowledge is no more esoteric and becomes open to all.

Development of general education by the sophists, appearance of the illustrious schools of Philosophy: Plato's academy, Aristotle's Lyceum.

Development of mass education, public schools.

Relations with the external world: Explosion of the movement for colonization. Complete submission of all old enemies, control over maritime routes. Worldwide hegemony. Economic, technological and scientific supremacy. A peak of civilization is attained.

The Greek movement for colonization of the coasts of the Mediterranean Sea intensifies, Greeks dominate the Northern side (and after Alexander the Great[5] the whole Oriental half).

Colonization of two thirds of all world lands, destruction of the Ottoman Empire, worldwide supremacy.

Methods of warfare: Massive armies, highly disciplined infantry. Development of conscription. War becomes increasingly costly in terms of human lives lost.

The Hoplite citizen-soldiers are no more sufficient in order to conduct wars, which are becoming increasingly terrible. Enrollment of non-citizens.

Popular sovereignty and nationalism cause the appearance of gigantic armies. Hecatombs of the revolutionary and Napoleonian wars, and then two World Wars, with enrollment of the colonial populations.

5) Late period—End of sovereign nations
(Starting from the IVth century B.C., *starting from 1945*)

Political institutions: Durable peace under foreign control between the States. Weakening of democracy to the profit of an oligarchy which follows orders from the dominant foreign power.

Pax Romana over all of Greece.

American domination and the increased size of new foreign powers strongly limit the actions of European nations. America tends to impose its will despite the will of other nations: push for the inclusion of Turkey into Europe, strong pressures over international politics and over the openness of markets…

Society/Law: Loss of dynamism. Control imposed by the foreign powers favors stability and therefore the stagnation of society.

Greek cities are governed by a pro-Roman oligarchy.

American domination forbids the establishment of a strong European power and favors internal divisions in order to keep European powers under control (entry of Turkey into the European Union…).

Arts/culture: Importation of the entertainment of the dominating power, influence of its standards.

Arrival of Roman games in Greece: gladiator combats…

Predominance of American films and audiovisual models in Europe, whose standards influence local productions.

Religion: Development of religious syncretism, relativism, as well as the appearance of new spirituality movements to the disadvantage of traditional beliefs.

Hellenistic period, marked by syncretism and a growing role for oriental cults.

Religious authorities are ignored. Individuals completely choose their religion, outside of any traditional frame. Importation of foreign cults (Buddhism, New Age, sects, progression of Islam).

Sciences: End of technological and scientific supremacy.

Slowing down of Greek scientific progress. The diffusion of Greek knowledge across the greater Greek world renders it impotent as a scientific edge over other areas.

Technical and scientific supremacy belongs to America. Europe retains an excellent level but is no more the example nor the engine of discovery.

Relations with the external world: Decolonization, loss of influence to the benefit of foreign powers. Unification attempt in order to resist to foreign powers. Switch toward a foreign tutelage model.

Greek cities completely lose control over their colonies, Greek colonies become Roman possessions. Greek cities attempt to group themselves in order to resist to new powers: Aetolian and Achaean leagues. Greece becomes a Roman province.

Decolonization, creation of the European union, American protectorate over Europe with NATO.

Methods of warfare: Interventions alongside the power in charge of the tutelage, with their agreement and participation.

Absence of military activities outside of the joint action between certain cities and Rome against Mithridates (and before that, joint action with the Macedonians of Alexander).

Interventions in Iraq (1991), Afghanistan and Libya are systematically executed under the command or with the approval of America.

B) RETURN TO CYCLE B

A similar method of analysis shows the same results for Cycle B. As was the case before, it is difficult to determine a cut-out that does not appear to be arbitrary. We propose one in four periods: the foreign monarchy (under the suzerainty of another power), the heroic Republic (marked by the conquest of the immediate vicinity and the creation of a national territory), the imperial Republic (establishment of an hegemony with the national territory as its center) and, finally, the Empire (transformation of the political regime and integration of the Republic and connected territories under its hegemony).

For this last period, we note that only the Roman historical fact is mentioned because America has not yet reached this stage of its evolution. We will thus seek to determine the pertinent elements that are likely to occur for the United States and we will later use these conjectures to develop a predictive tool.

In **bold**: Cycle B
In upright: corresponding Roman historical fact
In *italics*: corresponding American historical fact

1) The Foreign Monarchy
(VIIIth century B.C. —509 B.C., *XVIIth century-1776*)

Political institutions: Domination of a foreign monarchy.

Rome is dominated by the Etruscan Kings.

The American colonies are dominated by the British Crown.

Society/Law: Society is mostly rural and based on agriculture. Local communities are governed by assemblies that organize security under the control of the foreign power.

Roman society is founded on relationships of clientelism within local assemblies, the *curiae*.

Multiple systems of organization and exploitation of the lands: Charter colonies, Proprietary colonies, Crown colonies, with, according to the case, a governor or a colonial assembly.

Arts/culture: The culture is identical to that of the dominating foreign power

Art is based on the Greek-Etruscan model.

Art is based on the European model.

Economy: Agriculture by small farmers, beginnings of the development of commerce.

Exportation of the salt from the Tiber, collection of wood from coastal forests, cultivation of vine, fruit trees and cereals.

The Southern States live from agriculture, while the Northern States live from trade and fishing.

Religion: Specific religion that is not dictated by the foreign influence.

Roman religion and religious institutions are based on Latin culture with the Capitoline Triad.

Great awakening and development of evangelism, a specifically American form of Christianism.

Sciences: Mostly acquired from the suzerain civilization.

Construction of the sewers on the Etruscan model (*Cloaca maxima* produced by the Etruscan King Lucius Tarquinius Priscus), first architectural forms inspired by Etruscan technology.

The technologies employed by the American colonists under British suzerainty come mainly from Europe.

Relations with the external world: Foreign suzerainty.

Rome under Etruscan suzerainty.

American colonies under British suzerainty.

Methods of warfare: Based on the model of the civilization in charge of the tutelage, warrior militias that are more or less voluntary.

First, private militias serving nobles and then militias based on the Greek Hoplite citizen-soldiers model. Ideal of the citizen-warrior who pays for his equipment and provisions.

At the time of the colonial wars, private militias formed by colonists, and then joining to serve the king of England in wars against the French colonists. During the American Revolutionary War, American citizens take arms in order to reject British suzerainty. Combat methods identical to those of Europeans, with lined infantry.

2) The Heroic Republic
(509 B.C. to 272 B.C., *1776-1865*)

Political institutions: Independent republic, citizenship, suffrage, individual liberty.

Rome becomes a Republic, its citizens are free men given political rights and the right to participate to assemblies.

Formation of the United States of America, political and democratic system based on the suffrage of citizens.

Society/Law: Individual rights and liberties are guaranteed by a written system of Law, and magistracy is based on suffrage. Puritan morals.

Establishment of the constitution of the Roman Republic, *mos majorum*, writing of the Twelve Tables. Society founded on family and austere values: *pudicitia, integritas, reverentia* and the predominance of the *pater familias* whose authority is based on the values of *temperentia*, self-mastery and seriousness and importance of manner (*gravitas*).

Writing of the Constitution of the United States of America, Bill of Rights. Society is strongly dominated by the WASP community and protestant morals.

Arts/culture: Profound influence of Civilization A, which is the most advanced civilization of the time.

Greek culture influences Rome, directly through Greater Greece and indirectly through the Etruscan structure.

European cultural influence remains very important: fashion is European, American painters learn from trips to Europe. Neoclassical architecture and Georgian style.

Economy: Peasant exploitation by small owners, artisans, and trade.

Private properties grow but without reaching the size of the latifundiae. Introduction of Greek intensive agriculture methods: fruit trees, olives. Development of the export of Roman ceramics.

The Midwest is farmed by the migrants. First industrial developments. Beginning of standardization.

Religion: Development of a civil religion, the ensemble of beliefs and behaviors are not exclusively but significantly tied to a view of good citizenship and founded on the religion of original dominant ethnicity.

Official cult, organized by the State, ritual care for the stability of institutions supported by the Capitoline triad of traditional Latin religion.

American civil religion founded on the common deist foundations of the original protestant colonists and marked by American evangelism.

Sciences: Progress of production techniques, beginning of great innovations in the military and transportation domains.

Invention of the oil press. First uses of catapults, a starting point for artillery. Creation of the Appian Way, initiating a great realization in the network of transportation.

Beginnings of the mechanization of the manufacturing process (Cotton ginning machine of Eli Whitney). Major changes in artillery with the Gatling rapid-firing gun. Construction of the first transcontinental railroad.

Relations with the external world: Creation of a protection glacis by the subordination of neighboring peoples and the conquest of a strategic space; persistence of isolationism with no real imperialistic will.

Progressive subordination of neighboring cities and confrontation with the peoples of the mountains and the Greek colonies of the south of Italy. Slow conquest of the Italian peninsula for reasons of security rather than domination[6].

Manifest destiny, colonization of the American West and Monroe Doctrine. Great efforts are invested in controlling the American continent in order to protect the security of the United States.

Methods of warfare: Armies of conscripted soldiers developing an organization that is rational and adapted. Extension of the recruitment pool to non-citizens.

Army of conscription. Appearance of compartmentalized organization. Small units offer flexibility of use. First movement toward professionalization of armed forces. First integrations of allied troops.

Appearance of conscription during the American Civil War. Units are organized rationally: squads, platoons, companies, battalions and divisions. Integration of African Americans, non-citizens, in the army.

3) The Imperial Republic
(272 B.C. to 30 B.C., *1865-?*)

Political institutions: Extension of citizenship outside of the historical nucleus, appearance of a macro-Republic extending to the protection glacis.

Roman citizenship is given to all free men of Italy: Italy and Rome combine into one.

The United States form a single nation extending from the Atlantic Ocean to the Pacific Ocean, constituted under the leadership of Yankee power.

Society/Law: Industrialization, appearance of an urban society. Rapid growth in wealth destabilizes the mores, which become more permissive. Appearance of contestations of the ancestral sociopolitical consensus.

Luxury develops and wealth spreads, notably toward women. It becomes regularized, inducing undignified reactions by traditionalists like Cato the Elder. Appearance of opposition between the *populares*, partisans of ideas similar to socialism: debt cancelation and free bread distribution, and the *optimates*, who defend the traditional order of the *mos majorum* and *libertas*.

Emancipation of women, progressive weakening of the domination of WASPs over American society. Progressive development of a schism in American society between conservatives (neo-conservatives, and then Tea Party), who defend the traditional constitution as it was envisioned by the Founding Fathers, and the New Left as well as diverse socialist movements, partisans of a stronger economic intervention by the state, in particular in the domains of health and education.

Arts/culture: Appearance of mass entertainment. The culture of Civilization B becomes a dominant reference and an imitated model in foreign places.

Rise of circus games, development of theater with special effects (*Deus ex machina*). Exportation of entertainment in the ensemble of the lands surrounding the Mediterranean Sea.

Appearance of blues, ragtime and jazz. Golden age of Hollywood, after which American audiovisual and musical production dominates the worldwide market, becomes exported in all countries, and is imitated within other cultures.

Economy: Replacement of the network of small exploiters by greater entities, favored by the lowering of the cost of labor. Establishment of an economic domination founded on force.

Multiplication of slaves, appearance of big exploitations, the *latifundiae*. Imposition of a tribute to vassal nations. Rome becomes an important exporter of food and manufactured products.

Multiplication of machines, emergence of big enterprise by horizontal concentration, imposition of the dollar as the international reserve currency. America becomes the engine of world economy.

Religion: Diversification of religious beliefs, importation of foreign beliefs as the population residing in Civilization B becomes more cosmopolitan.

Rome is progressively conquered by foreign cults, in particular Oriental ones.

America becomes multiracial, exotic religions and syncretism develop, bringing America further away from the puritanism of the original colonists.

Sciences: Apogee of the creativity of Civilization B. Multiple and important technological innovations. Reflections are undertaken about the organization of human activity.

Invention of cement, plumbing, cranes, water mill, semicircular arch, siege machines and military technology, metal ploughshare. Rural economic treaties (Cato the Elder), agriculture, architecture (Vitruvius).

Invention of the lightbulb, household appliances, skyscraper, telephone, automobile, aviation, quantum physics, petrochemistry, nuclear energy, computers, robotics, the Internet, space travel, biotechnologies, nanotechnologies. Development of economic science.

Relations with the external world: Hegemonic position, multiplication of foreign interventions. An imperialistic attitude is adopted and justified by the appearance of a new discourse divorcing from traditional isolationism. There is a desire to assume the role of world police.

The Senate adopts an imperialistic attitude that is no longer defensive[7]. Punic Wars, Macedonian Wars, conquest of the lands surrounding the Mediterranean Sea, Spain and Gaul. Virgil, in the *Aeneid*, represents the imperial fate of Rome: *Parcere subiectis et debellare superbos* (spare those who submit and tame the proud ones).

Monroe Doctrine (the United States consider as an aggression any European intervention in America) modified by the Roosevelt Corollary (American defense interests justify foreign interventions). Expansion toward the Pacific, Spanish-American War, American imperialism in South America, participation to the two World Wars, Cold War against the USSR, and then neo-conservatism, defense of a leadership position in the world, preemptive wars, exportation of democracy and establishment of complacent regimes by force.

Methods of warfare: Professionalization of the army. Acquisition of a strike force over sea. Strong organization and technological superiority.

Strong movement for the professionalization of the army for long and foreign campaigns. Birth of a permanent army based on voluntary engagement rather than conscribed classes. Development of a powerful marine force against Carthage. Standardized armament and methods of combat, superiority of poliorcetic technology.

Disappearance of conscription (except for the Second World War), creation of a professional army. America acquires the most powerful worldwide maritime force and cutting-edge military technologies, notably in aviation and telecommunications.

4) The Empire
(30 B.C. to 476, ?-?)

Political institutions: Any form of democracy is abolished to the benefit of a central dictatorial power whose control grows, up to totalitarianism.

Abolition of the Republic, establishment of the Principate and then the Dominate. Transformation of the political regime into an autocracy.

Society/Law: The Empire appears as a remedy to the breach of the ancestral sociopolitical consensus. Individual liberties and judicial protections against the power disappear as the central power is reinforced. We observe a reappearance of castes with judiciary-political disparities and social mobility disparities.

The Empire comes to put an end to the conflict between the *optimates* and *populares*. The disappearance of the duality in magistracies reinforce the power with respect to individuals. Militarism and despotism of the power lead to a destruction of individual liberty. Economic and professional liberties disappear almost completely. Rupture of equality under the law due to the novel judiciary distinction between the *honestiores*, truly Roman *nomenklatura*, and *humiliores*, leading to a differing treatment in the tribunals of the State. Social stagnation.

Arts/culture: Official art supporting the power of the State. Art is marked by the absolutism of the central power and its increasingly totalitarian structure. Disappearance of the individual to the benefit of a symbolic and typical imagery. This systematic art, fixated and sterile, does not respond to universal sensibilities and loses its status of reference in the Empire, provoking the reappearance of local sensibilities.

Official art, disappearance of classical academic art. Resurgence of indigenous cults and disappearance of Roman cultural predominance. The tetrarchic period sees very specific individual portraits are replaced by "types," sign of a Roman collectivism in the Early Empire that strays away from the humanist individualism which had marked the Republic and the Late Empire.

Economy: The system evolves toward totalitarianism. The economy declines until complete crumbling, paralyzed by the authority of the central power and the control over production to the satisfaction of the needs of the State and the army.

Disappearance of economic and professional liberty. Imperial economic control, practically totalitarianism, puts all of the production to the service of the army and of fiscal revenues. Imperial law organizes into corporations the professions that provide support to the army, and imposes hereditary transmission of profession (the son will occupy the profession of the father) in order to ensure perennity. Appearance of the hereditary status of colonists. Legal attachment of peasants to their land, with which they can be sold.

Religion: Traditional civil religion becomes a unique cult imposed in order to favor central power.

Official cult of the *Sol Invictus*, and then State Christianism. The emperor is divinized (and then sacralized with Christianity). Civil religion is no more limited to the historical center of the Empire but imposed to all populations of the Empire.

Sciences: Stagnation of technological progresses, innovations are not used.

The absence of entrepreneurial liberty constitutes a break to innovation, despite advanced scientific knowledge. Hero of Alexandria, in the I[st] century B.C.[8], invents automata powered by water, the automatic opening of doors by compressed air, and the first fee-based automated water dispenser (for purification at the entrance of temples) and creates the Aeolipile, the first steam machine.

Relations with the external world: Transformation of the hegemony into an empire. Domination of vassals without further extension, except for punctual interventions. The more authoritarian character of the central government is felt in the way the power of B is expressed outside of the nation, leaving less autonomy to local governments.

Provinces headed by governors. Homogenized institutions and general rationalization of the central domination, leading to a loss of local autonomy, which manifests itself through the fiscal pressure exerted by the imperial state. The cult of imperial government is imposed to all inhabitants of the Empire.

Methods of warfare: Professional imperial army, important weight in the State apparatus, auxiliaries are employed.

Imperial army: enrollment at the local level, armies are very attached to their province of origin. Important increase in numbers of people serving in the military. Appearance of foreign auxiliaries.

2. Deepening the analysis with a zoom: Pythagoreanism and Freemasons

In order to show by an example that the models of cycles that we have described correspond so well to observations that they support equally important insight into the smaller scales of civilizations as they do with the larger scales, we will perform a zoom and focus briefly on the comparative role of secret mystic-scientific societies in the evolution of ideas and political events in Greece and Europe.

While the relevance of Freemasons to the evolution of societies and the planned or improvised aspects of their contributions remain debated, there is a broad recognition of their participation to sociopolitical changes of the XVIIIth, XIXth and XXth centuries. Their social circles have favored the diffusion of ideas of the Enlightenment, and their high level of organization has allowed some of their branches to implement these ideas in the institutions they have succeeded at grifting unto. The power of secret societies has generated much fascination for a long time, leading to fabulous theories as well as visceral hate. The very romantic concept of an occult influential organization attracts an interest by the broad public for works and documentaries dedicated to the subject, and it is not without reason that the press has many times dedicated headlines to the subject.

That being said, we often forget that ancient civilizations have encountered similar secret societies, sharing spiritual, scientific and at times political preoccupations. Importantly, these different secret societies share, across time, the same esoteric-scientific method: the school of Pythagoreanism. Our goal here will thus be to compare two secret societies separated by two thousand years.

The origins

Pythagoreanism, like Freemasonry, find its origins in a school of esoteric-scientific thought. The school of pythagoreanism was founded by Pythagoras of Samos, in the VIth century B.C.. Its doctrine was centered on the search for knowledge, in all domains, but knowledge was conceived from a very elitist perspective. The defenders of pythagoreanism thus organized in the form of an Order that was hierarchical and had initiation rituals. This organization was strongly influenced by Pythagoras and his disciples of Orphism, a religion with initiation rituals of Ancient Greece, which was naturally contestatory of the established social order centered on the individual and personal choice.

Heirs of Pythagoras, who was a mathematician, geometer and philosopher, the partisans of pythagoreanism, like their leader, strived to apply reason to all subjects, whether they be purely scientific, like geometry and astronomy, or spiritual such as was done in orphism. They transmitted knowledge within initiation rituals, and were organized in a form of sect.

The origins of Freemasonry are a subject of debate, but it seems clear that this organization is heir to the corporations of medieval builders, notably those who constructed cathedrals, which were themselves heir to corporations of workers at the time of the Roman Empire. These corporations practiced secrecy in order to preserve the exclusivity of their knowledge. Rosicrucian movements as well as eminent members of the Royal Society, the science academy of England, entered these labor organizations and adopted their rituals. Freemasonry is thus, at the onset, the result of a mix similar to that of Pythagoreanism, between esoteric and scientific movements, formed by people interested in knowledge in all domains.

During the XVIIIth century, Freemasonry elaborates most of the codes and modes of operation that remain alive today: initiation, hierarchy, great fundamental principles and the will to apply scientific curiosity to all domains, including the whole of the society formed by the non-initiated.

Thus we see that the school of Pythagoreanism and Freemasonry find their origins in the crossing of two schools of thought: intellectual and mystical, both oriented toward hermeticism.

Politics: the quest for rationalization

The proponents of Pythagoreanism applied their rational mind to the domain of politics: Pythagoras is considered the founder of political sciences. Because he believed that power, just like knowledge, could only be trusted to an elite, the great thinker was taking the side of aristocracy, and preferably a knowledgeable aristocracy, that is a government based on the model of Pythagoreanism. On its political front, Pythagoreanism was characterized by a search for equilibrium, notably in the ideas of geometric equality and proportionality.

Pythagoreanism was not limited to reflections, and certain of their branches actively participated to political life in Greater Greece (south of Italy), where its proponents lived. Notably, they exerted power in Crotone, where they had an important enough political activity that the people ended up massacring them in the Vth century.

Nevertheless, their ideas encountered a greater success than their actions. Political geometrism manifested in the reforms of Cleisthenes in Athens, which suggests a strong penetration of Pythagoreanism, beyond the restricted circles of the initiated in Greece. Cleisthenes, indeed, at the end of the VIth century B.C., initiated the reforms that would transform Athens into a true democracy, by replacing the old political system founded on families and ethnic groups with geographic cut-outs, that are more neutral in rational (demes and trittyes). We observe once more a mark of Pythagoreanism in the replacement of the religious calendar by a civil calendar and in the secularization of politics. Thus, it seems that while the mystical, esoteric and initiation-based aspects of Pythagoreanism did not spread, due to its hermetic nature, the intellectual and geometric aspects have strongly influenced Greek societies and the evolution of their institutional, social, political and religious considerations.

We find similar elements in Freemasonry. While it may not have been the sole origin for the Enlightenment, it certainly participated to its spreading: Freemasonry constituted, in societies where freedom of expression was not complete, a space for discussion and free debate. Furthermore, the equality implied—despite the presence of a hierarchy—between the initiated members of the Masonic Lodges introduced, in a society of orders like the French Ancien Régime, a new social paradigm: that of citizenship and isonomia. Nevertheless, we know today that the Freemasons were not revolutionaries: their care for the political was essentially for the harmony of the social group, notably in order to advance beyond the religious conflicts that had led to so much damage in Europe. The penetration of these ideas in the societies of the time favored a geometrical political reform, such as is obvious in the Declaration of the Rights of Man and of the Citizen, as well as its American and English equivalents. These documents tend to establish a constant relationship between the citizen and his freedoms in society, which are not tied to blood or to their belonging to a caste.

We find in the Freemasonry of the time two opposing currents, one more favorable to the Enlightenment and the other to religion, notably with Joseph de Maistre. It is no doubt in the former that we find the exaltation of reason and the desire for a secular society. These two currents progressively evolved into two loyalties: the one called "regular," traditionalist, respecting certain obligations such as the belief in God and the interdiction of political and religious debate in the lodge, and the other, called "liberal," progressive, rejecting precepts of regularity and as a consequence very much implicated in political and religious debates. While the deist Freemasonry remained preponderant in the world, the second movement triumphed in the XIXth century and the beginning of the XXth century, in particular under the Third Republic, i.e. the true establishment of democracy. The Grand Orient de France thus abandoned in 1877 the obligation for its members to acknowledge the existence of God, and the separation between State and Church, aggressively pursued, was a project led and supported by these "liberal" masonic circles (which is at the origin of a profound schism separating them from the "regular" Freemasonry). We note, by the way, that this anticlerical virulence found a response in the antimasonic hunt of the regime of Vichy, which echoes the massacres of the proponents of Pythagoreanism in Crotone.

Furthermore, at the same time and throughout the XXth century, we observe, in all of Europe, and more broadly in Occident, an important development of the methods for scientific research, which is based on the heritage of the members of the Royal Society and of alchemy, in that it is an attempt at mastering matter. As was the case with the other ideas first carried by Freemasonry, we observe a secularization as soon as they leave the Lodges: chemistry, for instance, separated from alchemy at the end of the XVIIIth century.

Pythagoreanism, just like Freemasonry, in their times, have carried and spread a form of scientism and encouraged the movements of secularization of societies, respectively Greece and Europe.

Pythagoreanism and stoicism, Freemasonry and globalism

With the spreading, in their respective time and place, of a form of rationalism, as well as their actions favoring the secularization of society, Pythagoreanism as well as liberal Freemasonry have pushed societies toward their political visions. Once these political visions were implemented in the real world, they were no more distinguishable other than through their mores and the occult aspects of their organization.

However, we observe that at a certain stage, these organizations have adopted new ideologies and favored the progression of these new ideologies within society, as they had done in the past. For Pythagoreanism, or perhaps we could refer to it as neo-Pythagoreanism, this new philosophy was stoicism. For liberal Freemasonry, it was globalism. Once again, this perspective presents important similarities in the development of these two organizations, separated by two millennia.

Neo-Pythagoreanism developed both in Rome and Greece. It turned out that some of the great stoics were also proponents of Pythagoreanism, such as was the case for Posidonius. While assuming the heritage of Pythagoreanism, they were adhering to the stoic doctrine which conceived of humanity as a great city (cosmopolitanism), and considered that all men were compatriots, and that the "city of the sage is the world," as Chrysippus would have it. Thus, we observed in Rome and Greece, in the two first centuries B.C., a partial mix between the old current of Pythagoreanism with the new Hellenistic philosophy, stoicism. We also note that the universalist doctrine of stoicism had, as its opposite, cynicism, a materialist current of thought that also acknowledged cosmopolitanism, but proposed an alternative to the stoics' love for order: a form of anarchism and disdain for the established authority.

Freemasonry still exists, mostly in Europe and in the United States of America. We know that as early as the XVIIIth century, it was a precursor in the resurgence of ideas from stoicism including the idea that men are citizens of the world, an ideal of fraternity which expressed itself in lodges by the banning of religious debate. Today, while "regular" Freemasonry still bans religious and political debates, the liberal obedience, more progressive, adheres to the globalist doctrine, according to which the world must move past nations and provide a unique government for all of humanity, while favoring exchanges, both economic and human, in order to lessen ethnic and religious differences, which are considered useless sources of conflicts. This is why this form of Freemasonry is profoundly relativistic and syncretic. Similarly to the stoics, current globalists are distinguished from alter-globalists, who are materialist globalists heirs of socialist-communistic internationalism.

Concluding this summary presentation, we can see a strong similarity between the ancient school of Pythagoreanism and modern Freemasonry, as it relates to their origin, actions and evolution. These esoteric "orders" have played an identical role in their respective places, defending sociopolitical conceptions that were similar and pushing for a similar evolution toward rationalization and secularization of the national political sphere. Both movements have then converged and worked toward a cosmopolitan vision and worked for the spreading of their visions after their initial implementation.

We can see through this example that the cycles can be informative at the smaller scale, using a zooming effect to compare micro-aspects of corresponding societies. We will now dig deeper in the sub-structure of cycles.

3. *The existence of subcycles: the case of ω, symmetry between Sparta and Prussia from Cycle D*

In Cycle A, we have described the following stage:

8) An antagonism appears within the civilization: a democratic, cosmopolitan and maritime bloc opposes a totalitarian, militaristic, autarkic and continental bloc.

The appearance of a bloc characterized by open society, democracy and openness toward the rest of the world through sea is the product of the first four stages of the general evolution of A, which we have reviewed. But where does this totalitarian, militaristic and autarkic bloc comes from? Since it is designated as a part of Civilization A, why is it so different from the rest of Civilization A? This is due to the fact that at a specific moment in the evolution of Civilization A, a nation bifurcates toward a different model. Here are the facts, respectively for Greece and Europe, which we have identified at Stage 8 of Cycle A:

Athens, an open and democratic society, opposes Sparta and its allies, a society that is totalitarian, militaristic, autarkic and continental.

France and England, open democracies as well as colonial and maritime powers, oppose Nazi Germany, a totalitarian, militaristic and autarkic regime with ambitions of continental domination.

Comparing the couple between France and England to Athens, as we have done, is relatively easy: their art and great philosophers, their open and democratic society and their great maritime empire are some of the similarities helping establish the resemblance.

The comparison of Germany with Sparta is more delicate. The difficulty does not show when one considers Nazi Germany, where the similarities with Sparta are obvious. The comparison appears to maintain its relevance for the German Empire of Wilhelm II. However, for the two centuries that preceded Wilhelm II, we must admit that many parallels do not seem to fit. In particular, the important cultural and artistic contributions, notably in the field of music, from Bach to Mozart, from Beethoven to Wagner, as well as philosophy with Kant and Fichte, literature with Goethe and Schiller, have allowed Germany to be featured as equal to its French and English neighbors in these domains.

Should the comparison between Germany and Sparta be therefore limited to political institutions, while putting aside cultural and social domains, in which Germany resembles more Athens than Sparta?

Partially, possibly.

But perhaps it is worth looking at things differently and seeing Germany differently from France and England: a nation that is born late, assembling heterogeneous elements that differentiated over three centuries of Catholic and Protestant traditions. Among the diverse regions that unified into Germany, the western half of the country is that which produced the great names of German culture. Meanwhile, it is under the power of a kingdom located at its eastern extremity that Germany was unified: Prussia.

This kingdom was described by Mirabeau not as a State possessing an army, but as an army that had conquered a nation. Thus, here is our working hypothesis: Sparta is Prussia. Germany, under the leadership of Prussian powers, is comparable in ancient times to the Lacedaemonian State, dominated by Sparta.

In order to test this hypothesis, let us return to our usual method and compare the history of these two entities.

A) HISTORICAL REMINDERS

Sparta

The city of Sparta, as it appears in classical Greek history, is born from the Dorian invasion of the Peloponnese. This people of warriors would have established itself as a class of lords ruling over the invaded local populations.

As a political entity, Sparta is first compromised by internal dissent, to which the reforms of Lycurgus puts an end by changing the aristocratic ideal of primitive society for a civic ideal. Sparta becomes a strong military power due to its new organization, and conquers Laconia and Messenia during the three Messenian Wars:

The First Messenian War occurred in the VIIIth century B.C.. During this conflict, Sparta sought lands to ensure its growth, disperses the Messenian aristocracy, and imposes its control over Messenia.

The Second Messenian War occurred in the VIIth century B.C. allowing the annexation of Messenia, whose population was converted into slavery in order to feed the Spartan masters.

The Third and last Messenian War occurred in the Vth century B.C.. Sparta, then, suffered from a weakening due to some natural disaster. The war extended, and ended with a compromise. Sparta was traumatized and the Helots (the slave class) were further oppressed: their massacre was organized as part of Cyrpteia, an educational test for the youth in which armed bands of young Spartans were sent on a mission to kill the Helots.

Sparta thus built the Lacedaemonian State, federating Sparta, Messenia and Laconia. The Perioeci cities (Laconia and Messenia) preserved a form of internal autonomy, but the Helot communities were directly subordinated to Sparta.

Then, came the Peloponnesian War, at the end of which, victorious, Sparta imposed the government of the Thirty Tyrants to Athens. This opened up a time of Spartan hegemony over Greece.

Then, Sparta became a champion for Greek freedoms and panhellenism, and turned against its Persian ally. The adventure went wrong, with the two failures of the expedition of the Ten Thousand, and that of Agesilaus II. A disastrous war followed with a second front in Corinthia, Greece.

Finally, Sparta was strongly defeated in Leuctra, lost its hegemony, and saw the dismemberment of its empire over Messenia. The Peloponnesian League, a network of allies of Sparta, was dissolved.

The weakness of Sparta allowed the rise of the Achaean League.

Prussia

962: Otto I restored imperial dignity for Germany. The Empire, then, was an aggregate of principalities in contact, on its eastern side, with important Pagan populations.

During the XIth, XIIth and XIIIth centuries, the land-based aristocracy of the Junkers colonized and Christianized the current Oriental Germany and Prussia. In 1224, the State of the Teutonic Order was founded. In the following years, the Order subordinated the Prussians (or Old Prussians). Through Papal bull, Prussia officially became a possession of the Order.

The Teutonic domination extended toward the East. This was the *Drang nach osten*, the drive to the east, and the *Ostkolonisation*, the colonization of the east, supervised by the Teutonics. This colonization movement was brutal: The Wends, a people of Slavs who were occupying these lands, were massacred, exiled or subordinated. Several Pagan revolts were strongly repressed.

The order reached an apogee of power at the end of the XIVth century. However, vanquished following a revolt of the Prussians, the State of the Teutonic Order became a vassal of Poland.

In 1525, the Great Master of the Order, Albert of Brandenburg, converted to Lutheranism and the Order became secular, allowing the appearance of the Duchy of

Prussia, which became, through a dynasty alliance with the House of Hohenzollern, Brandenburg-Prussia, in 1618.

In 1701, Frederick I became King of Prussia, a kingdom unifying all possessions of the Hohenzollern. In 1713, Frederick William I of Prussia rose as a king-soldier, the *Soldatenkönig*, making a priority of the army, based on the ancient land-based aristocratic model of the secularized Teutonic Order: The Junkers.

The rise of Frederick the Great in 1740 accelerated the ascension of the Prussian State among the concert of European powers while the chief doubled the surface of his kingdom through military campaigns.

During the Napoleonic Wars, Prussia allied with Germany and played a major role in the final victory of the coalition. It participated, notably, in the German uprising of 1813, and would know, after that, how to awaken the national sentiment in Germany in order to construct the Empire.

The construction of the Empire occurs mostly during the decade of 1861-1871. Otto Von Bismarck then sought to create German unity under Prussian leadership. In 1864, the Second Schleswig War, against Denmark, allowed Prussia to take over the Duchies of Schleswig and Saxe-Lauenburg. In 1866, the Austro-Prussian War consecrated the Prussian supremacy over the German world, and in 1871, following the French defeat and the Annexation of Alsace, the German Empire was declared as sovereign of Austria. Two thirds of the new Germany were Prussian possessions. Prussian provinces were often old German States that had been annexed (Hanover, Holstein…) and were under direct control of Prussian officials, while the attached German States such as Bavaria, retained a partial autonomy.

Under imperial leadership, Germany becomes more Prussian as things progressed. The defeat of 1918 traumatized the German people, in particular because that defeat was caused by the so-called German Revolution, when domestic troubles came to weaken the war effort. It is these troubles that led to the creation of the Freikorps, which later would come to garnish the ranks of the National Socialist German Workers' Party. Hitler, despite being Bavarian, thus inherited from "Prussianism," a military, statist and authoritarian spirit which forged the German Empire. The leaders of his army were Prussian. The *Lebensraum*, "living space," resuscitated the primitive impetus of the Teutonic Order (*Drang nach Osten*, the drive to the east), which was initially at the origin of the Prussian State.

During the Second World War, Nazi Germany crushed France and supported the anti-democratic regime of Vichy. Having obtained hegemony over Western as well as Eastern Europe, Nazi Germany built itself as a champion against Bolshevism and the Russian threat, which had been feared for a long time by Prussia. It turned against its old ally, USSR, in a catastrophic campaign, war becoming a conflict on two fronts, in particular with the entry of the USA into the conflict.

The final defeat was the end of Prussian Germany: Western Germany, after a century, was finally subtracted from the Prussian spirit, which from then on was confined to Eastern

Germany. It is a German renaissance as a civil state, with its past of culture, industry and commerce. The European community, and then the European Union, could appear.

Note on the Spartan social system: Citizens, Perioeci and Helots

Let us recall that after having been unified and structured by Lycurgus (whether the character is historical or summarizes the action of multiple individuals), Sparta conquered an important part of the Peloponnese: Laconia and Messenia.

The Perioeci were free but did not have citizenship and were not part of the political life of the city. They had the right to possess lands and participate to the army beside the citizens of Sparta. Most of the inhabitants of cities over the Spartan territory were Perioeci. As such, Spartan domination can be viewed as a forced confederation under exclusive control of the Equals, the citizens of Sparta with political rights. Contrarily to the Metics of Athens, the Perioeci were not foreigners but were subjects of the Spartan Empire, as indicated by the etymology, Perioeci meaning "those around the house," i.e. the populations living in periphery of Sparta (while Metic means "those who changed residence," i.e. foreigners who do not originate from the location they are currently living at). The Perioeci, like the Spartans, were called Laconians or Lacedemonians. Thus these terms designated all free individuals on the territory, whether they were citizens (Spartans) or not (Perioeci).

The Helots were not slave-merchandise. Sparta was not trading them. They were a population that were slaves of the collectivity. Constantly subordinated and terrorized, the apogee of their persecution seems to have occurred after the Third Messenian War.

Germany, as a XIXth century nation, is a profoundly Prussian achievement, one realized by the Junkers. This fact largely explains its fate until the end of the Second World War.

While Prussia has led (and even subordinated) Western Germany, it was itself under the control of the Junkers class, land-based aristocrats who were descendants of Germans who had colonized and Christianized the region at the time of the *Drang nach Osten* and the Teutonic Order. The Junkers were masters of the army and had, with their large agricultural exploitations, a corresponding economic weight. From the start, they were thinking as colonists taking over the lands of people reduced to slavery. The Teutonics employed thousands of Prussian autochthones in order to build their fortresses, after having crushed their Pagan tribes.

Note about the Junkers

They then formed the dominant class in the Kingdom of Prussia, supporting the monarchy and defending the military tradition. Vertebral column of the military culture of the Kingdom, they played an important role in the unification of Germany, largely established *manu military*. Prussia indeed conquered Germany militarily. They thus became the dominant class of Germany, and influenced the spirit of the new nation. This resulted in a Prussian spirit that was conservative, and even at times reactionary, militarist and antiliberal.

One can ask whether there was a continuity between this Prussian spirit, or Prussianism, and Nazism.

Many elements show differences rather than continuity: Prussianism was desiring of a strong, but not dictatorial State (while it was not parliamentary, and essentially governed by imperial executives, in particular high Prussian officials, and the right to vote was practically confiscated by rich classes with the three classes system). Nor was Prussianism supporting totalitarianism. It was a mentality of elites, not a popular movement, and it was conservative rather than revolutionary. Nazism disgusted many pure Junkers. Many enemies of Hitler are found among the ranks of this Prussian class, from the beginning to the end of his political path.

Nevertheless, we cannot oversee the important similarities: the model of the glorious military caste, which had produced Germany, certainly must have influenced non-Prussian minds, and the great numbers of Germans who were not Junkers. Through a phenomenon that was repeatedly observed, that is, the identification toward the victorious invaders, just like Gaul became France largely due to a Franc noblesse, and that the Gauls became French, the Junkers were the unconscious model for the German Man, and during the First World War, it was expected that any soldier would conform to it. The Nazi dream of the race of Lords and Warriors essentially meant making a Junker out of each and every German: Warrior-Lords having their lands cultivated by the Slav slaves, as was the case in the times of the Teutonic Order. Nazism was thus truly revolutionary, attempting to transform the people into a racial aristocracy. However, the model for the aristocracy that Hitler wanted to create was that of the military lord as it had existed since the *Drang nach Osten*, through the Teutonic Order (which was an object of fascination for the Nazis), and through the Junkers. Thus Goebbels was declaring: "*National Socialism can justifiably proclaim a Prussian origin. Wherever we are in Germany, we are the Prussians. The idea that we carry is Prussian. The values and symbols for which we are fighting are inspired by the Prussian spirit, and the goals that we hope to attain are nothing else than the actualization of the ideals pushed by Frederick William I, Frederick the Great and Bismarck.*"[9] The Nazis wanted to turn the German people into Junkers.

At the organizational level, we also observe a continuity between the Prussian spirit and Nazism, with the *Freikorps,* appearing as a reaction to the German Revolution of 1918-1919 in order to maintain the German Empire, and who massively joined the *Sturmabteilung* of Hitler.

Another demonstration of the importance of Prussians in Nazi Germany is the Night of the Long Knives, perpetrated in order to satisfy the Prussian conservatives who were afraid of a movement that would be too revolutionary. Hitler had understood that without Prussian support, he could not hold Germany.

Thus we find in German history, through Prussian history, the same spirit that animated the Spartan citizens, the same model of the warrior enslaving peoples and the same inequality in the social and political construction of the German Empire. Both the German Empire and the Lacedemonian Empire were produced by a similar mode of emergence.

Totalitarianism in Sparta

The crisis of the VIIth century B.C., that is, the Second Messenian War, could only be surpassed by the adoption of the new military innovation of the Phalanx. This moment corresponded to the creation of *eunomia*, which means the dissolution of the aristocracy into the popular masses of Sparta in order to create an army of Hoplites. The aristocrats renounced to their privileges, and the lands were pooled and redistributed in lots. Commerce was forbidden and the lands cultivated by the slaves, and citizens (*Homoioi*, the equals, or perhaps more precisely the similar, the same, the identical, in line with the collective ideals of Spartans) had to be dedicated to the war effort, around which the entirety of the educational curriculum was constructed: The Agoge, which would survive Sparta long after the end of its power. Spartan citizens had to consume their meals together. The values of the Aristocracy did not disappear, but the aristocratic ideology served as the new basis for the emerging civic ideology, citizenship becoming the new noblesse.

Sparta practiced eugenics, by selecting from birth the children who would live or those malformed or sickly who were killed. Money was theoretically banned.

The Helots, slaves of the State, were despised and constantly mocked in rituals. Their fate became even worse after the Third Messenian War, which was traumatic for Sparta. In 425 B.C., during the Peloponnese War, the Spartans deceived 2000 Helots by making them believe they would be freed only to massacre them.

Totalitarianism in Prussia and Germany

The Kingdom of Prussia and then the German Empire have not been totalitarian regimes. However, the Nazis, following the Prussian heritage, have attempted to transform the German people into Junkers.

After the defeat of the First World War, the economic and social context in Germany was favorable to revolutionary movements. Hitlerism, a synthesis of Marxism and of the Prussian spirit, pretended to make Germany strong, by making of every German an Aryan, a lord and a warrior. This revolutionary aspect displeased some Junkers, who became the enemies of Hitler since they were hanging unto their traditional aristocratic values. Others, such as Ludendorff (who came, from his mother side, from an important Junker family), followed from the beginning the founder of Nazism. Hitler created the Hitler Youth, aiming to provide young Germans with an education based on camaraderie, a spirit of wholeness and physical exercise. This trend existed in Eastern Germany well before the Nazis, since the end of the XVIIIth century, based on ideas from Rousseau and taking the form of the German gymnastic movement called *Turnverein*, a patriotic and paramilitary movement whose spirit would survive in Eastern Germany.

Nazi Germany practiced eugenics, by sterilizing and euthanizing the handicapped, those with incurable diseases, and by performing experiments in order to favor racial purity. The Jews and the Tziganes, who for a long time had been the target of a racism that existed throughout German society, saw their situation worsen after the defeat of 1918. Considered as inferior races by Nazi Germany, they were degraded, deported, reduced to slavery in concentration camps, and then massacred during the Second World War.

Let us note that one more aspect formed a distinction between Prussian Germany and the more open societies of England and France (and other smaller nations): nationality by blood. While the societies more inclined toward cosmopolitanism (France, United

Kingdom, USA) recognized the birth right of the soil as the main determinant of nationality, the German Empire, born out of Pan-Germanism, preserved the criteria of the right of blood which indicated a certain identitarian fixation existing well before Nazi fanaticism.

Let us now see if we can identify a pattern that would apply both to Sparta and Prussia, thus forming a subcycle.

Since Sparta, like the Prussian/German power were part of a Type A Civilization, this subcycle will be a process integrated to Cycle A. We will arbitrarily define the subcycle applying to Prussia and to Sparta as Cycle ω (Omega), ω designating the type of entity incarnated by Sparta and Prussia.

B) PRESENTATION OF CYCLE ω

In **bold**: stage of Cycle ω
In upright: corresponding Spartan historical fact
In *italics*: corresponding Prussian historical fact

1) Establishment of a warrior aristocracy in the lands where the original population is subordinated. They form the nucleus of nation ω.

The Dorians invade the valley of the Eurotas.

The Teutonic Knights and Junkers invade Prussia.

2) ω, a nation belonging to Civilization A, structures itself into a military nation.

Sparta becomes an hoplite nation (Lycurgus laws), based on the ancient values of the Spartan aristocracy.

Frederick William I, the warrior-king and the birth of Prussian militarism based on the Junkers, a Prussian noblesse dating from the Teutonic Order.

3) Formation, through war, of a federal hegemonic system of ω, led sovereignly, with a certain autonomy left to some political entities. Annexation and subordination of others.

Conquest of Laconia, eviction of the cities neighboring Argos, annexation of Messenia, creation of a federal system under Spartan hegemony. The Lacedemonian State is led by Sparta. Autonomy for the Perioeci, subordination of the Helot communities.

Series of wars (Second Schleswig War, Austro-Prussian War, eviction of Austria) creation of a federal system under Prussian hegemony, the German Empire is led by the Prussia of Junkers. Autonomy for German states (ex: Bavaria) or pure and simple annexation of other political entities (Hanover, Hesse…) into provinces under the control of Prussian officials. The Prussian government is characterized by political authoritarianism and economical statism.

4) Following various crises, hardening of the regime, which becomes increasingly totalitarian and brutal. Identitarian withdrawal.

At the end of the Third Messenian War (uprising of Messenian subjects opportunistically benefiting from an earthquake that destroyed Sparta), violence toward the Helots intensifies, massacres become common, in particular with the practice of Crypteia and the organized massacre of 2 000 helots in 425 B.C.[10].

The German revolution of 1918 (worker uprising due to social tensions and war-related austerity) leads to the birth of the Freikorps, a paramilitary group which will feed into the Nazi movement. Defeat by "knife in the back" betrayal, the idea of an enemy inside develops into a trauma which leads Germany to the establishment of Nazi totalitarianism, a caricature of Prussian militarism. Fanatical Junkerization of the people as a whole, mass massacres, in particular the Shoah.

5) Great war against a maritime power from an open, democratic and maritime civilization.

Peloponnesian War: Sparta opposed to Athens.

Second World War, 1939-1940 against France-England.

6) Victory of the foreign power, occupation of the territory, support for the establishment of a complacent non-democratic regime.

Athens vanquished, garrison of Sparta, establishment of the regime of the Thirty Tyrants.

France vanquished (and England pushed back), German occupation and support for the regime of Vichy.

7) ω establishes its hegemony over Civilization A, and becomes a champion for the fight against foreign powers to which it had previously been an ally.

Sparta establishes its hegemony over Greece, becomes the champion of Pan-Hellenism, and turns against its ally, the Persian Achaemenid empire, in the name of Greek liberty: Expeditions of the Ten Thousand and Agesilaus II.

Nazi Germany establishes its hegemony over Europe, becomes a champion of the European fight against Asian Bolshevism and turns against its Soviet ally: Operation Barbarossa and war on the Eastern front.

8) The war against the foreign power leads to a situation of a war over two fronts; weakening of the position of ω and defeat in the external war.

Sparta is weakened in its fight against the Persians which turns into a defeat.

Germany leads a war on two fronts, and the Eastern one turns to disaster.

9) This initial weakening allows another power, in alliance with the formerly-vanquished enemy, to defeat ω.

Thebes helps Athens to liberate itself and puts an end to the Spartan power in the Battle of Leuctra.

The USA[11] help England, liberate France and defeat Germany on the western front.

10) ω loses its hegemony and falls into a state of crisis. Rise of a confederate alliance of the other powers of the same Civilization A.

Sparta sees its empire dismembered, loses Messenia and its alliance system crumbles. Rise of the Achaean League.

Prussia loses all of its occidental possessions in Germany (provinces that had been annexed in the previous century), the control of the Germanic States of the Empire, as well as its hegemony in Europe. The allies dissolve the Prussian state; the Junkers are eliminated in the new communist system of Eastern Germany. Appearance of the European community.

Our working hypothesis is thus confirmed, and the exercise above helps us realize the depth and degree of resolution that can be attained from our broader description of the cycles. This reinforces the idea that the "echoes" that can be observed through history indeed form a system, and that they could be subjected to modelization. Perhaps we can even dream of laying it out into equations? With this exciting advance, we must now have a look at the dynamics of History and attempt to identify the foundations of these historical cycles.

III: THE DEEP NATURE OF THE CYCLES AND THE RANDOM (OR NOT) NATURE OF HISTORY

How could complex series of historical events have unfolded into a complex and recurring patterns, with structures that are stable, periodical and self-replicating? Would the laws of history extracted from these pattern support a form of determinism that would deny human liberty and the ability of men to influence the course of existence?

We will attempt to provide certain intuitive lines of approach to these questions. We begin by reminding that History is first and foremost a global phenomenon in which individuals are merely inserted. The broader fates are the product of a collective movement, and as such, they cannot be steered from their normal course beyond a certain degree. We will then attempt to identify the degree of variability allowed by these mechanisms.

1. Laws of History, determinism and individual freedom

The idea of Laws of History is often connected to the idea of historical determinism, and often draws critiques of its negation of human free will. A common objection is that of the example of a "great man," that is, an individual whose spectacular accomplishments would have "changed the course of History."

Importantly, there is no form of historical determinism, or conceptions around Laws of History that would constitute a negation of human freedom or of the ability of men to influence history. This is due to the simple fact that human freedom is part of the equation, in the same way the Law of large numbers does not negate the truths applying to the unitary level of specific numbers. Determinism is merely statistical.

The corollary of this statement is that no individual can modify the course of History, because the fate of History, no matter how spectacular, will be the realization of a probability based on circumstances.

An individual story may influence the course of History in that it can provide a color to events that they wouldn't have had otherwise. However, in no way can it change their deep nature, since these individual stories are merely an expression and realization of some probability.

Consider the example of Napoleon. Few individuals in history had such a flamboyant fate and as much influence as he had in his time. Yet, if we properly analyze the situation, what do we find? The periods of revolutionary anarchy are often followed by a military dictatorship. Napoleon's France was highly populated, and lived under a foreign threat since the beginning of the Revolution. When Napoleon imposed his dictatorship, it was positioned as a strong power in Europe, which created a favorable environment for Napoleon to rise.

Even if the military abilities of Napoleon, while incontestable, were not as exceptional as to be considered unique, these abilities would not have shined as they did, had he not inherited from a regenerated army after the revolution, an army that had experience and organization that were adapted to a moving war, which could be led successfully against the enemies of the Emperor. History has almost forgotten, perhaps due to Napoleonian propaganda, that the day Napoleon decimated, with a total of 80 000 men, the 60 000 men of the Prussian army, Louis-Nicolas Davout crushed as many Prussians with less than 30 000 men! This spectacular victory could have created a shadow over the Emperor, who had, in Marengo, claimed the merit for the victory which was attained thanks to the help of Desaix, who had died in the process and therefore could not receive his laurels.

We can thus surmise that the context of the power that was to be headed by Napoleon, giving him the means to control Europe, was pushing him in that direction anyway; and that another man, in his place, would not have acted much differently. This is even more obvious if we do not ignore that the true instigator of numerous wars of the Empire was England, who could not allow, in accordance with its traditional strategy position, to let a dominant power rise on the continent. Thus if we admit that England could not have done otherwise than encourage war against France, knowing that it disposed of a large human reserve and of an experienced and equipped army, then a great share of the history of the French Consulate and the Empire can be explained without specific considerations of Napoleon. In a country that is strategically positioned as a strong power, the presence of a strong foreign threat is such that it reinforces the legitimacy of the dictator as well as the growth of his military power, thus increasing the chances that it can come out victorious against the threats, while also increasing the chances that the dictatorship will engage into founding a new political regime.

Furthermore, in addition to these geopolitical facts that are independent of the individual, we must consider that in such circumstances, the very personality of the one who would become the master of France was following principles that would be quite easy to predict. In the context of a country threatened from every side and a society in mutation, we can guess that through some form of natural selection process, anyone who would become a military dictator would have the remarkable capacities having permitted him to reach that status. Whoever rises among crowds of other formidable individuals, as soon as the time comes for these personal values to be tested, would be expected to show energy, ambition, and having survived the revolutionary enterprise while playing a role within it. He would also be expected to be favorable to revolution.

After such an analysis, what remains unexpected in the highly probable character of Napoleon? Too little. What is left does not seem very important in the face of a context that seems bound to a certain fate. The individual might modify the particulars of the unfolding of historical events, lead to fascinating or terrifying anecdotes that historians will enjoy reporting so they can feel like storytellers for a moment, but the general sequence of History will not be significantly changed with respect to a similar situation in which some other man would have endorsed his role and would have added his own nuances.

It would barely be a caricature to state that Napoleon, in his role as a post-revolutionary military dictator, has really brought nothing else than the Corsican accent, his love stories with Josephine and his own face on the portraits of the time. By saying so, we do not negate the historical role of the Emperor of the French, we simply relativize the importance of the particular individual who occupied it: Napoleon Bonaparte. If Napoleon had not existed, we would study, in the History of France, the story of another man. Perhaps less flamboyant. Perhaps more. Certainly different in his anecdotes. But the unfolding of history would be broadly similar.

Let us consider another type of case: individuals who have a punctual role that appears to be major. This is the case for the Arab Revolutions and Mohamed Bouazizi. This man, who has immolated himself on fire, was a trigger for the Tunisian riots, and following that, the riots of the rest of the Arab world.

Does this mean that, without him, there would have been no Arab revolutions, or that a geopolitical event of this magnitude can hang unto the fate of a single man?

We could, out of laziness, adopt this idea. Too often, we judge History in such a way, as if it hanged on a single thread at all times. However, I would argue that while it is possible to adopt this perspective for certain smaller aspects of history, it is impossible to do so for its broad unfolding.

The case of Bouazizi was one among many others. How many revolutions, wars, and important events seem to have been caused by the action of a single man, a man from the revolted people, a man spreading a false information, or an influential thinker having impacted the theories defended by generations of ideologues? For such events, it is always hard to determine the true share that is attributable to the individual.

It is said that Norbert Wiener, the founder of cybernetics, and John von Neumann, a mathematician and physicist, have discussed a long time ago the possibility of predicting, though calculations, a future situation based on the current situation. Notably, the two geniuses discussed the analogy of the snowflake and the avalanche. Wiener noted that a single snowflake suffices to trigger an avalanche, but Neumann argued that it was not the case. According to Neumann, it would suffice to be able to predict which snowflake would cause the avalanche to keep it from happening. Neumann's view was denounced by Wiener, who noted that the avalanche-about-to-happen was in a hypercritical state, a state of extreme probability in which we should not consider that the avalanche depended upon a precise snowflake, but simply upon some snowflake, out of them all, that would be occupying a certain role. Intercepting a snowflake would not keep the avalanche from happening, since another one would replace it[12].

It seems fair to surmise that at the edge of revolutions, societies are in such a hypercritical state, where the probability to witness the initial sparkle is so high that it is certain that it will happen. In 2010-2011 Tunisia, we must consider the probability that a Mohamed Bouazizi would emerge was very high, and that if Mohamed Bouazizi had not put himself on fire, some other individual would have committed some other act, more or less similar, which in the prevailing social climate would have had the same triggering effect.

This leads us to conclude that History obeys a probabilistic logic, as much at the level of human masses as for the emergence of remarkable individuals. This is true whether we are talking about an individual having had a simple triggering role such as Mohamed Bouazizi, or a more important character, a "Great Man." The Law of large numbers is thus, in some way, applicable to History.

Thus we can surmise that the emergence of a Caesar or Napoleon, just like a Bouazizi, are the expression and realization of a probability, as much as is the case for the English and French revolutions. In a similar probabilistic way, an idea can be born in the mind of a man, leading to a written work that will have immense consequences on the future.

Consider, for instance, Marx and Marxism. It seems, at first glance, that this idea has had the most spectacular consequences on the history of the XXth century; it has engendered the Soviet Empire, the Cold War, but also, in reaction to Bolshevism, Nazism. We might be tempted to say that History could have gone differently without Marx. But we would be wrong.

What would have happened, had Marx not existed? It is often said that fictional history, or counterfactual history, is a perilous exercise, but nevertheless one can extract from such a process results that are quite obvious, as long as one does not adventure himself unto this territory with ideological presuppositions.

A first observation is in order: in the history of ideas, Marx is not alone. In addition to the fact that the communistic ideal that he has expressed is as old as civilization, we must consider that it is natural that an industrial revolution and a period of demographic explosion (European population having doubled in the XIXth century), would lead to an overcrowded, and therefore miserable proletariat, which would in turn lead to zealots of the labor cause. Others have preceded Marx, like Proudhon, and others could have easily elaborated an economic thought similar to his, particularly given the intellectual effervescence of the time around these questions. Someone else would have attempted to justify communism if Marx had not done so. Thus Marx was not absolutely necessary to the appearance of communism as a theorized political ideology in the XIXth century; nor to the success of such an ideology, since, as we have pointed out, the socio-economical conditions of the XIXth century were very favorable to the appearance of communistic theories, and just as much to their reception.

Secondly, Russia and the USA would have come to confront each other for the control of the world, even if Marxism had not been there to add an ideological element to the antagonism between the two powers. If one needs convincing, suffices to read the prediction of Alexis de Tocqueville, almost a century and a half before the beginning of the Cold War: *"Today, two great peoples on Earth, having started from different points, seem to be advancing toward the same goal: Russians and Anglo-Americans. Both grew in obscurity; and while men were occupied elsewhere, they suddenly became leaders in the rank of nations, and the world has learned simultaneously about their birth and their greatness.[13]"*

Without Marx, the Empire may not have been Soviet (although we have seen that Marx was not necessary to communism), but it still would have been an Empire, and it still would have met America, another imperial Republic, in its global ambition.

Thirdly, Nazism, or at least some movement close to it, would have appeared without Bolshevism. According to Ernst Nolte, opposition to Marxism is a foundational ideology of National Socialism. However, we have seen in our comparison between Sparta and Prussia that the totalitarian and racist foundations of Nazism and of Sparta were both the product of similar historical inheritances and social shocks. Thus, we can surmise that in the absence a reactionary position toward Bolshevism, some other form of ultra-nationalistic totalitarianism would have risen instead of Nazism[14].

What should we conclude from these observations? That History would be the same without Marx? Of course not. But it would be equally erroneous to believe that History would have been very different without Marx. In reality, it would have been slightly different, and only over a certain "thickness" of History. Without Marx, it is probable that the designation of the current defenders of the proletariat would have another name, but it is very improbable that in his absence, communism would not have existed at all as a force opposing capitalism. It is equally improbable that Russia would not have faced America for global supremacy, and that no form of totalitarianism would have taken over humiliated Germany, which had a strong industrial and human potential, and had been plunged into the disarray of a Dantean economic crisis. The appearances of the History that would be taught today would be different, but the real developments would be very similar.

Thus even in the history of ideas, either in action (Bolshevism) or reaction (Nazism), and their impact on geopolitics, we must conclude that Marx, as was the case with Napoleon, was a prominent character, but we must refute the idea that he was a determining one.

This nuance is what we must focus on, because it defines the difference between the appearances of History and its fundamental movements, the difference between allure and trajectory, and therefore between the unpredictable and the predictable.

This important difference is that between Contingent History and Necessary History.

2. Necessary History vs. Contingent History: deterministic and probabilistic considerations in History

There would thus be two main layers[15] to History: a deep layer, which remains essentially protected from randomness, and a superficial one, resting on the former, and more likely to be affected by randomness.

The first layer is *Necessary History*, that which will certainly occur. The second layer is *Contingent History*, the particular way in which *Necessary History* will come to be.

Going back to the above examples: Russia was necessarily destined to become a superpower and to enter in a rivalry against the United States of America. The particular form that this superpower would take and the form that the conflict would take between the two was contingent.

The reader will recall that this opposition corresponded to the following stage of Cycle B:

5) Confrontation to a powerful conquering nation. A fight for survival and supremacy leaves Civilization B without rival and able to dominate the world.

Similarly, Germany was necessarily destined to encounter totalitarianism, as the heir of a long militaristic and nationalistic tradition, which would lead to the war against France and England. The form that this regime would take was contingent.

This necessary fact was found both in Cycle A:

8) An antagonism appears within the civilization: a democratic, cosmopolitan and maritime bloc opposes a totalitarian, militaristic, autarkic and continental bloc.

And Cycle ω:

4) Following various crises, hardening of the regime, which becomes increasingly totalitarian and brutal. Identitarian withdrawal.

5) Great war against a maritime power from an open, democratic and maritime civilization.

What is our conclusion? That the cycles, these civilizational patterns which we have previously established, are models of Necessary History, and that it is the way in which they unfold that is contingent.

In order to be perfectly clear, let us imagine an imaginary cycle comprising the five steps noted as 1, 2, 3, 4, 5. These steps will form Necessary History: they will occur, one after the other, in this order. What will be contingent is the way in which they occur: a war could be more or less murderous, a revolution could be more or less violent… and also the speed at which they occur. The cycle will always ensure the occurrence of the steps, through some constrained randomness, 1, 2, 3, 4 and 5, but it could unfold as follows:

```
1-__------__-----2-----___----------_------------3-------_____---------------4----___----5
```
or
```
1-_---2--------_-------3--------__-----------------_____--------__----4---_____---5
```
or
```
1---------_____---------------2---__----------------3---4----__----------------------5
```

For example, we have seen that Jewish history, since Moses, until the confrontation of Rome, lasted between 1100 and 1300 years (according to the dating for the life of the prophet) while Arab-Muslim history since Muhammad until the confrontation with the

USA has lasted between 1400 and 1500 years (depending on whether we are seeing the actual defeat of Islamism against the USA or that a greater conflict would come in the coming decades).

Similarly, there is about one thousand years of Greek history between the end of the Mycenaean Empire and the Roman conquest, while there is about 1500 years between the fall of the Roman Empire and the transfer of Europe under American domination.

What we observe, therefore, is a path with a unique destination, but that includes random possibilities of acceleration, slowing down and some temporary detours.

How can such a mechanism exist? Perhaps as follows: a political, economic and social situation is established, which, given the tendencies that apply to the individual and the collective behaviors of humans (distribution of wealth and power in society, economic and demographic evolution, defense of acquired advantages, officials inclined to act in their own interests, corporatism…) will necessarily evolve in only one direction. This social context will not make punctual evolutions in the opposite direction impossible. Some other trends may take the forefront, but the system would ensure that these punctual evolutions are less common and less probable (altruism, ability for compromise, ability to voluntarily renounce to particular advantages for the common good, statesmen able to sacrifice their career for what they believe is just, geopolitical or environmental accidents erasing many years of evolution).

The mechanism can thus be summarized as the opposition between two trends, one with more numerous and frequent occurrences, thus being stronger, leading to the necessary outcome, and the other, with rarer occurrences and therefore less influential, leading to a slowing down of the general movement but never to a definitive reversal. These major and minor trends regroup elements of various societal dimensions: economic, demographic, sociological, political and environmental. The mix between the two trends vary, but not their nature: minor trends will have more effect at times when they become stronger, but may only constitute a temporary obstacle in the production of effects by the major trends, and will not be able to affect the final outcome. The limits of historical indeterminism, beyond the share of events that are irremediably linked to some individuals, must be found in this variation of the precise mix between the trends.

Let us consider the example of a progression from a feudal society to a democratic one. Power first belongs to a warrior aristocracy, culturally inclined to neglect production activities in general, and trade in particular. When economic progresses occur, the aristocratic class will fail to be the first beneficiary of these progresses (even if it collects various tribunes or taxes). Rather, it is the classes fully involved in the economic process that will be the first beneficiary. Subjected to the fiscal pressure from the dominant and non-productive class, the nascent bourgeoisie will develop a class reflex, claiming a reduction of the pressure, some liberties, and if needed, will foment an insurrection to get what they want. As their wealth accrues, they will be more and more powerful. Suddenly, a patterns appears into society where the aristocrat is perceived as the useless parasite, since it does not occupy its protective role anymore, which is better handled by private militias funded by the bourgeois. The aristocrat remains unproductive, because its culture keeps him from engaging in commerce, finance, etc. This social organization has only one possible outcome: the complete disappearance of this feudal aristocracy following its banishment from power.

Nevertheless, this outcome can be slowed down by various social and political events, sometimes caused by the drive for survival of this aristocratic class. The most obvious example is that of the extension of the caste: through marriage, or elevation toward noblesse, the aristocracy can deprive the bourgeoisie from its most powerful and dynamical elements while having them join their cause, thus perpetuating the aristocratic sociopolitical model.

However, this counter-trend can only constitute a temporary slow down, because in doing so the aristocracy is effectively acknowledging the essential fact that military force and the role of social protection, fundamental to the feudal regime, is no more the main characteristic of the aristocracy, but rather it is now wealth and merit that form the distinctive character of the noblesse, thus denaturing the very concept. In other words, the caste separation, in becoming so opened, disappears, and the very idea of separate classes in society loses its sense and becomes progressively more contested. Indeed, while in a feudal regime no peasant can hope to become a noble, due to insurmountable barriers of caste, in a society where wealth and work allows one to rank among elites, there are no more fundamental differences between a poor and a wealthy man, other than the degree of wealth.

Of course, it would still be possible that the noblesse never opens up and remains closed to nascent social forces. In this case we would expect the transition to be more violent. As soon as the force ratio between the aristocracy and the bourgeoisie equilibrates, it becomes more efficient for the bourgeoisie to hire its own militias in order to protect itself from the aristocratic power instead of paying taxes to the aristocratic power. A civil war would thus emerge that results in the eradication of the aristocratic class[16].

In both cases, whether the transition operates through progressive opening or through force, the final result will be the same. There are no cases where the aristocratic power will maintain itself indefinitely by parasitizing the productive bourgeoisie. The situation is thus a one-way street in terms of where it is headed, but with some degree of uncertainty about the path to reach the destination.

It is most likely based on the principles discussed above that a cycle appears, as a series of uncertain trajectories with certain destinations. The system of cycles that we have discovered is probably the product of the clashes between various necessary historical schemes which have progressively agglomerated and influenced one another until it morphed into more complex, stable and cyclical structures. This synthesis mechanism operates similarly to how complex structures emerge from cellular automata.

The cycles we have described constitute necessary history, formed by inevitable global developments, but which realize themselves following a contingent mode, due to the random facts encountered in the process. Among these random facts are the free will of men who live and make History. Men are not completely free to make any history, since they collectively carry instincts and predominant tendencies which dictate necessary history, but they also have some freedom of action, a conscience and an ability to counteract their own tendencies. The tug of war between the major trends and the minor ones, according to their force, will produce contingent history, which is real History, that which we can study as it relates to the past, and that which will happen in the future.

Necessary History can realistically be predicted. Suffice to compare the current state of the march of the world for civilizations for which we know one cycle, and develop a prediction according to the data characterizing the cycle.

Can we predict contingent history? This would seem contrary to its very definition. Nevertheless, as we have stated, contingent history is the product of an inner tug of war in human groups between major and minor trends. While their simple existence dictates necessary history, their level of magnitude seems to dictate contingent history. If it was possible to measure these trends statistically, then even contingent historic could be predictable, at least partially and probabilistically. We would be closer, then, to turning History into equations. We could thus predict the probable delays within which an element of necessary history could effectively occur, or the specific brutality with which the events would unfold.

3. Historionomy as a new interdisciplinary field of research

As we are concluding this first part, we have reached certainty around the existence of a pattern in the evolution of civilizations over long periods of time. We have observed the repetition of this pattern. While the elements at our disposition are limited in terms of applying this pattern to what we have referred to as Cycle Zero, and therefore no certainty can be attained on this subject, nothing that we found contradicts the hypothesis of such a cycle existing, and when some evidence is available, in the case of the Cretan-Mycenaean evolution, it seems to corroborate and support it.

This long-term pattern allows us to consider the existence of historical models in the same way we speak of models in economics. Such models would constitute an analytical tool that could untangle the causality chains underlying the evolution of civilizations, and weed out the determinant or epiphenomenal nature of a given historical fact.

For historical science, the patterns we have identified also give us a chance to rethink chronology in light of the structure of these cycles. A question which often generates debates is how the current period of history should be called. After all, we won't be able to call it modernity forever! Yet, it is the last period after the Antiquity, the Middle Age and the Renaissance. Based on what we have seen, new terms would be possible: The protocyclic age, in the times of the Minoans and Mycenaeans, The First Cyclic Age, from the beginning of Greek history to the fall of Rome, and The Second Cyclic Age, currently in progress.

But beyond the study of the past, would it be possible to apply the patterns we have developed to future History, that is, predict the coming social, political, economic, scientific, religious and artistic trajectories of our civilization, similarly to the probabilistic predictions generated in economical science[17]? We have sufficiently demonstrated the existence of long cycles. These cycles are repeated on human ensembles that are ethnically and culturally diverse and apply broadly over large spatial extents of civilization and over extended periods of time. Despite the important differences, these cycles succeed at repeating which demonstrates the permanence of the social laws that underlie them, since it would seem absurd that these cycles could be anything else than the organized agglomeration of societal laws. This is the decisive progress brought by the theory of cycles, which allows us to start identifying these laws, having demonstrated that they do exist.

We have, in this essay, proposed only intuitive elements as it relates to the behavior of human groups and the course of History, which may seem jittery when compared to hard statistical sciences. Having no competence in the mathematical and statistical domains, we will not attempt to propose a method to determine the precise probability of realizations of an event, or even to measure the forces at work within society. Our ambition, in concluding this essay, is much more modest. We hope to have incited interest for a promising field of interdisciplinary research at the intersection of economics, demography and history, a field aimed at developing a true physics of History. As is the case in economic sciences, where the maximization of utility seems to present certain analogies with physics, we find in social developments numerous analogies that seem to extend beyond simple pedagogical tools. For instance, when the rapid growth of wealth of a society produces inequalities in the ownership of resources and a social differentiation, we see various tensions appearing between the different social classes, tensions which act as physical forces and engender effects, including social movements and changes of political paradigms. We still lack methods and measuring instruments for most of these forces and effects, but five hundred years ago, no one knew about Volts, Amperes or Watts, which are currently used to measure electricity, nor about the Newton, which measures gravitational force. The Antiquity and Middle Age have never developed the idea of Force, which became fundamental in physics in modern times. We could thus soon define forces and social energies as central notions of a physics of the social world, forming a science of humanity that sociology has always failed at becoming. Already, the French Physicist Serge Galam has shown how the tools of physics could be used in order to apprehend the social behavior of masses[18].

Historians and writers have often been comparing wars to storms, due to the violence and destruction that they produce. But the origins of war seem to be as poorly grasped as meteorological phenomena. At the bottom, these phenomena belong to physics only due to their specific aspects: a storm is produced by the convergence of masses of air with radically different characteristics, which leads to a release of water until a new equilibrium is reached. A war is born between two human groups (from the same society for civil wars, or from two different societies for other wars) with radically opposed interests, leading to a confrontation, which transforms the energy of the political, social, economic and demographic tensions into a fight, as a sort of transformation of human matter (deaths, population displacements, modification of mores, cathartic phenomena…), thus producing a new state of equilibrium. If we succeeded at measuring these factors, could we not generate some sort of geopolitical meteorological predictions? By using the models of necessary history as a foundation, could we construct complementary models allowing to predict, even with some margin of error, contingent history?

Without claiming Historionomy to be a perfectly predictive discipline, in addition to its value as an analytical tool, it could perhaps become a very powerful prospective tool. Thus, in the following chapters, we will attempt to use our understanding of the cycles described above in order to predict the upcoming decades, and then centuries, of the coming History.

_____

1. We can also mention the concept of fractals, implying homothety, which is applied, notably, to other domains in the world of Laurent Notalle, Jean Chaline and Pierre Grou, *Les Arbres de l'évolution*, Paris, 2000.

2. This sends us back, intuitively, to the mathematical concept of recurrence relationships, defining each term in a mathematical series as some expression of the preceding one. It Is not the first time that a mathematical mechanism is identified in History, cf. *supra* note n° 18.

3. The recurrence, in space and time, of social, political and economic patterns has been shown for a long time, since Arnold J. Toynbee, *A Study of History*, Oxford, 1934-1961 and Christian Grataloup, *Lieux d'histoire : essai de géohistoire systématique*, Paris 1996.

4. Numerous didactical articles are available on Wikipedia, as well as about the Game of Life, the most well-known cellular automata.

5. Alexander the Great, the conquest of the Persian Empire and the entire Hellenistic period come after the Peloponnesian War, and thus after the limit of the IVth century given for the period. It is a problem of chronological inversion which we have seen above, an anomaly which is made even harder due to the fact that Alexander the Great has dominated the Greeks in Macedonia and conquered the Persian Empire as a Greek.

6. On this subject, see Paul Veyne, Y a-t-il eu un impérialisme romain ? In : *Mélanges de l'École française de Rome. Antiquité*, t. 87, n° 2. 1975. pp. 793-855.

7. Paul Veyne, *L'Empire Gréco-romain*, L'identité grecque contre et avec Rome, Paris, Le Seuil, 2005, p. 196.

8. Much of his knowledge was inherited from savants of mechanical sciences: Philo of Byzantium and most importantly Ctesibius, a true genius in the domain of mechanical sciences, IIIth century B.C..

9. Quoted by Georges Bulit, *Prussianisme et nazisme : le Regard des Intellectuels Français sur l'Identité nazie de 1933 à 1940*, Paris, Edilivre Édition Universitaire, 2010.

10. Let us note that 2 000 Helots being massacred is a considerable number for Greece at that time. It was indeed the number of Spartan *homoioi*, the citizens that could be mobilized for combat. Proportionally, the data appear to be equivalent or even superior to that of German history: the Wehrmacht was formed of twelve million mobilized citizens, for ten million victims to the Nazis' crimes against humanity (counting the extermination of Jews, the Tzigane victims, the Polish civilians…).

11. We note that at stage 9), for Europe, the USA have played the role that Thebes has played for Greece, and not Rome. This should be considered with respect to our earlier remark on entities that are external to the cycles and the possibility of single entities playing multiple roles that are played by separate entities in other instances.

12. This can be found in the Wikipedia article dedicated to Chaos Theory: http://fr.wikipedia.org/wiki/Théorie_du_chaos#Prédictibilité_et_calculabilité The free encyclopedia does not provide a precise reference for this anecdote. True or false, it illustrates our statement very well.

13. Alexis de Tocqueville, *De la Démocratie en Amérique*, I, II, X.

14. Benoît Malbranque has identified, in *Le socialisme en chemise brune*, Éditions Deverle, 2012 (an edition that is available online), the profound Socialist roots of Nazism. And Friedrich Hayek, in *La Route de la servitude*, had shown the statist and socialist tradition of Germany since Bismarck. If communists, instead of Nazis, had taken power in Germany during the crisis of the 1930s, History would probably have resulted in a Second World War, and a conflict between Germany and the USSR. During the Cold War, multiple conflicts between China and its communist neighbors (Vietnam, USSR) do demonstrate that ideological communion does not keep socialist countries from entering wars between one another. Other geopolitical factors can play a role, and a German communist regime, given the situation, would have been largely nationalistic, and thus, in practice, very close to the Nazism that we have come to know.

15. Fernand Braudel was dividing historical time in three categories. Firstly, geographical time is linked to the relationship between man and his environment and evolves slowly. Secondly, social time relates to the evolution of deep societal movements. Thirdly, individual time relates to historical events. However, Braudel saw this distinction as merely an analytical tool for History, and had not quite asked the question of the distinction between the inevitable and the evitable—although he did begin to approach this problem in *Grammaire des civilisations*, Paris, 1987.

16. This idea was developed by economists, Daron Acemoglu and James A. Robinson, *Economic origins of Dictatorship and Democracy*, Cambridge University Press, 2005. These authors have attempted to apply game theory to the fight between the elite and the people, and explained that a revolutionary reversal occurred as soon as the cost for the elite to maintaining its regime is superior to the cost to switch toward democracy, and inversely when the benefits for the people to switch to democracy is greater than to accept the established regime. This illustrates another example of the application of mathematics not only to pure economics, but to social evolutions. The economist Nicolas Bouzou gives a good summary of these theories and of their applications in *On entend l'arbre tomber mais pas la forêt pousser*, JC Lattès, 2013, pp. 314-319. The author references the works of Lawrence Stone, *Literacy and Education in England*, 1640-1800, *Past and Present*, 1969, proposing that alphabetisation and demographics may play a role as a factor favoring a revolutionary reversal. These two types of works show that the study of Laws of History can only be an interdisciplinary work, and lead us to believe that the major and minor trends are quantifiable, and thus their product, Contingent History, must also be predictable.

17. The mathematician Erik Zeeman has also attempted to apply to social sciences "catastrophe theory." We can refer, notably, to Jean Petitot, based on the historical model of Thom-Pomian, *Mathématiques et sciences humaines* n° 64, n° spécial, pp. 43-70, Paris, 1978.

18. Serge Galam, *Sociophysics: a Physicist's Modeling of Psycho-political phenomena*, Springer, New York, 2012.

PART II

Prospective essay

Chapter III

Futurology of the coming century, method and practice

Before we take the big leap and propose some predictions about the medium to long term future, let us first take the time to establish some methodological principles on which we will rely.

It is important to note just how superior the use of Laws of History is in comparison to other predictive approaches based on analogies. Indeed, numerous authors, historians, journalists and commentators often use historical comparisons, sometimes extensively, in order to generate predictions. In this line, it has been proposed that the USA would crumble in the same way Spain crumbled in the XIXth century, or that the European Union was encountering a series of difficulties that were similar to those of the Roman Republic in the Ist and would therefore evolve into a Pan-European dictatorship[1]. Such reasoning always consists of an analogy between a current and a past historical situation, and in the elaboration of a predictive scheme, it is generally supposed that the current situation will progress in a similar way to that of the past. The central idea is thus that from a given stage X at some time t, we should expect the situation to be followed by stage Y at time t + 1. This kind of historical parallel is very appealing to a number of thinkers because it provides quick results, ready for delivery and communication, and it has the appearance of reason. Yet while they can be very useful in order to understand a current situation, by attracting attention, for instance, on elements of current society that may have attracted no attention otherwise, their predictive power is, in reality, inexistent.

Indeed, the great weakness of this type of reflection is the insufficient depth of historical perspective. Historical parallels, properly understood, would be similar to an attempt, in geometry, to prove that two lines, AB and XY, are parallel when one knows only two coordinates for one and one coordinate for the other. Since any two points are necessary aligned into a line, it is easy to demonstrate that some complementary point Y must exist that has the same relationship to B as X has to A. But such a reasoning would be tautological if it affirmed to have found that point, because it would be assuming the postulate that XY is parallel to AB, which is what needed to be demonstrated. Similarly, we can always find in the past a situation that is broadly similar to current facts and surmise that similar causes must have produced similar effects. This will give the illusion of a valid demonstration, without having proven anything of significance.

On the other hand, continuing with geometry, the idea that any three given points are aligned is not self-evident. If we have two lines, AB and XY, which are verifiably parallel because we have the coordinates of A, B, X and Y, then if one takes a Point C on AB, we will be able to affirm that there must be some Point Z on XY that corresponds to it, and determine its coordinates[2]. The demonstration would be solid and significant.

Similarly, if we show in advance that a past historical trajectory is parallel to an on-going trajectory, and not only similar to a punctual state at t, but also at t - 1, t - 2, then our prediction of t + 1 will be much better supported, and its realization even more probable. This is where our method is most interesting, and much superior to conventional historical parallels. Comparisons over longer durations are in a different class of significance, and the long cycles that we have observed are, as such, the first step of the reasoning demonstrating the similarity between multiple past points.

How can the patterns and principles which we have established in the first part be used to predict what the future has in store? The goal of this chapter is to propose a few elements of prospective method based on the identified cycles and apply them to the coming century.

The cycles we have observed constitute evolutionary trajectories. In order to make a prospective use of them, we must begin by determining at which point of the trajectories we are located, and then determine which are the evolutions to come, the following steps of the cycle toward which history must necessarily converge. We have said, indeed, that the cycles constituted Necessary History, that is, the History that must occur with high certainty.

Thus, we must consider these stages in view of the iteration of the current cycle, and apply these patterns of necessary history to the world that we observe. This will allow us to project the model unto reality.

This application must allow to identify the important lines of the coming developments, which constitute the share of high certainty predictions that the cycles allow. These predictions thus form the skeleton of our prospective work, a first sketch of the future. It allows us, among other things, to exclude any alternative scenario. That is the true contribution of Historionomy, and this is where it can truly change the way we operate historical prospection.

Then, we will attempt to detail this skeleton by relying on classical prospective tools. For this, we will study geopolitical data in line with what we learned from the cycles. The predictions thus generated will be less certain, more random, since they touch upon the domain of Contingent History. However, by carefully studying the political, military, economic and social aspects of current societies, we should be able to rigorously fit these facts to our cyclic model. We will thus obtain a range of predictions that might vary between more calm or violent scenarios, which in total will draw a reliable portrait of the evolution of the world over a long period. Beyond our skeleton, we will thus develop an idea of what will be the flesh of History.

In order to predict these events with greater acuity, it will be interesting to attempt to deepen our comparative analysis, for instance in Greek and European history, in order to identify other similar elements and in social matters that we have not yet integrated to our models.

Let us now attempt to apply these methods to the current world in order to find lines of predictability and their corresponding future developments.

1. Europe, Russia and America: where are we at in the AB cycle?

Here is a reminder of the last stages of Cycle A as it relates to European history:

9) All-out war internal to the civilization, relentlessness from both sides, disappearance of conventional prohibitions.

First and Second World Wars. All-out wars, massacres of civilians.

10) All-out internal war results in a weakened civilization, leading to the crumbling of its colonial empire and the loss of its global hegemony. The Empire is taken over by an emerging power of a superior size.

Europe is exhausted by its "European civil war." It loses its colonial empire and the Russian power threatens its independence.

11) All of the states forming Civilization A are taken under tutelage by the superpower of Civilization B.

Europe becomes a protectorate of Americans who triumph against Soviet power.

The current situation of the world, and its comparison with the ancient world, leads us to believe that we are at the stage where the two cycles form a single one, due to the passing of Civilization A (Europe) under tutelage by Civilization B (America). Yet this transition can occur in multiple stages, for instance as it relates to Greece, and thus we cannot determine whether this transition is already over for Europe.

The presence of most nations of occidental Europe inside the American military ensemble, particularly with NATO, places them within what we could call the American Empire. But should we consider Europe as still independent from America, i.e. as a sovereign, or not?

The question is important since the integration of Greece to the Roman Empire occurred in two stages. First, at the end of the Second Macedonian War, in 196 B.C., Rome withdrew its troops from Greece (194 B.C.). The Greek cities remained in the Roman influence zone, and under the protection of this power, while not really subordinated to Rome, but integrated to its Empire. Then, there was the Third Macedonian War (172 B.C. to 168 B.C.), during which Perseus of Macedon, as a king, attempted to restore the hegemony of his kingdom over the Greek peninsula, by supporting demagogical movements in the cities, against the pro-Roman elites. After having vanquished Perseus, the Romans re-established hegemony and divided Macedonia into four distinct political entities in order to protect themselves against a new awakening of it. Nevertheless, new tensions had appeared between Romans and Greeks, the latter having not shown much enthusiasm in supporting Rome against Macedonia. It is only at the end of the Fourth Macedonian War (146 B.C.), initiated with Andriscus' unification of Macedonia under the authority of a single king, that the Greek cities, after having rejected the Roman Power, as they were united under the Achaean League, became possessions and provinces of Rome. This happened the same year that Carthage was demolished.

Thus let us consider these two stages of Roman expansion:

- First, the Roman situation between 196 B.C. and 146 B.C.: Carthage is still standing and independent, while diminished due to its defeat in the Second Punic War, and Greece is *de facto* subordinated to Rome (in particular due to its romanophile elites), although theoretically free. We already observe the extraordinary expansion of Rome, whose power did not extend any further than over the Italian peninsula one hundred years earlier. It now covers the Illyrian coast, half of Spain, and the Maghreb, a neighbor of Carthage, is allied to Rome.

- Second, the Roman situation a little bit less than a century later, just before the great troubles and the end of the Republic. Anatolia, Egypt and Judea have become vassals of Rome. Syria has been conquered as well as the second half of Spain. Greece passed from being an ally to being a province after its revolt. The territories of Carthage and that of Macedonia were also annexed.

As it relates to current times in Europe and America, are we in a period corresponding to the IInd or the I^{st} century B.C.? In the first situation or in the second one?

A question remains about the Greek uprising and the war of a part of the Greek cities against Rome, having led to the fall of the Achaean League and the provincialization of Greece. Are these events part of a supercycle?

Two possibilities can be considered. The first possibility would be a hard repetition, in which History repeats in full, and a similar conflict would come to oppose Europe to the USA. Another, softer scenario is to consider that Europe is already a province of the USA, within a modern conception of relationships, that would simply be less rigid than those of ancient times. Let us see the arguments in support of either scenario.

The soft scenario would of course be preferable from a humanitarian perspective, since the idea of a war between Europe (or a part of it) against America would be terrible. Furthermore, it seems realistic to surmise that humanity has been pacified across the cycles, would be calmer now, and that the American Empire has extended with less violence than Rome. Europe is thus destined, as was the case between Greece and Rome, to live a few centuries in the shadow and protection of the American power. In such a scheme, however, we would have to take for granted that any conflict between Russia and America is over. Yet we cannot state that with high certainty: Russia is far from being subordinated to America, and remains very militarized and threatening to American advances. The conflict in Georgia in 2008 and in Ukraine in the current moment illustrate this. In addition, the Euro-American cycle has given only minor signs in support of the idea that humans have truly been pacified. Although progressive developments have occurred, the Second World War, notably, has shown that the potential for violence was left intact.

Let us now consider the arguments in favor of a hard scenario. They are numerous, and unfortunately, convincing. We have, today, a conception of Russia, from outside of the American Empire, that is similar to that which existed of Carthage, when it was outside of the Roman Empire in 150 B.C.. We know that there is a nationalistic movement that has increasingly won the hearts of Russians during the last decade, a form of nationalism that is particularly oriented as an opposition against American imperialism. Despite signs of concordance and collaboration, we know that some degree of animosity remains, which has particularly expressed itself in the war in Georgia, when the US Navy has moved its ships toward Russian coasts. Russia certainly does not have the means to directly confront the American giant, but it is also true that it uses any occasion to display some resistance toward American advances. It also seeks to gain every bit of power it can, in the hope of restoring the balance between the two nations. We know that the Russians have complained that they have been ridiculed by the Americans since the fall of the USSR, and they accuse the USA of having benefited from their problems in order to weaken them even further under the covers of friendships. As it turns out, study of Roman policies regarding Carthage between the Second and Third Punic Wars show a Roman arbitrage that is systematically in the favor of the Kingdom of Numidia, neighbor of Carthage, in the conflicts between the two bordering countries, an arbitrage that appears to always have weakened the old enemy. Finally, Russia remains the other great nuclear power, and America remains worried about this fact. This nuclear force is an entrenchment from which Russia succeeds at launching increasingly powerful and brutal attacks against the American global order. The current situation in Ukraine certainly surpasses the gravity of the Russo-Georgian War. In summary, we find all of the elements that were present in the strategic situation between Rome and Carthage during the first half of the IInd century B.C..

Let us return to Europe. Europe has been an ally of America since 1945 through its integration to NATO. On its domestic side, it has been confederated into the European Union. The situation is similar to that of Greece after 194 B.C., while the Consul Flamininus had proclaimed the liberty of Greek cities following the victory of Rome over Macedonia, and had ordered the withdrawal of Roman troops. The Greek cities were allied to Rome, and assembled into confederations, the Aetolian League and the Achaean League, within which the cities were abandoning certain sovereign rights in order to govern themselves together and form a common front, and to increase their weight against the Macedonian and Roman giants. This situation lasted half a century, at the end of which the leagues were dissolved while a part of Greece rose against Rome by taking the side of Macedonia. This uprising caused, among other things, the development of an animosity of the Greeks against Rome, inflamed by the pro-Roman attitude of the elites who had taken power after the first Macedonian crumbling. These elites were overthrown and replaced by Greek patriots and demagogues, favorable to the rejection of Rome. Let us read what Paul Veyne[3] has to say about Greco-Roman relationships at the middle of the IInd century B.C.: "*The poor, the crowds, were hostile to Rome, and the wealthy were pro-Roman or careless, abstaining from resistance.*" The analogy is, once again, striking. Is this not a portrait of the current rapport between Europe and America?

Let us recall what we have said about Macedonia: its role, as that of Carthage, seems to play in the Euro-American cycle through Russia. We know that, since the fall of the USSR, the capitalist economic model prevails in all of Europe, but that an anti-American sentiment is common within the populations of Western Europe. We also know that the European Union is seen unfavorably by the same anti-Americans, who see in its institutions a denial of democracy and a transfer of power to the elites. As folkloric as the burgeoning of conspiracy theories may be, they still capture an important sociological fact: people are taken by a feeling that a loss of rights has occurred as to their ability to govern themselves to the benefit of uncontrollable hierarchies, and exasperation is increasing. The same phenomenon is observable in Greeks faced with Roman hegemony, which has led to the uprising and the abolition of the leagues in the IInd century. Additionally, this trend, in Europe, was accentuated recently by the economic crisis, and the resulting austerity plans. People do not feel that they are being governed in their best interest. They are tempted by identitarianism. This is often referred to as the rise of populisms, linked to a new demand for protectionism by the people. The same attitudes have previously led, after 10 years of accumulation, to the Second World War.

The current European crisis, referred to as "the debt crisis," is perceived notably as a crisis of the welfare state as well as a questioning of the compromise of social democracy. This crisis was built around the following choice: liberalism (more or less limited by technocratic dirigism and democratic clientelism) or fascism (authoritarian corporatism toward which simplistic and popular reasoning always converge).

Liberalism would be a return to less public expenses and more budgetary rigor[4], and a confirmation of European free trade, which would keep Europe inside the circle of American friendships and would favor the soft scenario. Fascism, whose premises are observable in the rise of European populism, was defined by Hayek as the socialism of those abandoned by socialism; as the emergence of socialistic demands from the middle classes and small bourgeoisie who had been abandoned by social-democracy to the benefit of the workers and, today, of immigrants[5]. This second possible reaction would be protectionist, antiliberal and thus always anti-American, which might create a rupture between Europe and America, and precipitate a hard scenario.

Here again, multiple elements seem to support the hard scenario: while the negotiation of the Transatlantic Free Trade Treaty between Europe and America demonstrates the strength of the link that still unites the two continents, centrifugal forces are also at play, and are stimulated in reaction to this cooperation.

Thus we are seeing, in Europe, a rebirth of the "Russian party." This Russian party, during the Cold War, was essentially composed of European communists for whom the USSR, the leading communist power both in size and seniority, was a natural leader. However, as early as the end of the Second World War, a sovereigntist like Charles De Gaulle was dreaming of a Europe from the Atlantic to the Ural, which he thought would constitute a counterweight against the American Power. In the times of the General, numerous sovereigntists, often positioned on the right of the political axis, saw Russia as too much of an incarnation of the communist threat to share this Pan-European vision. The fall of Communist Russia and the return of an authoritarian regime based on traditional order, particularly on the Orthodox Church, has led to the disappearance of these reservations.

However, this new Russian party does not only assemble European ultraconservatives. Indeed, it tends to unite under its banner all of Europe's populisms, whether they are right-wing or left-wing. Similarly to the habit of old European democracies to govern at the center, by betting on a consensus between right-wing and left-wing moderates, that is, a model of exclusion of the extremes, the new European populisms contest the reign of the parties of the government and claim to go beyond the traditional left-right dichotomy. This dichotomy is denounced as an instrument of democratic illusionism. Since the denunciation of the governing parties tend to be a common point between the two extremes, we observe, at the European level, the birth of a populist movement that appears to seek centrism through addition of the extremes, as described by Fabrice Bouthillon[6]. Thus, Marine Le Pen has announced her desire for a victory of Syriza, a far-left party, in the Greek elections, because she agrees with this party on the rejection of the supranational institutions of the European Union. Furthermore, Syriza allied themselves with the Greek nationalist right. Marine Le Pen and Syriza also share a similarity in having defended the side of Vladimir Putin in the Ukrainian Crisis; just like Jean-Luc Mélenchon, who has the pro-Russian *habitus* of the communists through anti-Americanism, and Viktor Orban, a conservative right-wing leader in Hungary. In an article dated September 29th 2014, on the website Dreuz, Guy Millière has described this networking between European populisms as a Neo-Fascist International, noting that despite their differences in positioning on the political spectrum of their respective countries, these movements had a common ideology in pointing to liberalism as a global danger against which we must fight. Such an argument re-appropriates the conservative and sovereigntist idea of Europe from the Atlantic to the Ural, that is, a Russian-European alliance seeking to form a continental bloc that would be hostile to American thalassocracy. Such a bloc would be characterized by collectivism, whether it is traditional and nationalistic collectivism or a communist form of collectivism[7]. Russia is the epicenter of this movement, naturally, because this country is the only one which, in Europe, incarnates the complete political ideal in question: an authoritarian regime, very nationalistic, based on traditions (especially religious institutions), standing up to the American power. This gives it a certain pre-eminence, as was obtained by the USSR over the European communist parties. As in the times of Stalin, Khrouchtchev and Brejnev, Russia has a direct geopolitical interest in feeding, in all of Europe, a party susceptible to support its cause, notably in the media.

The period of relative European consensus which followed the fall of the USSR has ended. New difficulties in Europe have led to this schism: the negative effects of the Euro over the equilibrium between national economies, and, following the crisis of 2008, the discontent with regards to political austerity (by reductions of social welfare advantages and/or by increases of fiscal pressure). These factors have brought water to the mill of euroskeptics. The return of Russian vigor and the apparent strength of Putin have given a credibility to the populists. A schism similar to that of the Cold War has reappeared, with, on one side, the euroskeptic nationalist populisms, which tend to align or support Russia, and on the other side, the Europeanism of governing parties, and their favorability toward America. We observe more and more manifestations of this schism, in particular with conflicts like that of Ukraine, which seems to oppose one right to another in a confused way: legality vs. legitimacy, the right of peoples to determine their own fate and national sovereignty. As populists are coordinating and winning audiences, we can imagine, in line with our hard scenario, that the intra-European tensions will increase, and could result in a dissolution of the Union. Vladimir Putin probably hopes for this dissolution, since the European Union has been a tool of American diplomacy that has kept Russian influences away from Eastern Europe. It is already the case that Russian banks are funding euroskeptic parties such as the Front National in France. While the Americans are pursuing their containment strategy with respect to Russia, Putin is attempting to bypass this strategy and manoeuvers in order to cause a dissolution of the European Union and NATO. The situation in the European Union having been weakened by the economic crisis, a few well-placed hits could lead it to falter. No need for populist victories in a majority of countries. A few electoral successes, giving these countries some nuisance powers, could have important consequences on the integrity of the Union, by having an aggravating effect on its situation. The crushing victory of Syriza in Greece in January 2015 was a first strong blow for the European Union. As soon as they were elected, the leaders of this far-left party and their sovereigntist allies have publicly declared their support of Putin in the Ukrainian affair, and taken the opposite stance to the European consensus on this question. Furthermore, the economic measures planned by the party of Tsipras will only aggravate the Greek situation, and thus the European situation. In the worst scenario, a domino effect could result from the aggravation, and popular exasperation could give to the Spanish equivalent of Syriza, Podemos, the necessary boost for an electoral victory at the end of 2015. In its turn, Spain would falter, threatening France which could see a victory of populism in 2017. The rise of the Front National to power in France is the secret hope of Putin: France has already historically demonstrated its propensity toward rebellion against the American hegemony, when De Gaulle withdrew France from the commandment of NATO. The reversal of the second greatest country of the Euro zone, and one of the most well-equipped countries of NATO, toward the Russian camp would be an immense victory for Putin, and would allow an authoritarian France-Russia axis to dictate its conditions to an isolated Germany[8]. The European Union would not survive to such a wave of electoral victories and military defections. Vladimir Putin would probably use the opportunity to restore the Russian Empire as it was in the times of the Warsaw Pact. We know that in September 2014, the chief of the Russian state has declared to the Ukrainian President: *"If*

I wanted, the Russian troops could arrive in two days, not only to Kiev, but also to Riga, Vilnius, Tallinn, Warsaw and Bucharest[9]. " A crumbling of the European Union and the appearance of intra-European tensions would be a dreamed occasion for launching such a movement, by benefiting from the inability of Europeans to react in unison.

Such an adventure would not be surprising coming from Putin. We must not commit the traditionally European error of believing that a chief of State would be unable to engage into an escalation just because it would be too risky for him. Not all leaders have the aversion to risk that is common in the career politicians leading our democracies. Some are willing to take risky bets in order to achieve what they perceive to be a great enterprise, and even more so when they are surrounded by a state apparatus and a people who share the same vision. Thus we must not neglect the fact that, psychologically, Russia is in a situation that is similar to that of Germany in the 1930s. Vanquished and reduced in its greatness after a defeat in a long war. This long war seemed, especially for the old guard of the KGB, who are today in power with Putin, not to be a military defeat but rather a defeat on the domestic side[10]. Humiliated by American bullying for 15 years, just like Germany had been bullied by France, the progression of NATO is experienced similarly to the occupation of the Ruhr in 1923-1925 (with the difference, of course, that the countries of Eastern Europe do not legitimately belong to Russia). All of this has awakened a desire for revenge. Russia certainly has not, relatively to today's world, the power that Germany had in 1939, but this slight demographic and economic difference is compensated by its nuclear arsenal, which makes its territory a sanctuary from which it can launch strategic offensives. Notably, its irredentist policy regarding Russian-speaking people and the natural space of Russia resembles that of Hitler in the Sudetes, in Austria and in Poland[11]. Furthermore, for ten years, the regime of Vladimir Putin, by profiting of the rise of hydrocarbon prices, has acquired a lot of weaponry and military equipment, considerably modernizing the Russian army which was poorly equipped in the 1990s. The Russians have used the opportunity of the Russo-Georgian War of 2008, among others, in order to test their army, and have no doubt learned a lot when one sees the efficiency of their takeover of Crimea. The rearmament program of 2007-2015 is about to be completed, and Vladimir Putin finds himself at the head of a renovated army, capable of undertaking new projects. Certainly, the Russian army would be unable to directly challenge the United States of America, but it can hope for a moment of weakness in order to make some important moves. The opponent of Putin, Andrey Piontovski, has raised the possibility that limited nuclear strikes[12] could be launched by Vladimir Putin on cities of Eastern Europe in order to demonstrate the impotence of the American "umbrella," and in order to discredit NATO. Such a scenario, however, seems unlikely. The use of a nuclear weapon for an act of aggression would seem too counter-productive, and would unify the European countries whose governing parties could denunciate Russian barbarity. This hypothesis by Piontovski is thus improbable, notably because it does not correspond to how the Putin regime normally operates, which is to play over ambiguities in order to compensate for its strategic weaknesses. On the other hand, the simultaneous agitation of the partisans of Putin in numerous neighboring countries with a strong Russian-speaking component, specifically in the Baltic States, and the use of such agitation as a justification for conventional military invasion operations could give an opportunity to humiliate NATO (whose members include these countries) and obtain the desired effect. Such interventions could be cloaked under the habitual rhetoric of protecting minorities, a rhetoric which has already shown efficiency in seducing a share of the European public. Furthermore, Putin may believe that the Americans will not risk a war for the Baltic States, just like Hitler thought that the French would not want to die for Poland, especially given that Russia seems to have already forced the United States to step back in their Syrian invasion project in 2013.

Even in a less catastrophic scenario, in which populisms would be partially discredited by a quick and resounding failure of Syriza[13], and would become incapable of winning elections, we could witness sufficiently-grave internal troubles. For instance, the populists could claim a denial of democracy, given the multiplication of deals between moderates, such as that observed in Sweden, where the government parties have simply decided to cancel elections in order to avoid a progression of populists, and govern together through a national union, which resembles a parliamentary dictatorship by self-proclaimed leaders[14]. This attitude reinforces populisms, by feeding into the narratives of the democratic illusion, of political connivance as well as the perception of politicians as "all corrupted," and this could push them toward violence, with the support of Putin, as the hopes of changing the situation through the electoral path disappear.

In this alternative hypothesis, Russia could take advantage of the disorder in order to advance its pawns, with the support of populists, while economic difficulties lead to civil troubles. The populists would serve as a fifth pillar of Russia, just like the French Communist Party served as a fifth column to the Germans, allied to the USSR in 1940. Of course, in addition to the political and military hegemony of Europe, it is also the American economy which would be threatened, and free trade between Europe and America would be compromised. The Russian hope would be that the hit to American hegemony would turn out to be fatal, and that the power of the United States would be pushed back to the Atlantic Ocean, which would constitute a complete revenge. The accomplishment of this project would be manifested in the appearance of a European-Russian authoritarian-populist bloc, in which Russians guarantee energy provisions to Europe as well as military protection in exchange for their subordination, notably through the purchasing of influential elites, with contracts and jobs, as was the case for the former German chancellor Gerhard Schröder. Russia would count on the economic power of Occidental Europe in order to durably outclass America[15]. Before this occurs, however, the USA would likely attempt to restore control of the situation, notably, if necessary, through force and with more or less brutality depending on the scenario, and with support from a part of Europe that would have remained on their side. We would thus be in a configuration of war which, following the Greco-Roman model, would result in an American victory. This is not only what the example of Ancient Greece teaches us, but also what a simple analysis of current times seems to suggest. America would rather enter a total war instead of letting an adversary become so powerful that it would constitute a threat to its independence. As Hitler committed an error when he thought that England would sign for peace once Germany had realized its domination over the continent following the defeat of France, Putin and the anti-American Europeans are very wrong in thinking that an America rejected by Europe would simply come to accept this fact.

Indeed, for the USA, as was the case with Rome, there are only two acceptable options: be alone, or be the master[16]. Being alone was the first American geopolitical doctrine, the Monroe doctrine, established in 1823, which forbid any European intervention on the American continent. Such an intervention would have been considered an aggression by the young power. The other side of this doctrine was that the USA remained neutral toward Europe and would not intervene in its own affairs.

However, during the second half of the XIXth century, the first globalization occurred, which led America to realize it could not remain alone, isolated between its two oceans. Thus came the Roosevelt Corollary, a complement to the Monroe doctrine that practically inverted its effect up to then: from now on, the United States would consider themselves justified in intervening outside of America in any place where their interests would be threatened. Incapable of being alone, America would have to be hegemonic. Through the discourse of Roosevelt in 1904, the USA self-proclaimed their status as world police. At no moment in its history, since its independence, has America considered itself a mere nation among others.

This mentality comes from the Independence: for the American people, to face once again dependence against a new foreign power would be equivalent to death, and, when it boils down to it, the only way to be dependent on no one, other than by being completely isolated from everyone, is to be a universal suzerain.

That is the guiding principle, the principle of principles of American international policy. All other principles, including ideals, are subordinated to that one. It is for this reason that America has supported dictatorships during the Cold War. It is for this reason that the United States never will abandon the exorbitant privilege of the dollar, which they won at the end of the Second World War, whether it be to the benefit of China, or anyone else. It is for this reason that America would militarily invade Europe and crush Russia under a carpet of nuclear bombs before it allowed a hostile Euro-Russian bloc to appear. According to the doctrine of Zbigniew Brzezinski, which continues to dictate an important part of American geopolitics, the United States can only be truly hegemonic, and thus safe, if they control Europe.

In the hypothesis of a total war, or something close to it, America could not lose: its military forces are way too strong compared to those of Russia[17], and it can count on stronger support in Europe than Putin can. An American victory in such a war would result in the definitive vassalization of Europe, and the definitive crushing of Russia, which could, given the inviolability of the territory of Russia due to nuclear capacities, take the form of an overthrow of the regime of Vladimir Putin and a pact between Americans and the Russian oligarchy, preserving the fortune of the latter in exchange for its subordination. Such a scenario would no doubt be very painful for Europe, which would have to go through its most difficult internal struggles since 1945, and would definitively lose the relative independence that it has been successful, up to now, at preserving with respect to the United States.

This would constitute a repeat of the events of 146 B.C.: the conversion of Greece into a province and the destruction of Carthage and Macedonia.

The most likely hypothesis, in my view, is a scenario somewhere in-between the soft and hard hypotheses that we have presented. In this scenario, Occidental Europe will remain on the side of the United States despite internal contestations (which might cause some troubles), and will face the Russian power alongside the USA. This confrontation will manifest itself in a great war, which could be nuclear, or could simply correspond to a tactic of support of the internal European contestation movements that would help favor a power grab in Russia and exclude the former KGB circles from controlling the Kremlin. This approach would be combined to the isolation of Russia on the international scene by depriving it of its nuisance potential in Iran, Syria and the Sino-Russian axis.

Europe after the reduction of Russia

The Ukrainian affair is already the clash of two empires: the fundamental stake is in the belonging of Europe to one or the other camp, Russia or America. The shift toward the Russian camp, which will not occur or will be partial, painful and temporary, would mean the emergence of an authoritarian populism similar to fascism, based on the model of Putin.

The definitive integration to the American camp will occur and can be progressive. While the continuation of the alliance of Europe with the American power is a part of Necessary History, the exact way in which it will occur remains Contingent History.

The first possibility, which is the least desirable, would be the transformation of Europe into a sort of American province, with a great loss of autonomy and an oligarchic transformation of local power. This would be the closest scenario to Ancient Greece: the final triumph of Rome on the Carthage-Macedonian axis leads to the transformation of Greece into a Roman province, and the loss of the autonomy that had been left to it by Rome at the beginning of the IInd century B.C., thus allowing it to live half a century of peace and prosperity, with the cities largely gathered into leagues. After the Roman victory against Macedonia, the leagues were dissolved and Greece was subordinated to Rome. Democracy, which still existed in numerous Greek cities, was weakened and replaced by oligarchy, which was easier to control by the Roman ally, thus ensuring the stability of alliances, contrarily to democracies which had always allowed the rise to power of demagogues calling for the abolition of debts and the rejection of Rome. Let us add that Corinth, which had been the ally of Rome, was, like Carthage, completely destroyed at the end of the war, as a punishment for its treason.

Europe, and in particular France, will undergo a similar fate if its populations are showing themselves to be too seduced by Putin and if, as we have predicted, some important defections occur within NATO, to the benefit of Russia. Then, the takeover of Europe under American control would be more difficult, and America would feel for a moment that its geopolitical safety is threatened, and would thus develop a durable distrust toward Europeans, susceptible to favor the search for stronger ways of controlling their political regimes, at the expense of democracy. Yet, democracy is still the regime in which the state of rights degrades the slowest. Furthermore, the diminution of the number of sane democracies in the world is never good news for the remaining democracies. Democracies are stronger when they are numerous, and thus can criticize each other. An America that would attempt to preserve democracy at home at the expense of that of others would quickly see its own democracy turn into an oligarchy or in a demagogical and authoritarian regime.

The alternative scenario is that of a Europe in which Putin's ploys for destabilization, in particular through local populisms, would completely fail, and would thus never constitute a serious threat to the stability of Euro-American alliances. The trust of the USA in the stability of European democracies within the American alliance would be reinforced, and the partnership between Europe and America on relatively equal footing would be given a break.

Let us not entertain any illusion: this break would be only temporary. In the end, America will no doubt become increasingly authoritarian, in a stage that will be later described, in line with the Roman example.

Beyond this internal progression within America, despite the ability of democracies to criticize one another and to maintain certain requirements in terms of rights and freedoms, democracies appear to be destined to degenerate. Indeed, their supreme global positioning will protect them from any external critique of their consensus. United democracies no longer engage in war amongst each other. They develop international networks, either official ones like the European institutions, or private ones such as the Bilderberg meeting and the Trilateral Commission, which tend to uniformize modes of thought and to limit the benefits that could be obtained by political contestation. Thus, the Snowden affair has shown, paradoxically, that Russia, a doubtfully democratic society with a leader like Vladimir Putin, who certainly cannot be considered as a strong defender of liberty and human rights, was willing to welcome an individual who has become a whistleblower by alarming the citizens of his nation about the spying of their government over their private communications. Inversely, the great European democracies, allied to the USA, and enmeshed in a close network of relationships, have submitted to the American government and have supported them in their persecution of Snowden, against any principle of liberty. There is thus a benefit to the existence of a common enemy such as Vladimir Putin, in that he is truly independent and willing to use all available means to discredit democratic governments, notably by denunciating their actual flaws. A genuine counter-power is a form of insurance. While it may be dangerous in other domains, it remains useful and would disappear if Russia became too weak. Thus, let us remind ourselves of the total defeat of Macedonia, which liberated the Greek cities from a threat, but also resulted, in the long run, to a greater subordination toward the Roman power.

Furthermore, the authoritarian evolution of the USA, naturally, will also weight unto liberties in Europe. America would then no doubt show a preference for an oligarchy as such an oligarchy would offer more stable alliances than democracy. It would also establish permanent powers that can be made loyal through privileges, such as citizenship. The members of governing parties would no doubt find an interest in such a setup, by soliciting some title and place in the power structure, as it happened in the case of Sweden.

Thus, for Europe, there will be advantages as well as disadvantages to the definitive submission of Russia by America. On the one hand, it will be a good thing to see Russian propaganda and the ideas of "realpolitik[18]" to stop having an influence over our thinkers, but on the other hand the democratic unanimity and the oligarchical evolution will be unavoidable in the long run.

2. Arab spring, Islamic winter: where are we at in Cycle C and what should be expected?

Let us take a moment to remind ourselves of the two last stages of Cycle C, in the case of Arab-Muslim nations:

12) In the face of the rising provocations, which reach an intolerable degree, Civilization B, infuriated, opts for the military solution and crushes the fanatics in bloody wars, repeatedly.

Events of 1979, attacks in Europe, September 11th attacks. Afghanistan and Iraq wars, the War against Terrorism and the worldwide fight against Al-Qaeda. Military victory against Islamist terror organizations, resurgence of the Islamic State.

13) Confirmation of the dominance of the model of Civilization B. Civilization C is eradicated as a political power.

Secularization of the societies of Arab countries, hope for the establishment of a democratic model after the great revolutions of 2011, progressive disappearance of the remaining radical Islamic organizations, death of Osama bin Laden.

Have we been too optimistic in making of the Arab spring one of the premises of the disappearance of Jihadism? Some elements seem to plead the contrary, notably the idea that an Islamic winter would be about to fall unto the Arab-Muslim world, by allowing the return into power of the old opponents of secular regimes, the Islamists. Yet we have seen, in our modeling of Cycle C, that in Ancient Jewish history, the Pharisees and the Zealots have taken power following the overthrowing of Hellenistic kings, and that they then engaged their people in the war against the Roman Empire, which turned out to be very murderous and humiliating for the Jews and for their radicals, who had highly terrestrial, Millenarist and eschatological hopes. It is the shock of an unprecedented violence inflicted by the Romans to the Jewish people that has broken these fanatical dreams. By making of Israel a vanquished people, the Empire liberated, in the end, Jews from the most retrograde expression of their religion, in particular the ambition to establish a theocratic political order founded on a strict reliance on the Laws of Moses in all of society. The inflicted humiliation discredited the dreams of final domination of the Jews and opened the way for a more spiritual interpretation of the texts, as well as the reorganization of the doctrine into Rabbinical Judaism.

In approaching this problem, we have considered that the great war between radical Islam and the American Empire had started on September 11th 2001, despite some precedents having occurred before, such as the Islamic Revolution of Iran in 1979, the attacks on the embassies of Tripoli and Islamabad, and the Grand Mosque seizure by a Mahdist movement. Yet, since 2001, the terroristic organizations have been weakened, and in 2011, the great figure of Islamic terrorism, Osama Bin Laden, was executed by American Special Forces.

Many commentators, during the Arab spring which occurred in 2011, have noted that the young people who were protesting were not making anti-Israeli statements and did not have slogans supporting the establishment of Islamic republics like the theocracy of Iran. It may have been tempting, if one was limited to these analyses in the moment, to think that the political-religious model proposed by radical Islam had been discredited by the incapacity of Islamists, demonstrated over 10 years, to win any confrontation with America, and their propensity to massacre other Muslims in attacks across the Arab world. In this setup, the revolutions would constitute the beginning of a rejection of the Islamic terroristic vision within the Arab-Muslim world. Thus, a modern Islam would be expected to develop within the coming years, which would abandon radical interpretations of the texts to the benefit of a more spiritual one, as was the case in the transition between Ancient Judaism and Rabbinical Judaism. In this case, we would have expected to see a rise to power, through democratic means, of (moderate?) Islamists like those of the Ennahda Movement or the Muslim Brotherhood in Tunisia and Egypt. Such movements would constitute a stabilizing conservative force after the revolutionary upheaval, which would allow a progressive evolution toward more modernity and less religious identitarian crisping.

The other possibility was that the revolutions would be largely recuperated by those who, for a long time, have been the main opponents of the defunct regimes: The Islamists, who support the establishment of a political regime in accordance with Islamic law. Then, the arrival of Islamists to power would not be a conservative temporary step in the evolution toward a secularization of society and a spiritualization of Islam condemning the Millenarist vision and theocratic objectives. To the contrary, this consecration of Islamists by popular support would be a prelude to a vast movement of identitarian withdrawal throughout the Arab-Muslim world, following the model, despite the Sunnism/Shiism distinction, of the Islamic Republic of Iran. The ensemble of the Arab-Muslim world would thus become the backers and supporters of a reinvigorated Islamic terroristic vision for years to come, leading to new occidental military interventions, of which the violence would be proportionate to the intensity of the new tensions[19].

The Muslim world is vast, and as such, we observe evolutions in the two directions. In some places, the Arab spring seems to be followed, despite certain difficulties, by a real democratic transition, which are punctuated by returns to authoritarianism. In Egypt, one can remain doubtful in front of the election of General el-Sisi. He could be compared to the military dictatorships of Napoleon in France or George Monck in England, which were merely transitionary steps in the revolutions of these two countries toward the final establishment of a durable parliamentarism. Furthermore, General el-Sisi seems to behave like Flavius Josephus. This Jewish general was revolted by the barbaric nature of the zealots of his own religion, so much so that he had joined the Roman camp. el-Sisi made, in 2014, a historical declaration at the Al Azhar University, one of the global centers of Muslim theology: *"This corpus of texts and ideas which we have sacralized for many years, to the point where detaching ourselves from it has become almost impossible, induces hostility toward us in the entire world [...] It is impossible that the thoughts we hold as the most sacred may be for the community of believers a source of anxiety, danger, murder and destruction for the rest of the world [...] Is it conceivable that 1.6 billion people do think that they must kill the other members of humanity, which totals to seven billion people, in order to live? ... I speak these words at Al Azhar, in front of this assembly of ulemas... What I'm telling you, you won't understand it if you remain stuck within your mode of thought. You must get out of what you are in order to be able to appreciate the benefit of a more enlightened spirit. I say, and I repeat, that we are faced with the need for a religious revolution. You, the Imams, are responsible in front of God. The entire world, I repeat, the entire world is awaiting your next movement... because the community of believer is ravaged, destroyed; and it is so because of us".[20]*

In other places, to the contrary, Jihadism is more vigorous than ever. The world was shocked by the appearance and brutal rise of the Islamic State and its restoration of the Caliphate, replacing Al-Qaeda, which had been weakened, by an organization that generated much enthusiasm in the fanatics across the world. This rise provoked Jihadist emulation, motivating even more Islamists from other areas, such as Boko Haram in Nigeria. These trends also gained grounds through older but still active organizations such as Al-Qaeda in the Islamic Maghreb. Europe is afraid that parts of its Muslim populations, who left to join Jihad-dominant areas, would come back trained to combat in order to perpetrate attacks. Already, the propaganda of Daesh, accessible on the Internet, radicalizes isolated individuals in Occident, leading them to commit terroristic actions. These lone actors are often pointed to by authorities as mentally insane, so that civil peace can be maintained. It is true that in Occident, the violent nihilism of Jihadism seems to offer a turnkey ideology for anyone seeking violence, taking the role that was once occupied by anarchism in the XIXth century and communism during the Years of Lead. From this point of view, the idea according to which these terrorists would not be "true Muslims" is not entirely false, but it cannot be considered completely true either. The murderous Zealots of Antiquity were Jewish, even if not all Jews were Zealots. However, through the game of radicalization, in this type of situation, the individuals are quickly required to choose a camp. When the fight begins to hurt family and friends, the choice can quickly be driven down to a simple question of belonging to a given community rather than adhering to a specific doctrine. It is this mechanism that causes the worst mass movements, like the religious wars of France in the XVIth century. It would be absolutely possible that, similarly to the ancient war of Kitos, which was a generalized revolt of Jews across the Hellenistic world, we would observe a rise of Islamism outside of the Arab world, where Muslim populations constitute a significant minority, that is, Europe. In France, the riots of 2005 have already provided an idea of what an uprising with a strong ethnic and religious component could look like.

We have explained above how much the community tensions between "native" occidentals and Muslim populations resemble those between the Greco-Romans and Jews in the first century of our era. Here again, the same causes could lead to the same nefarious consequences. In 2014-2015, two best-selling books were fully or partly dedicated to the fear of Islam, perceived as a threat to civilization: *Le suicide français* by Éric Zemmour and *Soumission* by Houellebecq. These literary works reflect a genuine occidental preoccupation that is similar to that of Cicero toward the Jews. The multiplication of acts by "mentally unstable individuals" or other incidents, such as those that have occurred in 2014 around synagogues, could suffice, in Europe as it is still affected by an economic crisis, to open the way for dramatic events. Small riots could incite other, bigger ones, or even attacks that would cause spontaneous reprisals from the population. Such disorders have not been encountered to that extent since the religious wars of the XVIth century. Worrying signs appear to be in line with this prediction. In Germany, on January 5th 2015, 18 000 Germans have protested in Dresden against "Islamicisation," and a recent movement, the "Patriotic Europeans Against the Islamicisation of the Occident," has the sympathy of half the population. The size of its audience is growing steadily as attested by its weekly meetings. These movements are developing in response to troubles to public order caused by Muslim individuals, notably the conflicts between several hundreds of Kurds and Salafists in Hamburg, on October 7-8th 2014. Across Europe, similar movements have been appearing for a couple of years, such as Stop Europe Islamization. The Charlie Hebdo shooting, on January 7th 2015, is another event in line with this progression.

Another scenario could involve a major conflict between NATO and Israel with a part of the Arab-Muslim world. An importation of such a conflict unto European soil should not be excluded, especially given that a large quantity of weapons of war circulate in the underground networks of certain cities. In January 2015, the Imam of Drancy, Hassen Chalgoumi, noted that 80% of Muslims, the peaceful majority, sees in the Quran a book of peace and a source of spiritual inspiration, while recognizing that for the remaining 20%, the Quran is seen as a book of war and intolerance, a license to kill in the name of Allah[21]. The statistic may appear to be reassuring from a proportional standpoint, but from an absolute numbers standpoint, it is worrying: 20% of the Muslim population would represent a million people in France, three million people in Europe, and three hundred million in the world. Even if only a percent of this radical minority was to take action, this would represent thirty thousand terrorists on the territory of the European Union. Would pacifist movements such as "I am Charlie," or the legitimate institutional and popular refusals to engage in ethnic judgment, survive such attacks? Or may we witness a radicalization pushing a greater share of Muslims with radical sensibilities to a form of radical action in which they would take more moderate Muslims as hostage, persecuting them for not being fervent enough while they are also being persecuted by non-Muslims for being too fervent? Sinister memories indicate that even in civil wars, such as the religious wars of the XVIth century in France, radicals from one side and the other are never only a minority. Their nuisance power lies in their ability to force the moderates against each other in order to provoke a general confrontation. Such a general confrontation, in Europe, could cause tens of thousands, perhaps hundreds of thousands of victims.

In any case, it seems probable that the political and religious dream of radical Islamism may not be considered as fully broken as long as the Islamic State or perhaps even the Islamic Republic of Iran will stand and provide the impression that the American Imperial power can be defied in impunity. Along with the Sunni Bin Laden and the Islamic State, the Shia theocratic regime of Iran constitutes the other great symbol of Islamic resistance to the American world order. Born in 1979, simultaneously to Sunni Mahdism, was the Great Mosque of Mecca. The fall of these symbols is certainly the *sine qua non* requirement for the final liberation of Muslims from the Millenarist fanatical vision of Islamism with respect to the dream of a final domination of Islam and the establishment of a global Caliphate. Furthermore, it is not impossible that these various trends would mutually destroy themselves, or that the United States would benefit from internal antagonisms in order to open up Iran and prepare a transition away from the regime of the Mullahs, while militarily crushing Daesh.

Concerning Iran, it seems that the Americans are in the phase of relaxation, as it occurred during the Cold War with the Soviets. The totalitarian aspect of the theocracy in Iran is different from that in Saudi Arabia. In Saudi Arabia, religious obscurantism characterizes the mentality much better, because it is a country whose mechanisms have remained very feudal. Iran, to the contrary, in the 1970s, was one of the most developed countries in the world, with an Occidental way of life. The Iranian regime is much closer to a Soviet regime with Mullahs leading the country instead of a Communist Party. It does not operate like a backwards theocracy. It is a totalitarian regime with very modern structures, inherited from its Occidental period. In other words, the same difference exists between the Russian absolutism of Ivan the Terrible and the Soviet totalitarianism of Brejnev and between Saudi Arabia and Iran. One of the pair is closer to Occidental Civilization than the other, and for this reason, it is possible that the USA will come to see Iran as a better ally than Saudi Arabia. This would be an extremely consequential change of perception because in the return to the Cold War that is building up between America and Russia, having Iran as an ally rather than an enemy is one way to limit and perhaps even threaten Russia from the South. The idea that this ally is more "natural" would facilitate such a transition.

However, all of the Middle-East is now unstable. We cannot tell whether the current stagnation of the Islamic State signifies there will be a drawback or new advances to come. There is also the potential for a blaze to take over the region beyond what is already happening.

Another factor determining the reconfiguration of alliances in the Middle East is the production boom of fossil energies in the USA, thanks to the important progresses in extraction techniques making accessible and economically viable reserves of oil that were previously unusable. Already in 2014, the restructuration of the energy market has led to an important drop in the price of gas and oil. Such a disruption in the production of fossil energy will profoundly modify the set of global interests involved in the Arab-Muslim world, reducing the possible paths of funding for radical Islam and diminishing its potential audience. Saudi Wahhabism will lose its influence and the fall of the regime of the Mullahs could be precipitated by increased economic difficulties.

Although it is difficult to predict the particular path of the future history of Islam, the completed analogy with the Judaism of Moses of Antiquity informs us about its destination. In the end, all regimes inspired by Islamism, and all Jihadist movements will be militarily vanquished and ideologically broken. There will no doubt be other painful combats, possibly of a terrifying size, on the territory of Occident itself, before the Muslim world can evolve toward a more spiritual, less political and materialistic version of their religion. We can expect that the question should be resolved by the middle of the XXIth century. If historical repetition was pushed to the extreme, then it would be possible (in a very hard scenario) that as the Temple of Jerusalem was destroyed at the end of the first Jewish-Roman war, leading fanatical Jews into desperation, the Mecca might be destroyed, for instance by bombardment, during a terrible confrontation between the USA and the Muslim world. A complete reversal of alliances, with an America that would have become allied with Iran, perhaps after the fall of the Iranian regime, could make this scenario credible. According to American intelligence agencies, a part of the Saudi army would already be seduced by the Islamic State[22]. We should note that, in reality, the Saudi conception of power and the rule of Sharia is not very different from that of the Islamic State, the only difference residing in the familial and patrimonial aspect of Saudi power, which has maintained a dose of rationality and stability in the Saudi Arabia regime, counterbalancing fanatism with money-making. A reversal of a part of the army and a revolution that would be favorable to the Islamic State would constitute a geopolitical cataclysm, providing the Islamic State with the military capacities of a modern power which could set ablaze all of the Middle East. In such an event, where Saudi Arabia would turn toward Jihadism against America, a bombardment of great Muslim religious centers would seem possible.

Other possibilities exist: an internal conflict similar to that of the Grand Mosque seizure of 1979, or a destruction as part of the execution of the Samson Option by Israel as it would be threatened of destruction by its neighbors (the Samson Option would be a last resort strategy for Israel consisting in a massive nuclear bombardment of its enemies[23]).

3. The starting point of the next cycle: China conquered by America

There is no reason for the American Empire to last forever. In our study of the fall of the Roman Empire, it is easy to find similar causes to those that threaten America today. Economic weakening of the center (the economy of Italy, filled with wealth from the Empire and paralyzed by excessive dirigism, progressively lost any dynamism, a phenomenon that was accentuated by the cost of wars, while the old Orient remained prosperous), political conflicts, weakening of the central power, political competition from a new center (The Oriental Empire of Greece for Rome; we can imagine an equivalent situation for America with a possible return of a unified Europe), mass immigration leading to pillaging due to insufficient management (resulting, itself, from financial difficulties), lack of security in the communication and transportation channels due to robbery by immigrant barbarians, various uprisings having negative impacts on the economy... All of these factors (and many others) interact and accentuate one another, in a gigantic vicious circle, that seems to have afflicted the Roman global order just before its fall.

We can surmise that, if we have properly formulated Cycle B, America is bound to encounter the same difficulties and will dissolve itself into its own power, as was the case with Rome, which was not the center of the Empire in its late period. Its position as a keystone disappearing, the Empire would thus crumble into pieces. It is also not over the top to predict that, when this happens, a phenomenon of de-globalization would occur, as was the case after the fall of Rome. Lack of security in the communication and transport channels, end of the *Mare nostrum*, crumbling of state power, reduction of trade, supply difficulties, de-urbanization and the emergence of multiple and unstable political entities are to be expected. In summary, after the world order, the world disorder. This progression would not occur instantaneously, but as a result of a progressive degradation, with punctual recoveries, until the final fall.

Who will be the heir of Greece and Europe?

The fall of the American Empire would not, however, constitute the end of Occidental civilization, because, if we believe our theory of cycles, the Occident was born again twice following the disappearance of an empire: in post-Mycenaean Greece and in post-Roman Europe. We can thus predict that Occidental Civilization will pursue its course in a new place.

Indeed, Cycle A starts as follows:

1) Invasion of the territories of the future civilization by a more civilized foreign empire (from the preceding Cycle B).

The question is: where? What will be the territories invaded by Americans to form the starting point of the next iteration of Cycle A?

We have already mentioned the difficulty posed by the application of Historionomy to precise places. Nevertheless, we can attempt to find a hypothesis by looking at the past. For Mycenae, this is difficult because the history of this empire is not known in great details, and the very discovery of this civilization is recent. Our main tool will thus be once again the Roman and European past.

It has been said that the center of European Civilization, its starting point, was Gaul, a crossroad for Western Europe. What was so special about Gaul?

The first important characteristic of Gaul was its people. There were about 20 million inhabitants at the moment of its conquest by Caesar[24]. Meanwhile, the population of the Italian boot, the natural borders of Rome, was three or four times smaller: five million, in addition to one or two million slaves[25]. Gaul was very dynamic economically, and had industrial centers producing iron, pottery and wine. The Terra sigillata (ceramic) of Gaul was mass produced in a standardized manner, in shops employing many hundreds of workers, such as that of La Graufesenque; a quasi-industrial method of production. Numerous important inventions are attributed to Gaul, including soap, the art of barrel production, wine maturing in barrels; some of its inventions, like braies and chainmails, were even adopted by the Roman army. Gaul, on the other hand, did not master writing. By its mere mass of population, it constituted a threat to Rome. It already had to face the attacks of the Celtic invaders, and had almost lost to them (Brennus, 387 B.C.). Politically, Gaul was divided in 90 peoples, often competing and in conflict between one another, but linked to each other by language (three main languages, divided into several local dialects). It was led by feudal nobles but relied on a trade bourgeoisie on which the Romans relied in order to pacify their conquests. At the time of Caesar, a part of Gaul, Gallia Narbonensis, was already integrated to the Roman Empire, and its inhabitants were very Romanized. Yet, before the Roman conquest, Gaul had been almost unaffected by Greek influence, and when such influence did occur, it was mostly through the colony of Massalia (today, Marseille) along the coast of the Rhône.

In summary, a strong population that didn't know writing, a strong economic dynamism, a certain level of technological innovation, a danger for Rome with political divisions, a partially Romanized territory before its conquest, and a civilization that had not previously undergone much influence from the Occident (Greece) are the important characteristics of Gaul in those times.

Can we find in the current world, outside of the American Empire, a country with many of those characteristics?

Russia? We have already seen that it would play multiple other roles, and its population is much smaller than that of the USA. It does not shine economically, its success being based mostly on its soil and reserves of fossil energies, and it is led by an authoritarian political regime. It does not constitute a very plausible candidate.

Brazil? Its population is also much smaller than that of the USA. The country is an emerging power which is performing well economically, but with important occidental roots. Could the candidacy be extended to all of South America? Its population wouldn't be much bigger than that of America. On the other hand, the criteria of linguistic unity would be met. Latin America, however, does not constitute a serious threat to the USA. Indeed, for a long time, it has been considered as a zone exclusively under the direct influence of America.

What about Africa? Its population is almost triple that of the American population. It is divided, but does not have a good economic performance, and its languages are very diverse. It does not constitute a threat to the USA and has been, for a long time—almost forever—a subordinated occidental colony.

Naturally, our sight turns toward Asia. Two giants draw our attention: India and China.

Is India a good candidate? Its population is almost four times greater than that of the USA and is young. India's economy is dynamic and the country is making its way in world rankings. It is rarely seen as a threat to the USA. It has 23 official languages, was a European colony for a long time, and Occidental authority has had its effect there.

What about China? The population of China is four times bigger than that of the USA. Its economy is on its way to take back its natural position, which it has occupied during the last millennia, as a leading nation. This great country is also known for its multiple inventions that benefited the Occident: compass, paper, printing... The USA consider China as their only true military rival in terms of conventional warfare, especially given the constant growth of the Chinese military budget. Furthermore, America is worried about the incredible economic progression of China. Additionally, the margins of China have already been partially Occidentalized: Taiwan, South Korea and Japan. These countries have been influenced for a long time, with the latter two being integrated to the American military empire. Throughout its history, China has never been faced with deep penetration of the Occident. It has a sovereign and old civilization that considers itself as such. Finally, China does not know phonetic writing, which it only employs in its relationships with foreigners, continuing for itself the use of ideographic characters.

China would thus appear as the best candidate. However, not all factors are supporting the hypothesis of China. China is not, at the moment, politically divided. It is entirely subordinated to the government of its Communist Party (the small exception of Taiwan is quite thin to talk of "division"). Yet, it contains 56 nationalities in the Chinese sense, that is, ethno-cultural identities: The Hans, who form a majority, are themselves heterogeneous in the domain of language and customs.

China, American conquest and the future heir of Occident?

Can we imagine a scenario of an American conquest of China? At first glance, this might seem complicated. Chinese power seems to be in constant growth, and the two powers would have a lot to lose in a war. Strong economic ties are linking the two countries. The size of their conventional armies would lead to a high casualty war, and China has nuclear weapons to defend itself.

However, numerous situations can be considered. The first would be that the USA would panic at the possibility that China is about to really surpass them economically, and would be on its way to develop a superior military power. They could then choose to intervene before the balance would turn to the favor of China. This scenario of a Chinese-American war would without a doubt be the most murderous.

A similar type of war could be induced by the problem of Taiwan or some incident around Korea or Japan. This would not be quite different and would result in a very murderous Chinese-American war.

Another possible scenario would be much more favorable to Americans and potentially much less murderous: the crumbling of the Chinese regime and a period of internal troubles. China, across its history, has encountered periods of order followed by the fall of the central power. The end of a Chinese cycle of order could provide an opportunity for America to solve its delicate strategic problem. However, is such a fall plausible in the coming decades, before China surpasses the USA, which is estimated for 2030/2050?

For anyone who knows the Chinese situation in detail, it is indeed very probable.

Indeed, it is important to note that China is what we might refer to as a geopolitical bubble. The world is stunned by its growth which seems to be on its way to elevating the country to the first rank, globally. As a consequence, the Occident tends to see China as what it seems to be headed for, rather than what it currently is: a country that has not undergone its democratic transition. We know how costly such a transition can be. China is a country with a real estate bubble that is ready to pop, as a consequence of the overinvestment of the State in infrastructures and useless habitations (around sixty million housing units are unoccupied). The country will be facing, in the medium term, a demographic problem linked to its one-child policy. On the one hand, its male population is greater by many tens of thousands of millions to its female population, which can create important social tensions. On the other hand, around 2030, China will have one working person for every non-working person and at this moment it will fail to produce enough to ensure the subsistence of its people. Finally, the country is dominated by a one-party regime, and thus highly weakened by corruption.

All of these problems are cumulative and multiply the effect of one another until they will form a mortal cocktail for the Chinese regime. There will be, in China, a population of millions of single males without hope of finding a partner and building a family. There will be a crumbling economy due to the popping of the bubble and the resulting displacements, which are already affecting the industries on the Chinese coast due to increasing costs. That is, the communist regime will lose the only thing that gives it some degree of legitimacy: good economic results. We have already seen, in January 2015, that the 2014 growth of China was merely 7.4%, the weakest numbers since 1990. This is taking for granted that the numbers provided by the communist regime are anyhow reliable. Since the rise to power of Xi Jinping, which occurred during the confirmation of the slowing of economic growth, the authoritarian measures to take back the ideological control of the country have been multiplied, and the Umbrella Movement of Hong Kong has been repressed. With the economic difficulties that are to come, it will be increasingly difficult for the Chinese government to maintain control.

There will thus be two possible scenarios. Here again, a soft one and a more violent one, which form for China the fork of possible future developments.

The most violent scenario is that of Asian conflagration: faced with a population agitated by economic difficulties, China could attempt to distract the people by exciting nationalist sentiment, as it was done before with the Senkaku Islands. The Chinese leaders may not be crazy enough to engage in a premeditated manner into a military adventure, but the nationalist excitement might very well, given the circumstances, prove to be uncontrollable and result, with or without their initial consent, in a war. It is not very likely that the war would only concern Japan. The USA have recently gotten closer to the neighbors of China, including Vietnam, a country that fears Chinese imperialism. All of Asia is worried about Chinese ambitions since, for a few years, they have been engaging in an arms race. This conflict could not possibly be won by China, even if it was to occur during a Russia/USA confrontation as described above. It would be facing not only the USA, which are much better equipped, but also a coalition between South Korea, Japan, the Philippines, Vietnam and likely Taiwan, to whom an opportunity for revenge would show after more than half a century. But the fact that it won't be able to win does not mean that the conflict will be brief. This could constitute a conflict as bloody as that of the Great War for Europe, and the great victor of this conflict would be America, naturally.

A softer scenario for the transition of a new order in China is essentially an internal scenario, in which the political system of the country would implode, before having the chance to engage in an external adventure. In this case, the social tensions would end up disrupting the equilibrium of this country and throw it into a civil war. This time, the movement could not be effectively countered, as it was in 1989, but would constitute a deep movement of the entire Chinese population, the movement of a billion souls that cannot be subordinated.

The USA would then have the ideal occasion to perform actions aimed at restoring order under the mandate of the international community, with additional justifications as it relates to maintaining the world economy. The weight of China would make such a crisis extremely dangerous, especially given that it is a nuclear power and that its neighbors, South Korea and Japan, would be very worried about the economic repercussions of a fall of China. Furthermore, Taiwan would have a candidacy for final sovereignty from Chinese powers while a complacent regime is established by America in China in the midst of this chaos. The troubles would keep any efficient reply organized by China from happening, including the use of nuclear weapons. The conflict would, as a consequence, be much easier to win for America. It would also be less murderous. Additionally, this scenario would reproduce ancient history: The Americans' help to Taiwan would parallel the help of the Aedui to Caesar, which provided a justification for the war of Gaul.

In order to impose their control and prevent a future awakening, the USA will most likely divide China into smaller political entities with numerous capitals: Beijing, Shanghai, Hong Kong… These administrative and political modifications will likely be facilitated by internal troubles and civil war. Tibet would gain its independence.

China, subordinated to the American Empire, would likely meet the fate of Roman Gaul. It would develop a Chinese-American culture, and its economy would be dynamical under American peace, without further military ambition (a little bit like Japan after the war). When America falls, China would become the heir of Occidental culture. From such an evolved and refined country, having been civilized from such ancient times, it would be expected that they would be able to enrich occidental culture with their own culture, and carry forward the civilization that was once Greek, Roman, European and American to heights that would be hard to anticipate today.

3. The domestic policy of the USA: toward an American Emperor?

We are currently most likely at this stage of Cycle B:

6) **The states of A become dominated by B.**

The following stages should be expected:

7) **Absolute hegemony over the known world, absence of rivals.**

8) **The Empire, a militaristic and autocratic regime, succeeds to the Republic.**

9) **Decline and dismemberment of Empire B.**

We have already seen how Stage 7) should occur through the relationships between America, Russia and China

The future of the American Empire consists, to begin with, in the developments that we have described in the preceding paragraphs: the maintenance or increase of American control over Europe, the definitive subordination of Russia and China to the American authority, and the final victory over radical Islam. We have already presented possible scenarios for the establishment of this new world order. Let us now reflect on its consequences.

After the resolution of the conflicts with Russia, China and the Muslim world, America will control on its own a good half of global lands. It is hard to see, however, what would lead Americans to engage in Africa, India, or South America. With the degree of power accumulated by America, it is more probable that no other country would constitute any threat to its hegemony, and that the USA, finally having gotten rid of any threat to their way of life, will be content with their empire. The subordination of Russia and China will give full power to the US over the UN (with the neutralization of any contrarian veto rights from any permanent members). Thus, the UN would be nothing more than an American instrument. America would then even be able to afford the luxury of attributing a permanent seat to Japan or Germany, which would be integrated to its empire.

How will America govern its empire?

Most likely (as it has done before) in the Roman way: leaving local governance to provinces of the empire, Rome would intervene with its governors only in cases of malfunctioning of local authorities (conflicts between localities, social disorder…) and in order to coordinate the great imperial enterprises (infrastructure, etc.). This style of governance maintains local elites in positions of power, turning them into loyal allies. The system is obviously poorly democratic, even if it can maintain appearances. We observe today in Europe, as we have noted, a relatively constant government on the part of European institutions, and as a consequence a similar consistency in the governance of European states, despite democratic rotations. Some interpret this phenomenon as the sign of a globalist conspiracy, which is not the case. The stability of governance simply reflects the adherence of the elites to an order that suits them, protects them, and appears to them as relatively profitable for their country. We observed the same phenomenon in wealthy Greeks with respect to Roman domination. Well-off people like political order, because it is necessary for the safety of goods and prosperity. We should thus not expect the complete abolition of conquests. Americans, just like Romans, conquer like Genghis Khan. They integrate the conquered country to a system, not merely by imposing full subordination by force. Thus, if America conquers China, we should expect the establishment of a few American bases, a monitoring over the administration, but not a full involvement in the micro-management of Chinese society, at least not at first. Indeed, the Roman governors, during the strong days of the Empire, intervened only in case of problems, or as a last resort. Meanwhile, under the Principate, we see Greek authors appealing to good behavior in their compatriot, so as to avoid tempting the Roman governor to meddle in the affairs of the city. The American Empire would thus have to act, and already does so, with this *modus operandi*.

This leaves open questions around the two last stages, which remain to be covered:

8) **The Empire, a militaristic and autocratic regime, succeeds to the Republic.**

9) **Decline and dismemberment of Empire B.**

An American Emperor?

The idea might seem mockable at first glance. However, we have seen that the American Empire, despite the democratic ideal, remains very undemocratic as it relates to the peoples subordinated to America.

The American people itself is governed by the Constitution, and only then by Democracy. This phenomenon is not always easy to understand for Europeans, in particular for the French, where constitutional reforms are common, and where the Constitution itself is just as rewritable as the rest of the judiciary corpus.

The central importance of the American constitution and the Bill of Rights must be properly understood because it will inevitably have a central role in the evolution of the country toward the Empire.

Let us remind ourselves of the establishment of the Principate in Rome[26]: in the I^{st} century B.C., as Rome had become master of most of the known world, Italy encountered an economic disruption linked to the mass arrival of slaves on the market which benefited wealthy owners and ruined small owners and artisans, who were reduced to unemployment. This economic crisis led to a social crisis, giving birth to a populist current, the *populares*, who carried socialistic ideologies (debt cancelation, bread distribution…). This movement was directly opposed to the *optimates*, a party (not in the modern and institutional sense, but in the form of a sharing of common ideology or interests) formed by wealthy aristocrats and their clients, and more broadly by Roman conservatives, partisans and defenders of the *mos majorum,* the customs of the ancestors, the set of traditional Roman mores and values. These traditional values included the Roman political constitution as a fundamental principle: separation of powers, control over magistracy, regular elections, state of rights. The goal was not merely to defend the interests of the wealthy. Individuals such as Cato the Younger were mostly concerned with the defense of the Republic and the concept of *libertas* linked to it, that is, the ensemble of all fundamental rights connected to Roman citizenship, guaranteed by the Republican structure of the government and the equality before the law. This schism formed the ideological basis that eventually built into a civil war and destabilized the very foundations of the Roman Republic. There were two opposed visions, one in which the interest of the people had to be prioritized, and another prioritizing traditional individual rights. What killed the Roman Republic is the end of the consensus around the *mos majorum* induced by socio-economic disruptions. The Principate of Augustus was a kind of fascistic response to this challenge.

This evolution allowed the establishment of the kind of social peace ensured by a Police state and led Rome toward a dangerous cliff: what had led to the success of the Roman model did not exist anymore, that is, a constitutional regime that was perhaps less democratic than Athens, but where the protection of individual liberties was guaranteed by a venerated constitution. All of the great minds of the time: Cicero, Lucretius, Seneca the Younger, have encountered a violent death. Ovid was exiled by Augustus. Roman proto-liberalism ceded to the Principate, a dictatorial socialistic regime, and from there, the trend toward statism strengthened until the Diocletian Dominate, a regime of dirigism, practically totalitarian, creating closed corporations, extending labors from father to sons, attaching farmers to their land, all in accordance with the needs of the army. The religious persecutions that victimized Jews and Christians under the Empire are quite revealing: not only did they result in the followers of these religions to worship the official divinities of the Empire, but they also resulted in a true weakening of religious tolerance which had for a long time be a Roman characteristic. We cannot consider that these persecutions had nothing to do with the authoritarian character of Roman power, especially given that the violence of the persecutions increased proportionally with the strengthening of the imperial power. The more the empire grew into indifference toward Roman liberal traditions, the more repressive it became. Furthermore, there was the inevitable corruption inherent to any totalitarian or quasi-totalitarian state, which ruins the people and forbids the emergence of a middle class, while repressing anything that resembles it. Taken together, the fall of Rome occurred on the model of the USSR, a statist system stifling entrepreneurial spirit, negating economic liberty and suppressing social mobility while demoralizing individuals against invaders (who wants to fight for a tyranny?). A necessary fight against the foreign military threat eventually drained all resources, exhausting an empire that covered very different cultures under a common varnish. The dislocation occurred to the benefit of the *nomenklatura* of the Roman Empire, which took over public powers and initiated the evolution from a liberal Republic to the totalitarian Empire.

With these reminders, let us now see how this evolution could occur, and in reality has already started, in the United States. Since the election of Barack Obama and his push for a very statist vision of American society, the Tea Party has appeared as a conservative movement presenting itself as defenders of the Constitution and of individual liberties guaranteed in the Bill of Rights. In this context, Obama is accused of being a socialist, a very derisive term in the USA.

On the other hand, the economic crisis has also led to the rise of anti-capitalist movements: Occupy Wall Street and "We are the 99%." For the first time in the history of the United States, in 2009, the majority of American households has received more money from the State than it has paid in taxes, as noted on July 14th 2012 by the economist Greg Mankiw on his blog[27].

The crisis of 2008 seems to have caused the emergence in America of the schism between the proponents of the American *mos majorum* and the *populares*.

The USA are probably not at the edge of a civil war. However, the fracture has appeared and it is probable that it won't be repaired. In the coming years and decades, it will develop depending on the economic difficulties until the time where the liberal principles of the Constitution of the US no more constitute a consensus within the population. A time of great troubles would then come, which would necessitate the birth of a new paradigm. An event such as the Bundy standoff, in which an armed militia defended a ranch against the Federal State and highly-armed police troops, gives an idea of how such a civil war could start, and the way it could unfold, by opposing a militarized police and a reformed American army against militias equipped with weapons of all grades, from knives to assault rifles.

It is possible that the troubles will only occur once America has become a true master of the world and of its foreign enemies, as was the case with Rome. As long as there are foreign enemies, the nation can define itself in the negative, and for a few years America has seen itself as the country of liberty opposed to foreign tyrannies. When the USA will have reduced Russia and China into docile vassals, and will have successfully broken Islamic Fundamentalism, these landmarks will no more exist to sustain American identity. Furthermore, the existence of powerful adversaries, even enemies of liberty, is paradoxically an advantage for the defense of liberties against the growing powers of the State. Edward Snowden, who has denunciated the NSA spying over the American population, has not found protection in Europe, with the allies of the USA, but only in Russia. While the regime of Putin may not be a great defender of individual liberties, it has found an interest in the denunciation of the violations of liberties by those who claim to be in a position to give them lessons. *De facto*, the enemies of the USA have the opportunity to serve as an external counter-power to the American State, broadcasting information that the government would prefer to hide from its own population. When America has no more rivals, this counter-power will disappear. The governments of the allies of America will never find as much interest as Russia did in supporting a contradictory stance, and even less as the elites of these various countries will tend to be internationalized, as they are already tending to be. They will be the local members of the same universal body. The path will thus be opened to the strengthening of governmental powers in all occidental democracies, to the detriment of individual rights. An important characteristic of the maneuvers of Caesar, as a precursor of Augustus in constitutional experimentation, has been to rely on the Roman Empire to take Rome itself, along with the Empire. Two facts demonstrate this strategy: he put an end to Roman electoral campaigns that were funded by wealthy financiers who extorted money from the provinces, and he allowed the entry into the senate of the Gauls and Spaniards.

We can imagine that the appearance of one or many individuals using a similar strategy could take over the leadership of the USA and the American Empire, by relying on the margins of the Empire rather than the center. Perhaps such a strategy would make use of the UN, in order to pass above the American Constitution, and create a global government for the Empire. Meanwhile, the American government would have an interest in favoring, within democracies, an oligarchical and technocratic evolution, which would be seen as more stable and less likely to foment anti-Americanism.

Once this new paradigm is established, the rest is easy to imagine: the same statist and socializing slope that occurred in Rome. We would see a growing concentration of power, which becomes increasingly arbitrary and turns its back to the recipes that had made the initial success of the USA, leading to the very birth of that Empire. However, as was the case with Rome, the fact that this development would occur only once the great rivals are vanquished leaves place to a slow decline, since no one is there to benefit from the moral weakening of the central power. Thus, the disappearance of liberalism will induce the progressive corruption of new institutions toward a sterile statist authoritarianism which will, as it did in the case of Rome, induce the death of the Empire: the economic power of Rome and Italy could not be maintained under the Empire, which was one of the causes of the fall. Starting at the IInd century A.D., the Roman metropole has been faced with the competition from its own provinces, and it lost its markets, leading to a reduction in the productivity of its lands, some of them being abandoned, and a diminishment in the value of these lands, leading the heart of the Empire to become poorer. It was only able to compensate in appearances for its economic difficulties by replacing its own productivity with a predation over its provinces. It had been the capital of the Ancient world in the domains of technology and commerce, as well as a major exporter, but it eventually became an importer and became more dependent on its regions. The unfortunate monetary interventions of the emperors have only made the situation worse. The standard of living was only maintained through the money collected from the provinces through taxation. The economy became increasingly managed and therefore decreasingly dynamic.

Have these developments already begun in the USA? The country has made its fortune with its industries, but they are progressively de-industrializing, allowing others, like China or India, to enrich themselves by becoming in turn the workshops of the world. The trade balance of the USA is already in a deficit. Is that simply a bad moment or have they begun to decline economically?

It seems that it may simply be a bad moment: the progresses of robotics seem promising, for the few decades to come, and could lead to a re-industrialization of the USA, since domestic production would become more profitable. The French economist Charles Gave noted on December 12th 2011 on his blog[28]: "We are at the eve of an industrial revolution. Ten years ago, robots could compete with men if the cost of the robot was below $50/hour. Today, it is $2/hour, which is below the cost of labor in China. The industries installed in China will thus be repatriated closer to consumption centers. Due to this, the American trade balance will be in surplus again." Thus it seems that new technologies, for which America remains a center of innovation, will be able to guarantee the dynamism of the American economy for a few decades to come. If we follow the reading of economic cycles by Kondratiev, the American economic power would still be protected for four decades, the new Kondratiev cycle beginning with the exit from the crisis of 2008 and the arrival of new technological inventions linked to automation (home automatons, driverless cars...)[29].

The phenomenal progresses of automation will also cause a revolution in the military domain. While telecommunications have helped develop networks for armed forces, the progresses of robotics will allow to transform the methods of war of industrialized countries, with those of the USA first. The American army already equips certain infantry troops with exoskeletons allowing quicker traveling and the carrying of heavier loads. This is only the beginning. The prototypes of military motorized exoskeletons such as the XOS of Sarcos provide a peek into the American army in ten or twenty years from now: a man enshrined in an armored suit, capable of displacement without fear from light weapons (even those with penetrating projectiles) in difficult terrains, carrying superior caliber weapons. Such combinations lead simple soldiers to become equivalent to a whole squad, a squad that would be indifferent to obstacles that would block conventional ones, which would facilitate options for urban or guerilla wars in the mountains such as those that Americans have faced in Afghanistan. Yet, human losses remain haunting for governments in the age of information, and this might constitute an important break to military interventions, even with an improved army.

A Kondratiev cycle lasts about four decades. This is interesting because we have already noted that the great geopolitical changes and the extension of the American Empire to Russia, China and the Middle East would have to occur from now to the beginning of the XXIst century. Thus, the next Kondratiev crisis should occur once America has vanquished its rivals. We would then be in the situation of Rome in the first century B.C., a situation of political reversal that we have just described briefly. An America that would have gone through its robotics revolution would be, in a time of crisis, similarly positioned to Rome, flooded by slaves replacing the labor of free men.

Toward an authoritarian America: the socio-political risks of robotization

I would like to pay attention to the parallel between the mass arrival of slaves in the Roman economy with the mass robotization that is to come, and produce a scenario for the American conversion to authoritarianism.

Economic progress is characterized by a process that we call, since Schumpeter, creative destruction. Technical progress leads to the disappearance of certain forms of employment, but the resources liberated by gains of productivity lead to new activities, new markets and new forms of employment toward which the workforce can be directed. We can thus surmise that, as was the case in the industrial revolution throughout the XIXth and XXth centuries, during the robotics transition that should occur within the next twenty to thirty years, progress will virtually abolish certain forms of labor and replace them with new ones.

It is unquestionable that humans have the ability to create new jobs that will allow people to earn a living as well as train individuals so that they are able to undertake important tasks. However, there may be issues of timing. Indeed, creative destruction and creation are not simultaneous, and the more massive and systematic the destruction is, the more destabilization of the system is to be expected. This is due to the inability of societies to compensate for destruction through creation in a timely manner. A revolution such as that of robotics will constitute a period of mass destruction that resembles few events in History.

Let us return to the socio-economic crisis of the IInd and Ist centuries B.C., at the origin of the Roman Empire. Economically, the arrival of masses of slaves, in an unprecedented proportion, was a true upheaval. All markets were impacted simultaneously. Crassus, who was the wealthiest man of his time, dedicated a significant part of his activities in the commerce of slaves. This was not limited to purchasing slaves in order to sell them. He was purchasing slaves, training them to diverse tasks, ranging from builders to scribe, and was then selling them or renting them. His slaves were able to undertake any imaginable task on the labor market. In Roman Italy, anything that could be done by a free man could be done more cheaply by a slave. It was, of course, mentioned that the productivity of slaves was smaller than that of free men, but the lower costs were largely compensating for that.

The free men of Roman Italy, in a manner that was *rapid* (a few decades) *massive* (the proportion of slaves in the population of Italy was multiplied by ten within a century) and *systematic* (a majority of professions were affected) lost their jobs. A small minority became fabulously wealthy. A part of the population saved its position in the economic system by purchasing slaves in order to work for them, and when artisans had a workforce, they enriched themselves by replacing them with slaves. A large part of the population was simply ruined: those who, at the moment of this revolution, had no capital (the proletariat), or whose capital suddenly lost any value (small landowners incapable of exploiting the land as efficiently as the large exploiters, even using slaves).

Leaving aside the moral problem of slavery, one must admit that, in a proper economical logic, the mass liberation of capital and workforce should have led to economic progress, a creation responding to the destruction. The Romans were an industrial people; they should have been able to bring this state of affairs to fruition. They had invented the oil press, the semicircular arch, and concrete. Their ingenuity in terms of developing machines, cranes and scaffolds of all kinds had allowed them to develop siege engines that became famous: catapults, scorpions, mobile towers. Furthermore, at the theoretical level, the Ancients did not lack inventiveness: Ctesibius, in the IIIrd century B.C., had invented the hydraulic system which still operates within the doors of all buildings, named the groom, as well as the piston, the keyboard, and the first functional automata. The Antikythera mechanism, which is dated to many centuries before our era, shows that the Ancients were capable of putting together complex metal gears. Two centuries later, Heron of Alexandria invented the first steam engine, the famous Aeolipyle, and proposed an automated system for the opening of doors using steam.

The Greco-Romans were successful at putting together many major innovations. At the end of the I^{st} century A.D., the water mill appeared, and at the end of the IInd century, the first crank rod system transforming a circular movement into a lateral one.

However, the reality is that the Ancient world did not greatly benefit from these inventions, which came to be used commonly only in the Middle Ages, and eventually to a much greater extent after the Renaissance. Nevertheless, there was a manifest interest into these innovations as soon as they appeared. In the IInd century, the industrial water mill of Barbegal was producing 4.5 tons of flour every day. In Hierapolis, Turkey, the mechanical saw, combining the crank rod and the water mill, functioned on the same principle as those which flourished millennia later, and this beginning as early as the IIIrd century. It seems that the mechanism was known and used in Switzerland as early as the IInd century. These saws, which were some of the technological marvels of those times, were not used to cut wood, but stone. Yet, we had to wait for the XVth century to see the association between the water mill and wind tunnels allowing furnaces to reach higher temperatures, thus resulting in important progresses in metallurgy. We had to wait for the XVIIth century for Denis Papin's rediscovery of vapor and its mechanical potential, and the XVIIIth century so that, in combining all of these innovations, the European man could initiate the industrial revolution.

Why did we have to wait two thousand years for these progresses to be made? Certainly, the Ancients did not have coal, a combustion material that was much more efficient than wood, and they may have been lacking sufficiently solid metals and joints, but despite their mastery of steam engines, hydraulic energy was barely exploited. Is it a matter of ingenuity, no one having thought to associate a wind tunnel to a water mill to increase the temperature of furnaces for more than a thousand years?

This would not explain the weak spreading of revolutionary inventions which we have described above (taking for granted that this weak spreading is not an artefact of the incompleteness of our archeological records). Logically, even if further progresses would not have been made at first, we should have expected the machines to multiply throughout the Roman world. Then, their use might have diversified.

However, this is not what happened. Many have tried to explain the technological shutdown through some sort of failure of the Ancient to think in terms of progress, suggesting that they were imprisoned in a cyclical view of the world, which would only have been challenged by Christianity and its linear conception of History. This absolutist conception of Ancient mentality is radically at odds with the numerous technical progresses that Romans had been able to achieve in the preceding centuries, but then what, in the late Ancient world, created a mentality that was so obstructive to innovation?

I have already described this mentality in my book on Rome: the regime and the imperial society were refractory to progress. The Emperor Vespasian rejected an invention, which was revolutionary according to Suetonius, allowing transportation of the stones for building the temples of the Capitol at a lower cost. The emperor paid the engineer so that he would not reveal anything and would destroy his plans, in order to ensure that the workers would not lose their job. This kind of decision, horrible for anyone who cares about technical progress, was coherent with the nature of the imperial regime.

Indeed, the economic upheaval of the IInd-Ist centuries B.C. had grave political consequences. It was too rapid, massive and systematic to give the chance to economic structures to adapt, or for creative destruction to occur. A great number of people became discontented more rapidly than the market could adapt. Starting on the second half of the IInd century B.C., the practice of public redistribution gained ground, which rapidly took the form of welfare. These redistributions gave to the Roman State an increasing power, unequaled previously, favoring political clientelism.

In summary, the economic upheaval occurred as follows: the arrival of slaves deprived free men of their jobs, while those who had the means to invest in this market enriched themselves considerably. This brutal economic divergence was compensated by massive recourse to public redistribution, which produced a society dependent on social welfare, occupying public functions and abandoning the culture of labor which had characterized the Romans for centuries. Thus was the original social pact of the Empire: a population conceding supremacy to the State in order for free subsistence.

Therefore, we should worry about the transition toward an era of robotics in the modern world, and in the United States in particular, which is the equivalent of Roman Italy in the Ancient world. Economically, the multiplication of robots and their adaptation to all tasks could very well have similar effects to the exponential development of slavery in late Republican Rome, in line with the following scenario:

1) Within a few decades, in a great boom of robotics, robots will massively replace humans in jobs where they remained necessary to assembly lines, but also in transportation, and increasingly, in intellectual activities. The active population will be impacted with an intensity that it hasn't encountered since the crisis of the Greco-Roman world. Some studies lead us to believe that, in France, three million jobs could disappear due to robotization from now to 2025[30]. In the United States, it is estimated that 47% of all jobs could be delegated to computers within the next two decades[31]. The phenomenon will be so massive and systemic that a large share of individuals excluded from the workforce will have no chance to find new jobs, because the progress of computers will be quicker than their own ability to be trained or to innovate. As soon as they would be trained in a new job, the job could be found to be practicable for computers, and for cheaper. The proportion of the excluded will be such, in our societies, that it will have an immediate impact. Indeed, the distribution of wealth can only operate in three modes: through the capital markets, the labor market, or political coercion. In the economic situation that we are predicting, the entire proportion of the population which will have too little capital to live from its investments, and no access to the labor market due to the progress of robotics, will only have political coercion as a lever. Since it will be so numerous, it will obtain what it wants. The only political remedies that a State would be able to propose will either be to block technical progresses by forbidding the replacement of humans by robots, in order to maintain some access to the labor market, or, alternatively, to redistribute the wealth of the owners and exploiters of robots toward those who don't have any, through direct coercion (taxation and redistribution).

2) The result will be a growth of the intervention sphere of the State in the economy, and the creation of a welfare society.

Admittedly, one could argue that the industrial revolution has not led to such extremes. Creative destruction, up to now, has kept afloat. However, the industrial revolution did not occur as quickly as it is often believed. In France, the population living from agriculture in 1789 represented 66% of the total population. It is only in 1880 that this proportion went under 50%, in 1950 under 25%, and in 1960 under 20%. Thus, it took more than a century and a half to replace 50% of the active population by machines. During this time, across generations, populations were trained and professional occupations that were exclusively human have developed.

The robotics revolution to come could replace close to half of the active population by machines within twenty or thirty years. That is between five and seven times quicker than the industrial revolution. As was the case with Rome, it is probable that the labor and training markets will not have time to adapt before social tensions induce harmful political mutations such as those considered above.

Thus will appear, as we have described, a new form of government in the United States, which will govern the American Empire in a more integrated and authoritarian fashion. The progression of socialism in the economy and the recoil of liberalism will make it less dynamic, and State intervention, probably in the Keynesian style, will only make matters worse. The central power will evolve toward a cult of personality which, as was the case in Rome, will reject any ideology that are hostile to the idolatry of the State, starting with monotheistic religions: Judaism, Christianity and Islam. Progressively, the American imperial government will end up resembling the Brezhnevian Soviet Empire or North Korea. Having attained complete extenuation, worn by centrifugal forces linked to the persistence of local identities: European, Asian and South American, the Empire will dissolve and, as we have stated above, the next Cycle A will probably begin in China, or more broadly in the Far East.

It is hard to guess at what time this will occur. We can note that the Cretan-Mycenaean iteration lasted about 1 600 years, and the Greco-Roman iteration lasted just as long. If the Euro-American AB iteration is reproduced in the same time scale, knowing that it has begun in the VIth century, then the American Empire will fall in the first half of the XXIIth century.

Thus, we will have in the end (in **bold**, Cycle B, in *italics*, predicted American historical fact):

7) Absolute hegemony over the known world, absence of rivals (it is at this step that Stage 1 of the next Cycle A occurs).

Grave social, economic and political troubles at the middle of the XXIst century, establishment of an authoritarian regime at the head of the USA and over all of the American Empire.

9) Decline and dismemberment of Empire B (corresponds to Stage 2 of the next Cycle A).

Economic and cultural weakening of America, loss of dynamism caused by authoritarianism, dismemberment of the American Empire (China and East Asia emancipate from American tutelage)

As well as:

4) The Empire (around 2040-*?*)

Political institutions: any form of democracy is abolished to the advantage of a central dictatorial power whose control grows, up to totalitarianism.

The American democracy disappears *de facto*, leaving place to a socialist dictatorship that is at first moderate, and then increasingly authoritarian and autocratic.

Society/Law: The Empire appears as a remedy to the break of the ancestral sociopolitical consensus. Individual liberties and judicial protections against the power disappear as the central power is reinforced. We observe a reappearance of castes with judiciary-political disparities and social mobility disparities.

The empire establishes a new sociopolitical order by replacing the liberal order that had been in effect since the proclamation of American independence. The central power becomes a police state. Constitutional rights are increasingly violated. A soviet-style *nomenklatura* appears, with judicial privileges. Disappearance of equality under the law, separation of social classes and the disappearance of economic liberty put an end to social mobility.

Arts/culture: Official art supporting the power of the State. Art is marked by the absolutism of the central power and its increasingly totalitarian structure. Disappearance of the individual to the benefit of a symbolic and typical imagery. This systematic art, fixated and sterile, does not respond to universal sensibilities and loses its reference status in the Empire, provoking the reappearance of local sensibilities.

An official art serving as propaganda for the central power appears. Cinema exalts heroes sacrificing for the community and obeying to the orders of their superior. The perverted American model does not seduce anymore and local cultural traits reappear in Europe, China…

Economy: The system evolves toward totalitarianism. The economy declines until complete crumbling, paralyzed by the authority of the central power and the control over production to the satisfaction of the needs of the State and the army.

The economy veers toward socialism and statism, similar to the Soviet model, and military expenses are increased.

Religion: Traditional civil religion becomes a unique cult imposed in order to favor central power.

Personality cult around the *Commander in Chief*. Distrust toward religions that are hostile to this cult: Catholicism, Judaism, Islam.

Sciences: Stagnation of technological progresses, innovations are not used.

Socioeconomic sovietization, with sate dirigism, corporatism, monopolies and obstacles to entrepreneurship sterilize any attempt at innovation.

Relations with the external world: Transformation of the hegemony into an empire. Domination of vassals without further extension, except for punctual interventions. The more authoritarian character of the central government is felt in the way the power of B is expressed outside of the nation, leaving less autonomy to local governments.

America puts an end to any form of democracy in its vassal countries and imposes officials applying the policy of the central government. Any inhabitant of the empire is subordinated to the imperial administration and pays taxes to the imperial treasury.

Methods of warfare: Professional imperial army, important weight in the State apparatus, auxiliaries are employed.

Completely professional army, major role of the army in the maintenance of the imperial power (the army is also the center of the economy). Increasing employment of private mercenaries.

Why the colonization of space will not occur in this cycle

Some readers with an interest in technology and current progresses or future hopes of developments may know that high level scientists at the NASA and elsewhere are seriously considering the possibility of interstellar travel, perhaps by escaping the physical limits of the speed of light. Faster-than-light travel, although the expression is not an apt descriptor, are already considered as theoretically possible and have been mentioned in peer-reviewed publications. The two technologies that are potentially achievable may involve either wormholes in the fabric of space-time allowing to temporarily shorten the distance between two points of the universe, or alternatively the warp drive or Alcubierre drive, which postulates another type of manipulation of space-time, less ambitious but potentially as efficient: the contraction of space in front of a spaceship and its dilation behind it, in order to propel the spaceship on a space-time wave, similarly to a surfer. The spaceship would remain immobile in the space containing it, just like the surfer with his board, while the wave would carry it with speeds equivalent to dozens of times that of light (several millions of kilometers per second). These technologies, for now, are essentially theoretical, but they are starting to draw the attention of NASA.

Furthermore, the private sector is increasingly interested in profits from the coming space conquest. The opportunities range from simple publicity, such as the sponsorship of the free fall of Baumgartner for Red Bull, up to ambitions in the developments of a true spatial industry, which is the case with Planetary Resources and Deep Space industries, who are preparing for the mining of asteroids that cross the path of the Earth. Private enterprises hope to compete with great state institutions by developing high efficiency rockets, such as the Grasshopper, a reusable rocket, capable of landing just like it launches, resembling a space elevator, or the project of Escape Dynamics to use micro-waves for propelling.

This convergence of a serious reflection around interstellar transportation technologies and the economic interests of entrepreneurs could lead one to believe in an imminent acceleration of space conquest. This would seem like an interesting parallel to the discovery of the New World a few centuries before. The first great expeditions, just like the conquest of space, had first been financed by States whose leaders hoped to gain prestige, and these first expeditions were rather sterile in economic terms. The conquest of the New World, and the opening of relations with India and the Far East, were a task for adventurer-merchants and the various Companies of the Indies, after the sovereigns had become uninterested in the subject. One could be tempted to believe in a possible repetition of this scheme in the decades to come.

However, I do not believe that these elements must result in a massive colonization of space by Humanity, in the way the world was colonized by Europe. Here are my reasons.

First, we have seen that the great historical movements of colonization are accomplished by a Type A civilization. We have described the European and Greek cases and their similarities. As a reminder:

3) Renaissance Period—Consolidation of the State (VIIth-VIth century B.C., *XVIth-XVIIth century*)

Relations with the external world: Decisive victory over foreign threats. The technological and economical gap is no more. Exploration movements are initiated, based on new navigational techniques, establishment of first colonies.

Greco-Persian Wars, victories against the Persian Achaemenid Empire. The colonization movement of Greece extends toward western Mediterranean territories and the Black Sea.

Defeats of the Ottoman Empire and end of its progression in Europe, thanks to the creation of new boats equipped with more advanced rudders and navigational instruments (compass…). Discovery of America, creation of colonies.

4) Classical Period—The Nation state (VIth-IVth centuries B.C., *XVIIth-XXth centuries*)

Relations with the external world: Explosion of the movement for colonization. Complete submission of all old enemies, control over maritime routes. Worldwide hegemony. Economic, technological and scientific supremacy. A peak of civilization is attained.

The Greek movement for colonization of the coasts of the Mediterranean Sea intensifies, Greeks dominate the Northern side (and after Alexander the Great the whole Oriental half).

Colonization of two thirds of all world lands, destruction of the Ottoman Empire, worldwide supremacy.

Yet, Cycle A has been completed. Europe has concluded its colonial history and has entered its withdrawal phase as a vassal entity of America. Thus, the colonial push will not occur.

This argument may appear thin, in comparison with the elements described above. It might be argued that such a statement requires a blind faith in the repetition of the cycles which we have observed. In reality, this argument can be expanded.

In the two cases of Europe and Greece, the vast colonial movement extending over an important part of the known world was the result of the union of two fundamental elements: decisive technological progress providing means of transportation that were significantly more efficient and allowed new types of traveling, and an irrepressible sociopolitical need. This need manifested in the Greek *stasis* and *stenochoria*, as well as in the religious wars and demographic push of Europe. In both cases, we observe a crisis resulting from overpopulation, and rapid social upheavals reverting the traditional order. Mere overpopulation is not sufficient; it is an overpopulation of a somewhat intellectual class, thirsty for discovery and understanding, which, both in Greece and in Europe, could only arise spontaneously after many centuries of dark ages.

This convergence will not occur in the decades to come. Emerging countries have the desire to imitate Europe, but the colonial push is not a movement of imitation, it is a very profound phenomenon which only strikes, as we have shown, certain societies after a long gestation period. Furthermore, the world, during the coming century, will experience an increasingly important grasp of American hegemony, which will be, as described above, sterilizing for technological progress, just like Roman power was in Antiquity.

Perhaps some readers may think it possible that the parallel between Rome and America may not reveal to be exact, and that the famous pioneer spirit of Americans will push them to be able to do what Rome has not done. This would be an error. Romans had a pioneer spirit similar to that of Americans which dominated over Italy during the first centuries of the Republic and expressed itself in the multiplication of Roman colonies controlling the national territory, i.e. the peninsula. It was imperative to do so from a strategic standpoint, just like the conquest of the West. In both cases, once a national territory was under control and strategically viable, there were no more important colonial movements, whereas in comparison, European nations as well as Greek cities have launched into colonization enterprises once their national territory was stabilized. Could the conquest of space be a counterexample? No. We must realize that the Apollo program was in reality an act of war, aimed at winning through prestige against the USSR, who had gained an earlier interest in space than America, and with Sputnik and Gagarin, had taken a considerable advance. Then, Reagan's Strategic Defense Initiative responded to military issues and, since the end of the Soviet Union, the USA seek to maintain their space technologies in observation satellites, but have significantly reduced their efforts for space conquest, which is limited for now to probes, robots and relatively restricted manned flights. Similarly, and contrarily to the Greeks, who were engaged in extensive sea faring, the Romans had only taken over the Mediterranean in response to the Carthage menace. They captured, during the First Punic War, a quinquereme of Carthage, imitated their technology and put their industry to work in order to industrially produce these ships and overpower their mortal enemy. Here again, we observe an even more detailed expression of the parallel between Rome/Carthage and America/Russia.

In the decades to come, the economic exploitation of proximate space will likely develop. Mining operations on asteroids crossing the path of the Earth, as well as the establishment of bases on the Moon, and perhaps Mars or Jupiter's satellite, are possible. Some exploration missions outside of the solar system may be launched but would likely turn out to be unsuccessful. All of these developments will be extremely limited, even if they feature technologies that appear to be promising at first glance. America will turn out like the Romans who, for centuries, have traded with India, as was described in the fascinating Periplus of the Erythraean Sea, dating from the first century B.C., without initiating significant colonial expeditions. We would have to wait for modern European nations, including England, which had at its disposal technologies far superior to the Roman world at its apogee.

The survival of a European Empire?

When the Roman Empire crumbled, the Oriental Empire, a Greek civilization, survived it. Should this historical fact be included as a stage of Cycle A? Should we note that the

Empire seeds, on its western side, a new country ready to engage in a new start for Occident, and on its Eastern side, the country from Cycle A, first civilization of the AB couple (Greece for the Greco-Roman cycle, Europe for the Euro-American cycle) as heir of the Empire that can extend its existence for a certain time? It's a possibility, but only the distant future will allow us to determine an answer.

Many facts appear to support this hypothesis. Europe, as was the case for Greece, remained a wealthy civilization at the intersection of three worlds: Occident, Orient, and Africa. If the United States were to lose their economic weight and as a consequence their military might, as it should happen at the moment of the fall of the American Empire, Europe could benefit from this vacuum in order to become once again the global center, by default. Furthermore, its strong population density could turn out to be an advantage in order to resist to the crumbling of the American Empire, since the maintenance of order and the defense of circuits of exchange will be doable at lower cost. Finally, Europe having attained the phase of Universal State, according to the model of Toynbee, it would be expected not to fall, but instead, like the Byzantine Empire (the Universal State of Greek Civilization), would encounter a series of decadences and restorations.

Is a "Dark Age" still possible?

Certain readers might wonder if, in our current stage of technological development and degree of civilization, it is at all possible to observe, on Earth, a period of five hundred or a thousand years without technological innovations, even perhaps a regression. Considering such a phenomenon seems to be an assault to intelligence. However, if we pay attention to the causes of progress, we realize their fragility.

For progress to occur, there must be a state of rights that protect individuals. They must have entrepreneurial freedom in order to benefit from technological innovations, and there must be communication and trade channels that ensure the free circulation of goods, persons and the meeting of the minds.

Human societies, like computers, only show their full potential within a network. A network allows an individual at Point X, whose research encounters an obstacle, to benefit from the research of another individual at Point Y, who has a solution to this obstacle while facing the problems that were already solved by X. The product of their talents gives more than the sum, because without each other they are in an impasse, but together they have a result. This is equivalent to a leap of infinite value, the passage from nothing to something. If X and Y had remained isolated in their intellectual islands, due to material or political barriers, then their work would result in nothing, and humanity would be deprived of a progress.

What leads to today's fast technological progresses is that the great research centers, despite industrial and strategic secrets, or questions of intellectual propriety, are globally interconnected, and respond to each other's questions, while sharing solutions. The networking of the talents of men is, incidentally, also the process at the heart of civilization. The rise of urban centers, which are platforms for encounters between individuals, allows the exchange of ideas. Then, it is the urban centers themselves who get together in networks, which leads to the appearance of national territories, unifying the urban centers who share a common language. What we call globalization is precisely the networking, in turn, between the local networks of national territories. However, the existence of such networks is conditional to the safety of communication and traveling channels, which is never certain.

The establishment of the American Empire, and its progressive evolution toward totalitarianism, will have very negative consequences, as was the case in the Later Roman Empire. The American Empire will have its Bagaudae, bands of thefts and insurgents composed by individuals fleeing the fiscal pressure and generalized servitude. Their guerilla will punish an already suffering economy, while causing increases in military expenses, increasing fiscal pressure even more, thus forming a vicious circle. The situation will worsen progressively and entire regions of the world will become war zones, which will lead to population displacements similar to those we observed in Syria and Iraq, but of a much greater magnitude. Dozens, perhaps hundreds of millions of people will be displaced in the world, who will, in turn be pushed into misery, and therefore into pillaging.

In order to protect themselves from the troubles, as was the case in Gaul at the end of the Roman Empire, the big agglomerations will build walls similar to those constructed in Israel at their border with Jordan and Saudi Arabia, in order to protect themselves from Daech. The population will accumulate behind concrete walls, abandoning the suburban areas which will turn to ruins. Inside cities, slums will replace public gardens, as they did when the Central Park became Hooverville in New York during the Great Depression. The stadiums will be transformed in citadels, their rows between transformed into confined habitations, the grass disappearing under constructions where the chiefs of the city will be seated, at the heart of the defensive system [32]. The major growth in population density and insalubrity of newly-constructed habitations will cause hygienic problems and a drop of life expectancy, as was the case in Russia after the fall of the USSR. The rules imposed by the municipal governments in order to ensure provisioning of the cities will aggravate penuries further, as the devastated countryside will not be able to sustain such population densities. Cities will depopulate, and there will be an urban exodus. The tax requirements of the American Empire will lead to insurrections, until the critical moment where the authorities will become unable to collect further taxes to fund the army, which will result in the fall of the Empire, and its balkanization into a multitude of entities of all sizes, from principalities to free cities.

When the American Empire falls in the way described above, after having sterilized the entire global network through totalitarianism, it will be the beginning of de-globalization. As a new form of feudalism arises, channels of communication and travel will be cut. The free circulation of persons, goods and ideas will encounter obstacles due to piracy and fees imposed by local "Lords." In some cases, these Lords may even forbid passage, in order to retain technological secrets as strategic advantages. This will add to the intellectual obscurantism that is inherent to these kinds of socio-economic situations. These conditions will cause a cessation of technological progresses, at first, due to the impossibility of sharing discoveries and inventions, and then, a technological regression, since the individuals, incapable to travel in order to acquire training in civilizational centers, or at least to benefit from their knowledge, will lose any capacity similar to the savants of our time, due to a lack of access to knowledge. It will also be hard to employ, as we do today in intellectual centers, a scientist coming from the other side of the world. In addition, the inability to obtain certain goods, machines and materials will accelerate this regression by limiting access to technologies that will still be known but hard to put in action.

An important share of current knowledge will disappear locally, in the sense that it will still be known or preserved by some, but lost everywhere else. A small share may be completely lost, in the sense that such knowledge, science, or know-how will completely disappear from humanity, and will only be obtained again through rediscovery rather than simple transmission. The disappearance of several large networks of computer servers will have a similar impact to the Burning of the Library of Alexandria.

Let us pause a moment to imagine concretely what this futuristic Middle Ages may look like. It will be a divided, feudal world where a new aristocracy will rise along with its clients. Take, for instance, East Asia: China, Korea, Japan, India and Indochina. These regions will be the equivalent of Northern Europe and Occidental Europe in the Middle Ages. Concrete fortresses will multiply, dividing the countryside where food will be produced. The smaller Lords will be limited to a Blockhaus, basic comfort, and some military exoskeletons with a few vehicles and heavy weaponry. More powerful Lords will have larger areas, a luxurious residence and garages filled with armored vehicles and helicopters. The very powerful ones may have an air fleet. The neo-feudal aristocracy will control certain economic tools, as was the case in the past with the Lord's furnace or mill. Such a lord in the future may possess an electrical plant, perhaps others might possess a manufacture and its machines, while others may control an offshore drilling rig, an oil processing plant or an airport. These lords will be at war with each other regularly, limited by the extent of their means and the instability of their alliances.

As for the people, largely exiled in the countryside to return to a subsistence economy, its standard of living will be greatly diminished. Nevertheless, this standard of living will not return to the level observed in peasants in the Middle Ages. Several technological advances will be transmitted, in an artisan rather than industrial manner. We are already observing on the Internet several videos from ingenious individuals describing how to construct a homemade exoskeleton, and several people in these communities are capable, if given the necessary materials, to put together homemade computers. The quasi-absence of these goods will encourage continuous recycling and do-it-yourself production, which will likely be transmitted across generations, like the plows and tools of the past.

The existence of these goods implies, of course, that electricity will not disappear altogether. We have mentioned that powerful Lords might own electrical plants, but it is not very probable that extensive electricity distribution networks will not survive the fall. The Lords who own these plants may use them to power up a city, and a few neighboring villages, but not much more. For most of the population, disseminated across the territories, other sources of energy will have to be used, probably through artisan exploitation and local technologies that are being developed today, such as anaerobic digestion as well as solar and wind power. There is no doubt that some of the low-cost technologies being developed today to help populations in underdeveloped countries throughout the world, such as the Gravity Light (which works with a dynamo and a counter-weight) and water purifiers, will come to be handy as solutions to failing infrastructure for supplying water and energy.

Illiteracy will likely become common. We have seen that between the Mycenaean Empire and Ancient Greece, during the Greek Dark Ages, the knowledge of writing was lost. Similarly, at the end of the Roman Empire, it is estimated that around 50% of the population was literate, compared to 1% around 1000 A.D.. It is possible that, through every iteration, the regression is lessened, especially given the increase of the level of literacy. Today, all countries around the Pacific Ocean have a literacy rate above 95%. This rate could fall under 30%, which is comparable to the least literate countries of Africa today. It is likely that, as the regression of the labor market following the de-globalization at the end of the Roman Empire has constrained individuals to become proficient at several task on their own (produce their own clothes, tools, etc.), this lost of knowledge by a great share of the population will be compensated by polyvalence in the domains of agriculture, mechanics, construction, plumbing, electronics and textile production... Only the elites of the social class which had always been responsible for knowledge in primitive and mystical societies, that is, the religious, will preserve some level of education. Neo-Christian clergymen (see our point below), the new copyist monks, will preserve in future abbeys the knowledge from the time of the American Empire, by preserving computer archives and maintaining servers with copies of that knowledge. The Neo-Christian Church will be maintaining hospitals in which it can apply medical knowledge, and might preserve observatories for preserving the knowledge of astronomy. That is what the American Middle Age will look like.

A return to progress will only occur, as it was the case in Greece and Occidental Europe, through a reappearance of the urban centers of exchange, and a networking of these centers, which will allow the preserved knowledge to spread once again, and to lost knowledge to be rediscovered by new researchers. This movement will take centuries to occur.

4. The future of Islam and of great monotheistic religions

Beyond the certainty of the final defeat of Jihadism as well as the Jewish zealotry of Antiquity, we must ask the question of the future of Islam as a religion. Indeed, the last stage of Cycle C has been described as follows:

13) Confirmation of the dominance of the model of Civilization B. Civilization C is eradicated as a political power.

Nevertheless, this political conclusion does not mean the end of the religion. Today, Rabbinical Judaism is still well alive, and Jewish identity is thriving. Jewish culture has taken a new form after its military and political crushing of the I-IInd centuries. Jewish faith has been reformulated, has abandoned Millenarism and the hope of global domination.

Judaism has then evolved into two branches. Proselytic Judaism was confounded with Christianity, and got absorbed by it. The figure of Christ, an exemplary man, incarnation of the divine, left very little in the religious competition for traditional Judaism, even after its conversion to the Rabbinic form in the first century. Similarly, it left little for the imperial cult of Mithras, parent of Mithraism.

The Rabbinical Judaism which exists today is the branch of Ancient Judaism which has refused to acknowledge Jesus Christ as the Messiah, as the Jews had imagined a triumphant war chief such as those on whom hopes were invested in the leadership of insurrectionist movements. The Rabbis have preserved, from their traditional texts, the prophetic figure that dominates the Torah, Moses, but they have adapted it to a more spiritual interpretation. In doing so, the Jewish faith has purged itself of the violence of the tradition of Moses, but, being incapable to replace the hope of a global domination with an alternative, as was done in Christianity through the concept of an imminent saving by Christ, this new Judaism practically lost any capacity for proselytism, and became essentially a common inheritance for the purpose of preservation, with no missionary pretention. Having failed at extending itself over the entire world, Judaism withdrew unto itself: of the three monotheistic religions, it is the most difficult to penetrate for outsiders, because of the goal of identitarian preservation, which imposes strict conditions on the acceptance of new converts by asking for guarantees on the profundity of their conversion. Today, there is, in the world, less than twenty million Jews, which, taking into account the demographic impact of the Holocaust, shows that this population has been ceiled in its growth for two millennia around the level that existed under Hadrian.

The abandonment of the spirit of Moses' Judaism, which was not integrated into Christianity, since Christianity was in essence, just like Rabbinical Judaism, a surpassing of it, allowed Muhammad to fill a void by presenting a religious message that went back to primitive Judaism, making of the Arab Muslims the new chosen people, instead of the Jews.

In total, post-Moses Judaism has formed the basis of three different monotheisms: Rabbinical Judaism, which renounced to terrestrial messianism in the face of all of its failures, Christianity, which has surpassed messianism by recognizing as Messiah a man who has ordered to renounce to worldly ambitions, and Islam, which is a reboot of the original Judaism. Those were the three attitudes toward monotheistic messianism, after its terrestrial realization had failed: spiritualization (an understanding that waiting never ends), the affirmation of its effective accomplishment in another way than the one that was traditionally expected (the Passion of the Christ, who died and was resuscitated), or its renewal under another prophet who recycles for himself the initial message (Muhammad). It is hard to see, logically, what other solutions could have been proposed to the problem of messianic disappointment. Either one faces its failure, and seeks to re-interpret the message in a vaguer way, toward a more spiritual goal, or the appearances were misleading and it was accomplished, but not in the expected form, or the revelation was not yet complete since it was still missing one prophet.

From here, having observed the identity between the trajectory of Moses' Judaism and that of Islam, we can surmise that the latter will encounter a similar evolution, once its modern messianism, Mahdism, will have failed like the former.

Thus, it is not very probable that the ensemble of the Muslim world would convert to the post-Mahdism version of Islam, which could be termed Ulemic Islam, based on the Rabbinical Judaism model, an Islam that would be reinterpreted, spiritualized, born from a doctrinal agreement among some Ulemas. This Ulemic Islam, like Rabbinical Judaism, will not be proselytizing, but rather will be characterized by the same kind of religious melancholy following fanatism, that is, disappointed Millenarism. As was the case with Rabbinical Judaism, it would not have a force of seduction, but would be essentially carried as an inheritance to preserve. In the centuries that will follow, the Ulemic Islam population would not extend much more than their population level in the XXIth century, and would become increasingly smaller relative to the rest of the global population. It is to be expected that Ulemic Islam, in the next two millennia, will be like Judaism in the last two millennia, a minority religion whose members will be marginalized, subjected to hostility and distrust, and pushed toward strong communitarian bonds in the societies welcoming them, as well as occupying positions in trade and intellectual work that would require frequent traveling, in order to protect themselves against persecution. Antisemitism will thus likely extend toward them. It is not impossible that Rabbinical Judaism and this Ulemic Islam would end up in some unified form, due to the proximity of their spirit, the substance of their faith, and the resemblances of their texts, as well as their potential interest in allying as persecuted minority communities. Furthermore, if Islam follows the trajectory of Judaism, then, in addition to Ulemic Islam, it should engender two branches destined to be of high importance for the history of the coming two millennia: one constituting a surpassing of Mahdism, and the other, a renewal of it. These two branches would respectively constitute a second Christianity and a third version of Ancient Judaism.

First, let us consider a second Christianity.

The hypothesis is not absurd. No doubt, there are Mahdi warriors in Islam who are emerging as the leaders of Muslim uprisings. The first of the modern era is probably Muhammad Ahmad ibn 'Abd Allah Al-Mahdi, chief of the Sudanese Dervish, in the Mahdist War, during which occurred the Siege of Khartoum, at the end of which Sudan was founded as a theocratic state equivalent to the current Islamic State. Others have followed. But beside these Mahdi warriors, who are carrying a Millenarist vision of Islam, we also find individuals who were advocating for a surpassing of the Islam of Muhammad.

The two main ones and probably the most significant are the Báb and Baha'u'llah, fascinating figures of Persian Islam in the XIXth century, on the one hand, and on the other, Mirza Ghulam Ahmad[33]. The Báb, born Sayyed 'Alí Muḥammad Shírází, has an impressive path similar to that of Jesus of Nazareth. Born in 1819, demonstrating impressive aptitudes in religious school where he studied as a child, he announces in 1844, to a Muslim mystic who was traveling across the country in order to find the Mahdi, that he was the one. The mystic became his first disciple, soon to be followed by others, for a total of 18. The Báb, which means "the Door," went in a pilgrimage in the holy places of Islam, Mecca and Medina. His preaching attracted the crowds and the governor of Chiraz ordered his arrest to please the Muslim clergy. His doctrine largely implied the abolition of Sharia. The Báb decided to deliver himself to the authorities. He was arrested, and transferred many times between fortresses due to his popularity. He was finally judged, and during his trial, he was asked who he is. He announced that he was the chosen one, awaited by Muslims, after which he was mocked, molested and condemned to death. His execution happened twice: first, he was suspended to the walls of the fortress of Tabriz with a young disciple. The peloton that was supposed to kill him fired, as the crowd watched, but he survived, one of the bullets having struck the ropes suspending him, which led some to believe in a miracle. A new attempt eventually worked, leading to the death of the Báb. His body, recovered by his disciples, was finally buried on Mount Carmel in Haifa, in 1909.

This story is comparable to the life of Jesus in many ways. A prodigious child, the preaching of a pacific doctrine, the hostility of the authorities, the trial leading to the affirmation of a prophetic mission, as well as the condemnation and martyrdom.

The Baha'u'llah is in line with the Báb. Born in Iran in 1817, Mirza Husayn-Ali Nuri, son of an aristocratic family, became an adept of Bábism at thirty years old, during the preaching on the Báb. In 1863, he declared to people close to him that he was the chosen one, a manifestation of God to come after the Báb, and expressed a desire to establish a global religion, a monotheism crowning all other religions. He traveled through the Ottoman Empire and communicated his preaching in writing. Frequently ending up in prison or exile, he continued preaching until the end of his life, in 1892. It seems that most Bábists, who have been extensively persecuted by Persian Power, have disappeared, or have joined the Baha'i movement. This movement is, in a way, structured like Christianity for which Paul had affirmed being a new prophet, and had to some extent supplanted the figure of Christ. This is odd, because the figure of the Báb, due to his life, would have seemed to constitute a more authentic prophet compared to Baha'u'llah.

The other case is that of Mirza Ghulam Ahmad, who founded the Ahmadiyya movement. Born in British India in 1835, he claimed to have received a revelation in 1889 and to have been entrusted by Allah with a mission of renovation and purification of Islam, proclaiming himself, in a spectacular syncretic effort, Mahdi, as well as the avatar of the Hindu God Krishna and Jesus of Nazareth coming back to Earth. He asked Muslims to abandon Jihad and to side with pacifism. Interestingly, he considered to be, with respect to Muhammad, what Jesus was to Moses. He died in 1908.

Bábism and the Ahmadiyya movement are two contemporaneous religious movements from the XIXth century, having emerged in Islam, and being founded around individuals who claimed to surpass the religion of Muhammad, not only as theologians favoring an interpretation, but as prophets invested with divine authority. In the two cases, we find a claim to the status of Mahdi, but without the warrior spirit that would normally be associated with the term, which is replaced by a sense of spiritual guidance.

Up to now, neither of these movements have encountered much success. Bahaism claims to have seven million members throughout the world, and the Ahmadiyya movement would have around ten million. This may seem small after a century of activity, and in comparison to the rest of the Muslim population which is estimated to more than a billion and a half individuals today, a population which has grown five fold in a century.

Of course, it could be said that the success of these recent religions, these Muslim Christianities, could develop in the coming years faster than Millenarist apostasy. When Islam, broken, would renounce to its dreams of conquest, just as the Jews did in Antiquity, it might become easier for the proponents of Baha'u'llah and Mirza Ghulam Ahmad to have their prophets recognized as servants of Allah, the chosen one, as opposed to the multiple Mahdis who would have succumbed to American and European attacks.

There seems to be, however, an obstacle to be surmounted in the weakness of these various characters, in comparison to the figure of Jesus of Nazareth. While the Báb does have a life that resembles that of the Christ, they remain distinguished on many aspects. The Báb was married, his life story does not mention miracles, and he is not believed to have resuscitated after his death. Baha'u'llah, on his side, only stated being on a mission after having his revelation. He was married, had children and died of old age. Mirza Ghulam Ahmad claimed to have been hearing voices, to have been able to predict the future and to perform miracles. None of them, contrarily to Jesus, are claimed to be a direct incarnation of God, nor to have been born from a virgin. Certainly, the historicity of the acts and realizations of Jesus of Nazareth, in particular the miracles, is impossible to establish, but historicity does not matter so much in the capacity of seduction of a religion. Rather, what matters it the content of the faith and discourse it proposes. Christian faith has seduced, and still seduces, through the figure of Christ. If Jesus was presented in the evangelical tradition as a man tortured and buried, having never resurrected, would his message still have the same echo? Would he have been acknowledged by such a great number of Jews, as rapidly as he was? Would Christianity have such a success if Jesus had only been recognized as Messiah by the Apostles and the first Jews converted to Christianity, but not recognized as God? Even Arianism recognized a divine part in Christ. One can surmise that beyond the beauty of the message of peace, the miraculous talk may play a role in the diffusion of a religious message. From this point of view, one can doubt the capacity of these pacific versions of Mahdism such as Bábism, Bahaism and Ahmadiyya to seduce, in the coming two centuries, as many people as Christianity did. Perhaps an embellishment and reconstruction of their prophets may occur, as it seems not to have occurred during the first century of their existence.

Most importantly, the main obstacle to the emergence of this second Christianity seems to be the existence of Christianity itself. Indeed, if Islam was able to appear, it is due to the disappearance of the Judaism of Moses. If Ancient Judaism had not disappeared, Muhammad could not have captured its message as he has done. That space would have already been occupied, and the original would have been preferred to the copy.

Yet there is no reason to believe that Christianity could disappear in the coming centuries. Today, it is the first religion of the world, with close to two and a half billion followers, a third of the global population. It is a dynamic religion in terms of demographics.

Furthermore, the great strength of Christianity is, precisely, the figure of the Christ on which it is based. From the strict point of view of religious anthropology, without presuming of the veracity of the beliefs or in the rigor of the texts, it seems that the figure of Jesus Christ is unsurpassable. Of all monotheistic prophets, none can pretend to equate the figure of Christ. Jesus Christ, as he is presented in Christian faith, does not have and has never had a single defect. His life is exemplary from the beginning to the end. He did not become a prophet; he is born as such. He does not commit any injustice in his life, and specifically, compared to Abraham, Moses or Muhammad, never lies or kills. A character such as Muhammad, for instance, has a history that can lead to certain critiques, that are regularly used by the detractors of Islam, for instance the massacres that he has committed, his marriage with the young Aisha, who was a child… Moses, on his side, is the assassin of an Egyptian. Jesus of Nazareth, however, is never criticized by the enemies of Christianity. They are limited to trying to demonstrate that he has never existed, and that is because Jesus, the man, is impossible to attack in how he is portrayed by Christianity.

Additionally, Jesus of Nazareth is presented by Christian faith not as a simple man serving as an intermediary toward God, but as God incarnate himself.

By unsurpassable, we mean that no religion could be founded by claiming to surpass Christianity, because this would require the appearance or invention of a prophet with attributes that would make him an ever greater authority than Christ. It is hard to imagine how a prophet, imaginary or not, would have more authority than the very incarnation of a unique and omnipotent divinity, nor how a man could pretend to be as perfect throughout his life, nor how a man could claim a greater perfection in his behavior as that of Christ as presented in the Gospels.

Thus, the figure of Christ is so unsurpassable that it is only through a partial negation of its veracity that another monotheism, Islam, could appear after. It took the negation of the divinity of Christ, through the denial of the divinity of his death and resurrection. This other monotheism turned out to be, in the end, a recuperation of pre-Christian Judaism. The Báb and Mirza Ghulam Ahmad, who have claimed the status of Mahdi, saw Jesus in the same way Islam did.

One would at least have to equate the figure of Christ in order to massively convince the Christians, who have historically rejected Islam, of a new faith. This seems impossible. Indeed, either Jesus of Nazareth was truly Christ, Christian faith is true, and then no man could ever appear and carry a different revelation from him; or the Jesus of Christians is a mythical reconstruction of the historical Jesus, but this reconstruction benefits from the advantage of dating from two thousand years ago, while new prophets acting today would be known first and foremost as men, with their defects. In both cases, it seems close to impossible that a Christ-like prophet (that is, a prophet carrying a message of peace and spirituality, and never acting, contrarily to Moses and Muhammad, as a political or military chief) would succeed at imposing himself in the face of traditional Christianism.

In summary, as it relates to the evolution of Islam in correspondence with the Judaic mutation into Christianity, there can be two possibilities.

If there were a prophet emerging from Islam (the Mahdi, as Jesus was the Messiah), then he will, fundamentally, be a replica of Christianity in his moral doctrine, his principles and his spirit, just like Islam is a replica of Ancient Judaism. But since Christianity already exists, and is demographically more successful than Islam, it is hard to see how this new vision of Islam, this post-Mahdism, like Christianity is a post-Judaism, could impose itself as an autonomous faith. In the unfolding of the cycles, that is the great difference between Ancient Judaism and Islam. The latter emerged and existed alongside the already surpassed Judaism, Christianity. In comparison, Ancient Judaism grew on the coasts of the Mediterranean Sea as the sole monotheism (leaving aside Greek monotheistic philosophies, that were too abstract to have convincing power over the people, and which was eventually absorbed by the Church Fathers, notably Saint Augustine). The only competing monotheism existed in the East, in Persia (Zoroastrianism).

If such a character does not emerge from Islam, then two directions for the evolution of Islam can be expected. On the one hand, a branch should develop into a reformed version of Islam, equivalent to Rabbinical Judaism, which we have referred to as Ulemic Islam, and which we have briefly described. On the other hand, a branch should massively convert toward Christianity during a complete renewal of the religion, since, progressively, with the trajectory of the Cycle B of America, the conditions for the initial rise of this religion under the Roman Empire would occur once more.

This second hypothesis seems to be supported by what has happened to modern Christianity, specifically Catholicism, since the middle of the XXth century, and the strong period of de-Christianization of the 1960s-1970s in Europe and North America. Catholicism seems to have returned to the same state that it had attained on the day following the death of Christ: a despised, persecuted religion delivering its testimony often in pain and in the blood of martyrs, but without violence. Through these challenges, Christianity, and especially the Catholic church, is restoring the advantages that it had in the beginning, erasing in the blood of current martyrs the past violence of the Crusades and the Inquisition for which, exceptionally, Pope John Paul II asked pardon. It is not to be excluded that, when the American Empire progressively begins to appear as a global USSR, certain leaders of the Church may end up being persecuted, leading people to forget about the dark side of Christian history and equipping Christianity with a crushing moral authority, just like the Shoah erased—temporarily, unfortunately—anti-Semitism, which became a social taboo in Occidental countries.

In the 1960s, Christianity became a religion concentrated on its role, its internal organization, and its means of diffusion. On this last aspect, the Second Vatican Council and its consequences formed the most important reform of the Church since the council of Jerusalem, in terms of its rituals, modes of operation and its self-perception. The council of Jerusalem was the first in Christian history, which led to the distinction between Judaism and Christianity, the end of circumcision, and the abolition of numerous nutritional restrictions. Vatican II, in modern times, had a similar effect by ridding Catholicism of a very distinctive cultural apparatus which constituted an obstacle to the universalism of Christianity as claimed by the Catholic Church. We saw a de-occidentalization and de-Europeanization of rituals and Catholic thought. Thus, Catholicism got rid of what made it appear as colonial, by pretending to have Africans and Asians celebrate evangelical faith in accordance with a liturgy that completely emerged from European culture. While these reforms had, understandably, a negative effect in Europe, where several followers did not recognize their traditional religion into this new form of Christianity, they have, for the same reasons, facilitated missionary work in the post-colonial third world, by adapting the expressions of faith to local cultures.

But other than this new pastoral orientation for the Church, as far as modes of operation and teaching of rituals of the Church go, it is a genuine doctrinal remake that occurred under Vatican II, and a passing of all other religions. For close to two thousand years, the Catholic Church has taught that all other beliefs were false. As a consequence, the conversion to the Catholic religion necessitated a denial of preceding beliefs. From then on, conversion required much less abandonment of previous beliefs, which is a considerable advantage. Indeed, since Vatican II, and in particular since the Declaration on the relation of the Church to non-Christian Religions, titled *Nostra Aetate* ("In our time"), of October 28th 1965, the Catholic Church says that other religions are partially true, stating: *"The Catholic Church rejects nothing that is true and holy in these religions. She regards with sincere reverence those ways of conduct and of life, those precepts and teachings which, though differing in many aspects from the ones she holds and sets forth, nonetheless often reflect a ray of that Truth which enlightens all men."*[34]. It is the doctrine of the "seeds of the Word," which, with respect to Catholicism, distinguishes between Christian heresies and completely separated religions. As such, the Church positioned itself as the religion overseeing all others, a kind of universal receiver of all the spiritualties of the world. The Assisi meetings, on the International Day of Prayer for Peace, on October 27th 1986, as part of the inter-religious dialogue, was in this vein a very strong symbol whose full meaning may not have been fully understood yet in the history of religions and of the Catholic Church in particular. In these meetings, representatives of all the great religions of the world were assembled around the chief of the Catholic Church. The goal of the meetings was certainly not to express any sort of Catholic domination, but the simple fact that the initiative and organizational effort, as well as the place, were decided by the Catholic Church, illustrates the new place that the Church is claiming as the heart of global religion. Vatican II has allowed the rise of Catholicism to the rank of a religion of religions[35], and has given a new sense to the word "Catholic." The Church has thus acquired a powerful doctrinal machine for the absorption of the other religions.

And this universality, for a religion, is unsurpassable, just like its foundation on a unique God-prophet. This was also what the Muslim prophet Baha'u'llah claimed to have founded. By claiming to crown all of the religions that had ever existed, Bahaism, while having a less perfect prophetic figure than Jesus of Nazareth, would appear like an Internet search engine emerging today that would attempt to compete against Google without offering a better service.

Thus, structurally, Christian religion, and specifically the Catholic Church, is increasingly well-prepared for the global religious changes that will affect the evolution of Islam. It is prepared internally (organizational reform, increasing openness to local cultures and traditions) as well as externally (its reputation and the improvement of the perceptions of the Church by the external world) and doctrinally (definition of Christianity as a religion capable of accepting all others). This preparation of the Church through continuous de-Europeanization, notably with the discourses of Pope Francis on excessive centralization and the necessity of reforms of Roman governance under Roman Curia, will be a decisive advantage.

Let us conclude on this possibility of a massive conversion of Muslims to Christianity with a very recent example, that of Adjara, a province of Georgia with approximately three hundred thousand inhabitants. In 1980, this population was 75% Muslim, and there was a single Church that was active in Batumi, the capital of the province. In 2002, 75% of the population had converted to Orthodox Christianity without any particular reason (and, notably, without any political requirement to do so)[36]. Every year, throughout the world, around six million Muslims convert to Christianity[37], and Christianity is the religion with the quickest growth when including both births and conversions[38].

In the end, if Christianity was to be absorbed into a post-Islam, a "Muslim Christianity," by being either completely replaced or integrated to it in a form of syncretism, then it will seem that Christianity, in and of itself, was merely a religious anthropological phenomenon, a belief that would not be truer than any other.

If, however, Christianity is reinforced by these developments, ends up serving as post-Islam, and absorbs an important part of the Muslims as it has done in the past with Jews, leaving behind a reformed Islam equivalent to Rabbinical Judaism, then the truth of Christianity would not have been refuted, but it would not have been proven either. This second hypothesis appears much more probable, for reasons of religious anthropology. On the one hand, the unsurpassable, and even difficult to equate character of the prophetic figure of the Christ, and on the other hand, the demographic weight of Christianity (today we count about one Baha'i for every 350 Christians, and 1 Ahmadis for every 250 Christians).

No matter where the world is headed, it seems certain that the great religion of the two coming millennia, that which will be dominating these millennia, like Christianity dominated medieval and modern history, the religion of the future Civilization A, will be monotheistic with characteristics close to Christianity in general, and Catholicism in particular. Whether it is a sort of new Christianity, emerging within Islam and surpassing it like Christianity surpassed Ancient Judaism, or an important Christian renewal uniting Christians with a part of the Muslim population as they resist together their political persecution by the American Empire and its totalitarian direction, we can encompass these two possibilities in the term Neo-Christianity, a term which includes the two possibilities of a new Christianity, born from a mutation of Islam through the teachings of a Christ-like prophet, or a Christian renewal profiting from the fall of Islam following the failure of Mahdism. This term will be used going forward in our description of the coming two millennia.

The third and last branch of Islam, after the Ulemic and Neo-Christian ones, will be that which corresponds to Ancient Judaism. This will thus constitute a third Judaism, which we could call Neo-Islam. Just like Ancient Judaism and Islam, it will not be so centered around a prophet, although such a prophet will have an important role as a founder and as a model, but it will be centered around a doctrine and a religious law. This law will adopt the traits that form the similarity between Islam and Ancient Judaism: a small number of strict religious prescriptions will allow believers to distinguish themselves from the rest of the community, notably, dietary restrictions. As was the case with Moses and Muhammad, the prophet carrying this religion will probably appear in a region that is distant from great civilizations. The rise of the new faith will be favored by the systemic crumbling of global civilization, like the Israelites benefited from the fall of Mycenae and its devastating consequences over the Mediterranean Sea and Orient, and like the Arabs benefited from the weakening of the Roman Empire of Orient, for which they were what the Barbarians were to the Occidental Empire. The people, seduced by this prophet, will rapidly establish an empire over the ruins of the American Empire, which will serve as the base for the diffusion of this new religion. This new belief will likely retain the prophetic lineage from Abraham to Muhammad.

5. *Summary of predictions*

We are reaching the end of this prospective essay for the coming century based on our theory of the great cycles of civilization, and it seems we should briefly summarize our predictions before the conclusion.

Between now and the middle of the XXIst century, the American Empire will pursue its conquest of the world and the USA will continue its economic and military rise.

Today, Iran is replaced by the Islamic State as the most visible representative of Jihadism, a movement in full expansion since 1979. Iran could make peace with the USA, due to fear of this novel enemy, which could lead to the reform of the regime of the Mullahs. The repeated military crushing of Islamic Millenarism (Mahdism), will lead in the end to the appeasement of the Muslim world by the development of a moderate and appeased version of Islam, which we have called Ulemic Islam. This Islam, characterized by less proselytism, will cease its historical expansion. Numerous Muslims, disgusted by Millenarist violence or disappointed by the failure of their hope for a global triumph of Islam, will distance themselves from the religion and will convert to Neo-Christianity (defined as one of the two alternatives expressed above).

In parallel, this return of Iran within the American sphere of influence will weaken China and Russia internationally: China, because the USA will then have their hand on the faucet of the petroleum industry, and Russia, because its attempt to build a system of control of energies that would be competing with the of the USA in the Middle East would have failed. This failure would be even graver given the fact that the exploitation of schists oil will diminish the importance of Russia in the global reserves. This ranking of Russia in the global reserves of fossil energies is what allowed it to recover in the last few years and resulted in a drop of energy prices: losing their position would mean a considerably weakened Russia.

Perhaps before 2020 or around 2030 at the latest, the Chinese regime (if it doesn't engage in a foreign adventure before) will implode under the influence of various economic and social factors which were described above. The USA will succeed at legitimizing an intervention, even if limited, within the country, perhaps with the help of its allies in the region, and to establish a friendly regime, similarly to Taiwan. Russia will thus lose its objective ally against the American global policy and will find itself weakened on the geopolitical scene. It will be isolated in the Security Council of the UN, which itself will become a leverage of power under the control of the USA, and will support any military intervention of economic sanction decided by the USA without the Russians being capable of opposing to them, because American propaganda will present them as the supporters of all inequalities. The Russian position is already hard to defend today with the support of China, and it will become indefensible without it. Thus, without a single bullet fired between the two nuclear powers, Russia could be neutralized, integrated against its will into the American Empire... conditionally to Europe not degenerating in the meantime, which is very much possible.

Additionally, the North Korean regime will disappear which will cause regional destabilization. The fall of China, the global model of State Capitalism, of the working authoritarian regime, could discredit the partisans of state interventions in the economy for a few years.

At this stage, the *pax americana* will be reigning over the world.

During the same period, the American imperial policy will have been sustained by a new, very favorable economic cycle, due to new technological innovations having appeared in the 2010s and having been perfected for many decades. However, in the 2040s, while America will be at an apogee of control over the world, an important economic crisis will occur, ending a very favorable Kondratiev cycle. At that moment, the uncontested and unshared domination of America in foreign places will lead to a fall of its institutions on the inside. The conservatives will have no more enemies threatening democracy and liberty, as is the case today with Iran, an enemy that they could use as a scarecrow to stop those who, hurt by the crisis, will seek to denunciate capitalism. The body of traditional values of democracy, liberalism and capitalism of America will be fragile, since it will have lost its contrast through the negative, i.e. the living counter-example of despotism and denial of individual rights. While today, we can still highlight the efficiency of the liberal model through comparison with the alternative models (Iranian theocracy, North Korean totalitarianism), the disappearance of these living images will weaken the discourse of the American conservatives. The danger having disappeared, the slope of limiting individual and constitutional rights will appear much less slippery.

A period of internal troubles will thus begin in America where the liberal-capitalist model will no more be subject to consensus, perhaps due to difficulties brought by the robotic transition. The proponents of the welfare state will reach numbers and political power that this country has never known, and socialist propositions will become increasingly common. The deep ideological fracture inside the nation will not be solvable, because of the absence of a basis of comparison with a foreign tyranny. American society will see a political realignment toward collectivism and socialism, and institutions, due to the tensions induced by these changes, will have to adapt to this new paradigm. Ambitious characters will emerge by benefiting from these changes and gaining power in order to establish a new regime by claiming the middle ground between American tradition and socialist concerns. They will develop an authoritarian power and a function similar to that of an American Emperor will appear.

America will thus be engaged on a gloomy slope. The existence of an authoritarian power, even if moderate in the beginning, will allow the progression of statism and economic dirigism, and a culture at the service of this power to replace the democratic and liberal critique. Interventionism will impede on the economy, whose difficulties will encourage even more interventionism. A slow decline will progressively weaken America, and the increasingly heavy yoke of the regime will exhaust the Empire. The imperial totalitarian ideology will make the American Empire look like the USSR, a USSR that would extend over almost the entire globe. As is the case with any totalitarian regime, it will repress religion as an obstacle to political unity and will combat the cult of leading religious figures: Judaism, Ulemic Islam and, most importantly, Neo-Christianity, the most dynamical and numerous, will be subject to prohibitions and persecutions. These persecutions will reinforce these religions and could, toward the end of the Empire, turn Neo-Christianity into the official religion, or the agitations related to these persecutions could be the origin of the fall.

Statism will establish a form of corruption that will increase the fragility of all institutions. The provinces of the American Empire will become feudal, some individuals choosing to take over, locally, the functions and institutions of the state. The American Empire will die like the Roman Empire, piece by piece. It may persist in a unified Europe for a moment, while feudalized and Neo-Christianized Asia enters its Dark Ages, a period of gestation for a new stage of Occidental Civilization, which within a few centuries will emerged in the Far East, having become the Occident, and will surpass all the past glory of Europe and America.

---

1. David Engels, *Le déclin. La crise de l'Union européenne et la chute de la République romaine. Quelques analogies*, Paris, 2013.
2. Hopefully the distinguished geometricians will pardon us for using an intuitive vocabulary rather than the idea of a vector.
3. « L'identité grecque contre et avec Rome », *L'Empire gréco-romain*, p.178. Numerous pages of this article echo the current situation between Europe and America.
4. Of course, the budget austerity measures which do not reduce public expenses but seek to reduce deficits by increasing fiscal pressure, as is the case in France, cannot be characterized as liberal. The United Kingdom of David Cameron has put in place authentically liberal measures, by drastically reducing public employment and by reducing taxes, which has resulted in a major growth and allowed the United Kingdom to surpass France in 2014 in the ranking of global economies. This also allowed David Cameron to triumph in the last elections.
5. Friedrich Hayek, *The Road to Serfdom*, 1941.
6. Fabrice Bouthillon, *Nazisme et Révolution, Histoire Théologique du National-Socialisme, 1789-1989*, Paris, 2011. The historian explains that there are two ways to pretend to surpass the left-right schism. On the one hand, classical centrism attempts the union of the moderates, the "two thirds of the population," by excluding extremists from the government. On the other hand, an intellectual discovery attributable to Bouthillon, there can be centrism through addition of the extremes, which seeks to create national unity by regrouping the extremists. In support of this thesis, Bouthillon mentions the case of Napoleon, who united the partisans of the authoritarian monarchy who were supporting the alliance between the crown and the Church, a rather far-right idea at the end of the Revolution, with the Jacobin heritage of the Revolution itself, a far-left ideology. Another example is that of Hitler, who while having emerged from far-right circles, has succeeded at seducing many electors on the far-left.
7. http://www.dreuz.info/2014/09/une-internationale-neo-fasciste-gagne-du-terrain/
8. Marine Le Pen has publicly announced her desire to withdraw France from NATO: http://www.nationspresse.info/mondialisme/atlantisme/marine-le-pen-il-faut-sortir-de-lotan
9. http://www.slate.fr/story/92303/poutine-troupes-russes-riga-vilnius-varsovie
10. For a naive observer looking only at maps, the fall of the USSR seems to involve a minor reflux of Russian borders, limited in comparison to the size of the Russian Federation. In order to properly understand the catastrophic nature of the fall of the USSR for the Russian elites, one must remember that the USSR included more than 290 million inhabitants, and dominated over Eastern Europe populations of around 90 million inhabitants as part of the Warsaw Pact. The Soviet Empire, which was a Russian Empire, thus reigned over more than 380 million individuals. Today, Russia has only about 147 million inhabitants, half of the population of the USSR at its peak. Politically, and, importantly, demographically, the fall of the USSR would be the equivalent, for America, of the defection of NATO and the secession of all western states of the country.
11. This obvious parallel, which adds to the deeper one of the ancient situation between Cartage and Macedonia with respect to Rome, is a good illustration of the fractal nature of History. That is, History presents similar schemes at different levels of analysis.
12. http://www.slate.fr/story/91837/poutine-guerre-nucleaire
13. Yet, this failure would have to be perceived by the populations as the failure of Syriza itself, despite the program of this party being pure economic fantasy. If the Greek party is to be kept from implementing anything by European authorities, the failure could be attributed not to populism itself, but to European authoritarianism, thus reinvigorating even further the populist discourse. The result of a failure of Syriza in the mind of the European peoples is thus uncertain, and depends on how it occurs.
14. http://www.contrepoints.org/2015/01/27/195862-coup-dÉtat-en-suede
The article summarizes the situation as follows: "*An atypical party has risen in the last elections […] With 12%, the SD could only be an opposition party, but when another party joined it to reject the budget, the government found itself in a minority position, and its budget was invalidated, a classical situation of governmental crisis. In any democracy, this leads to the resignation of the government,*

158

and here it would be a case where dissolution would be imposed. This is so obvious that, at first, the chief of the Swedish government, Stefan Löfven, has decided and announced, on March 22nd 2015, that there would be new elections. [...] However, the polls started to indicate a strong rise of SD, representing levels of support such that neither the alliance between the Greens and the Socialists, nor the center-left, could hope to govern. Afraid of losing, through this last effort, the places that they occupied in an amicable rotation, these parties have decided to keep the positions for themselves, but instead of rotationally, simultaneously and forever. Or at least until 2022, first date for revising their agreement. Stefan Löfven has thus reverted his previous decision: the elections planned for 2015 would not occur, and the result of those of 2019 are already neutralized due to the agreement between the people in place, who want to remain in place, and their alliance is organized until 2022. Sweden will thus have the "chance" to be the first democracy globally to know the composition of its government before the elections, and know that it will remain in place independently from the results."

15. Françoise Thom has shown, following the Georgian crisis of 2008, that this was the final goal of Russian elites. Cf. "Le grand dessein de la Russie poutino-medvedevienne," Commentaire, n° 125, Spring 2009. From the same author, "Russie-Europe : les risques du 'redémarrage'," available online at http://www.diploweb.com/Russie-Europe-les-risques-du.html as well as "Poutine : l'heure de vérité," Commentaire N° 147, Fall 2014, also available online at http://extremecentre.org/2014/09/22/poutine-lheure-de-verite/

16. Cf. Paul Veyne, "Y a-t-il eu un impérialisme romain ?", Mélanges de l'École française de Rome. Antiquité T. 87, N° 2. 1975. pp. 793-855, available online at
http://www.persee.fr/web/revues/home/prescript/article/mefr_0223-5102_1975_num_87_2_1034

17. While the US Air Force is the first global aerial force in the world (more than 5700 aircrafts) the second global aerial force is... the US Navy (3700 aircrafts). Thus the third and fourth global aerial forces, that is, Chine (2500 aircrafts) and Russia (less than 2000 aircrafts) sum up to less than half of the American forces. As for the ability to launch aerial attacks, in particular the network of US bases, America controls about 80% of the aircraft ports in the world. Finally, America and Russia are about equal in terms of their operational nuclear weapons, around 1 800 each, and China would have around 250.

18. Cf. Françoise Thom, "Russie-Europe : les risques du 'redémarrage' ": "The Russian expert Lilia Chevtsova was surprised recently of the ease with which certain Europeans become parrots for Russian propaganda. She noted an ecstatic remark sent to Putin by Thierry de Montbrial during the meeting of Valday in 2007: "Mister President, you are the first leader in the history of Russia who has attained this level of power, and at the same time has shown so much willingness to share that power with others ... This proves that you are a democrat." How many times have we heard that Russia was "humiliated," that every country had the right to defend its "values," that we hadn't attempted to impose our liberal democracy, etc. According to the ex-Chancellor G. Schröder, Russia has the right to defend its security interests, that is, the right to keep Ukraine and Georgia from choosing their alliances. [...] After the Russo-Georgian War, the French Prime Minister François Fillon has done everything he could to avoid sanctions for Russia, using word-for-word the arguments pushed by Russian propaganda for years, assimilating the proponents of a strong policy to old schoolers from the times of the Cold War (which, of course, would have been the responsibility of the Occident) [...] By repeatedly hammering that the defense of liberal democracy is the goal of American Neo-Conservatives, the Russian propagandists have thus succeeded at getting the Europeans to abandon the very basis on which Europe was constructed for more than fifty years. The idea of an equality of rights between European states, big and small, the idea that the use of force is excluded among Europeans, the idea of a European solidarity, all of this is rejected with disdain by Moscow. If this "philosophy" of the Kremlin makes progress, Europe is at risk of an important regression, and might forget the harsh lessons of the two World Wars."

19. Laurent Artur du Plessis has suggested that an important conflict between the Occident and the Muslim world, in particular between Pakistan and Iran, could lead to the systematic use of weapons of mass destruction. Cf. De la crise à la guerre, la faillite des élites, Paris, Jean-Cyrille Godefroy, 2011.

20. I reuse the translation by Guy Millière, who has highlighted the historical character of this speech: http://www.dreuz.info/2015/01/le-courage-historique-du-marechal-sissi/

21. http://www.atlantico.fr/decryptage/contre-terrorisme-verite-comme-force-frappe-hassen-chalghoumi-philip-roy-1949045.html

22. http://www.lefigaro.fr/international/2015/01/22/01003-20150122ARTFIG00459-washington-tente-de-revoir-son-alliance-strategique-avec-riyad.php: The American intelligence services are particularly worried about the question of the loyalty of Saudi armies, in the context of an internal fight for the succession of the King, who is very sick. Since the time of Roosevelt, Americans have always served as protectors for the royal family. However, the progression of the ideas of the Islamic State among the military institution of the Kingdom is judged as "worrying." "The assassination, by commanders of the Islamic State, of a Saudi general sent to the northern border of the country in order to evaluate the loyalty of certain units that were judged as unreliable illustrates the magnitude of the problem," adds the source, which is close to American intelligence circles, talking to the Figaro. An evaluation of the "magnitude of the Salafist virus" is "in progress." The attack, led by the Islamic State, through the border and against the General Oudah al-Belawi must have been well planned: "It was based on the communication of precise information from inside the army."

23. According to http://en.wikipedia.org/wiki/Samson_Option

24. Jean-Louis Brunaux, Nos ancêtres les Gaulois, Paris, Le Seuil, 2008, p. 63.

25. Paul Veyne, "Entre l'Orient, la Grèce and Rome," L'Empire Gréco-romain, Paris, Éditions du Seuil, 2005, p. 270.

26. For details on the political upheaval of Rome over a longer time period, see my previous work, Rome, du libéralisme au socialisme : Leçon antique pour notre temps, Jean-Cyrille Godefroy, 2014.

27. http://gregmankiw.blogspot.fr/2012/07/progressivity-of-taxes-and-transfers.html Quoted by Alexis Vintray on Contrepoints :
http://www.contrepoints.org/2012/07/17/90672-redistribution-des-revenus-nouvelles-inquietantes-des-États-unis

28. http://lafaillitedelÉtat. com/2011/12/12/parlons-dautre-chose/

29. The Kondratiev cycle, supplemented with theories concerning innovation and creative destruction from Schumpeter, lasts around 40 years. At the beginning, we observe a phase where the economy rises, due to ensembles of important innovations which become the engine of economic growth (for instance the appearance of railroads and the steel industry, or the automobile and the oil industry, or the Internet and telecommunications...), then a phase of recession and depression, once these inventions have reached maturity and begin to merely respond to existing demand rather than create novel demand. The crisis of 2008 is, according to Kondratiev, not only financial but also a consequence of the slowing down of innovation in telecommunication technologies, which has led to the last economic rise in the 1980s. Indeed, starting in the 2000s and the popping of the Internet bubble, despite the appearance of new gadgets such as smartphones and tablets, there was no revolution comparable to the appearance of the Internet and the mobile phone. We must thus surmise that we have begun the descending phase of the Kondratiev cycle since 2000, that the crisis of 2008 is a landmark for the failure of the American attempts, through manipulation of the currency rates by the Federal Reserve, to combat the economic slowdown due to the lack of innovation, and that the beginning of the next Kondratiev cycle and the economic rise associated with it are getting closer, with the innovations that will result from the progress of robotics. The premises for this innovations are already here: high-end vehicles are equipped with radars for when they move back, and sometimes of systems allowing the car to park itself, without the driver. However, these advances are still only gadgets for the wealthy which are coming before the no-driver car, of which Google has already presented a prototype, and which will constitute a true revolution. Traffic and related infrastructures, public transit and the very modes of use for the car will be massively impacted. Similarly, in the 1980s, the first wireless phones were only a precursor to the mobile phone revolution.

30. http://www.latribune.fr/actualites/economie/france/20141027trib64edc65c1/les-robots-detruiraient-trois-millions-d-emplois-d-ici-a-2025-en-france.html

31. http://www.01net.com/editorial/611702/47pour-cent-des-emplois-pourront-etre-confies-a-des-ordinateurs-intelligents-d-ici-20-ans/

32. It is thus that the Gallo-Romans did. For instance, the great stadium of Vésone (now Périgueux) was, in the early empire, transformed into a fortress.

33. I base my analysis on these subjects from information gathered from Wikipedia, where articles appear to be properly referenced. See the articles for Mirza Ghulam Ahmad, Ahmadism, Bábism, Bahaism, the Báb, and related articles. Much information on the Baha'is is also available on the French edition.
34. *Nostra Aetate*, 2.
35. This is an expression from my friend Julien Lalanne, which has also inspired this paragraph. I thank him deeply for this insight.
36. http://orthodoxie.com/interview-du-metropolite-de-batoumi-et-lazeti-dimitri-eglise-orthodoxe-de-georgie/
37. https://muslimstatistics.wordpress.com/2012/12/14/al-jazeerah-6-million-muslims-convert-to-christianity-in-africa-each-year/
38. Christianity grows by 2 500 000 converts every year, compared to 900 000 for Islam. There are 23 million Christians born every year, compared to 22 million Muslims. http://fastestgrowingreligion.com/numbers.html

Chapter IV

The two coming millennia: History of the Third Cyclic Age

It is quite daring to pretend to be able to give a preview of History for the coming 2 000 years, and this might seem like a gratuitous exercise, especially given that no one alive today will be there in a hundred years to verify the sequence of events, making it an easy game for the author to predict that the world will be this way or that way.

However, we are not attempting divination here, but merely trying to apply our understanding of cycles to a more distant future. The patterns that we have established can be tested through the predictions that we have made for the coming decades. If these predictions turn out to be correct, then we can consider that our methodological approach is sound and that our theory of cycles is confirmed.

Yet the cycles characterize what we have called Necessary History. Thus, although the appearances and contingencies might lead to small differences, we would still be able to consider these cycles as reliable tools for predicting the unfolding of history in the centuries further into the future.

The goal of this last chapter is thus to attempt to anticipate, based on Necessary History and the cycles, the broad traits that are to be expected of Contingent History for the two thousand years ahead. If, in 50 years, the broad strokes of our predictions from the previous chapter have come to be, then those who will read this book will be justified in believing that these further predictions will also come to be.

A warning for the reader before we go down this path. We have noted an increase in the size of entities described through each cycle, as well as a qualitative leap in terms of technologies. We should not, therefore, frown upon the considerations of space travel and the possibilities of colonization of other planets in the upcoming cycles. We must keep in mind that centuries of technological development separate us from the periods that we will be describing. Let us remind ourselves that discussing the cross of the Atlantic Ocean with a Roman would have made one look like a fool. We must keep in mind that the productive apparatus of humanity in one thousand years from now will be as distant from ours compared to that of the Year 1000.

1. The AB couple: Asia and new planetary worlds, the New Occident

A) THE COASTS OF THE PACIFIC OCEAN: THE AGAEAN SEA OF THE FUTURE

As we have seen, it is probable, according to the cycles, that Occidental civilization will find a new beginning in China, or more broadly in the Far East: China, Korea, Japan, Vietnam, perhaps also India (Germany is born from Germania, which was not a part of the

Roman Empire). After the switch from cities to countries, with Rome and the Italian peninsula, the United States will have allowed the passing of countries to super-countries: quasi-continental state entities. And then, as we will see, the sizes will get even bigger.

Thus, in bold, we will describe Cycle A and under each stage, a description of its next iterations.

1) Invasion of the territories of the future civilization by a more civilized foreign empire.

The United States extend their empire to China, following troubles and a civil war having led to the crumbling of the communist regime. American bases are established on Chinese soil, and a vassal regime is put in place to lead the country. China is fragmented into diverse political entities, with the great cities becoming independent capitals. Tibet becomes independent. All of Eastern Asia is under American control.

2) New invasion by barbarian populations revert the political order imposed by the first invaders.

Africa, India and Pakistan, all overpopulated, lead to millions of immigrants arriving to the flourishing countries of Pacific Asia, while America, weakened by its own authoritarianism and a socialist economy, loosens its grasp over Asia.

3) Period of disappearance of the ancient culture and gestation of a new order.

The varnishes of Asian Americanization start weakening, and de-globalization resulting from the disappearance of the unifying effect of the American power leads to shortages and disorder. The territories of Eastern Asia and America feudalize. Local governments become somewhat hereditary principalities, which leads to tensions, rivalries and conflicts. These problems negatively affect communication and trade routes. A large part of the population returns to a subsistence economy and cities diminish in population. Education levels fall, superstition comes to dominate, and great religious structures reappear.

4) Progressive appearance of political entities unifying into a common civilization.

Through wars, marriages and alliances, the principalities become larger, leading to entities that resemble States to ensure safety of the territory. This Asian "Middle Ages" is an opportunity for teaching and trade to begin developing again. We rediscover, in the Universities of the greatest lords or clergies, sciences and technologies from the Ancient American and European Empires.

5) Progressive cultural differentiation and competition between political entities for hegemony.

The appearance of great stable political entities that are competing favors a cultural differentiation, variations around the theme of the new Asian, or Asia-Pacific Civilization, since this Civilization extends partially over North and South America, heir of the Euro-American Empire.

6) Creation of a colonial empire stimulated by internal crises and technical progress.

Technological progress favors a demographic increase and urbanization. However, cultural and religious differences lead to conflicts between political entities as well as internally. The Asian-Pacific Civilization surpasses the technological limits reached by America in the domain of transportation and becomes capable to travel in space more efficiently, as well as establish bases with somewhat hostile living conditions. Colonies are founded on the Moon, Mars and Venus, and on other satellites of various planets in order to mine them.

7) Confrontation with the threat of a foreign civilizational superpower. War of resistance by Civilization A.

The Asian-Pacific Civilization bumps into the Swahili Empire and leads a difficult war of resistance in America and in the mountains and steppes of Central Asia. The final victory over this Type D Civilization leads to a colonization of all of Africa by the Asian-Pacific Civilization.

8) An antagonism appears within the civilization: a democratic, cosmopolitan and maritime bloc opposes a totalitarian, militaristic, autarkic and continental bloc.

The Asian-Pacific Civilization advanced globally toward democracy and the state of rights, international trade, but inside the land, a totalitarian, militaristic and autarkic political entity develops.

9) All-out war internal to the civilization, relentlessness from both sides, disappearance of conventional prohibitions.

The war that occurs with this bloc leads to hundreds of millions of deaths and ravages Eastern Asia.

10) All-out internal war results in a weakened civilization, leading to the crumbling of its colonial empire and the loss of its global hegemony. The Empire is taken over by an emerging power of a superior size.

The Asian-Pacific Civilization is worn out. It loses control of Africa, Europe, and of a part of America. The great planetary powers become those who used to be only colonies: Mars and Venus first, which became more viable due to human efforts.

11) All of the states forming Civilization A are taken under tutelage by the superpower of Civilization B.

The mother Asian lands pass under the tutelage of Mars[1].

Let us now have a look, through the century, at the expected internal evolution of this new Civilization A.

In **bold**: stage of Cycle A
In upright: corresponding Asian-Pacific historical prediction

1) Primary gestational period—Absence of State

Political institutions: Aristocratic order based on the ownership of land and war. Fragmented powers.

The lands surrounding the Pacific Ocean are under the control of local warlords, heirs of former official positions or bandits self-proclaimed as legitimate authorities. They exert their power over local areas that have been conceded by more powerful lords, on the model of feudalism.

Society/Law: Caste system, primitive modes of justice. Rural society, peasantry and communal populations.

A feudal order is established under the control of local lords. Individuals who are not members of the Noblesse are subordinated to members of that class. Cities have been emptied due to economic misery, insecurity and the lack of reliability in communication and trade pathways. The population is essentially rural and focused on a subsistence economy.

Arts/Culture: Art is almost exclusively religious. Theater, representational art, and architecture are limited to religion.

Art is only found in the architecture of the temples of the religion of the Asian-Pacific Civilization and in the representation of Neo-Christian dogmas.

Religion: Common religion for the whole of the nebulous Civilization (not yet structured with nation states). Religion is a factor of cultural unity for lands deprived of a central power. Superstition is dominant.

The disappearance of urban society and the regression of education levels favor a return to superstitions. A common belief, Neo-Christianity, structured around a unique religious center, the new Vatican of the Popes, is established in Los Angeles. It is shared by the ensemble of peoples of the lands surrounding the Pacific Ocean. The clergy of the new religion has an important weight in the sociopolitical order.

Sciences: Science is virtually confounded with religion. Nature is explained with myths and beliefs.

The return to superstition favors a return of religious explanations for several natural phenomena. The scientific knowledge that was most anchored in the persisting American Empire persists, but much of it is deformed through the prism of magical beliefs and the blurriness of general ignorance. Numerous technologies become poorly understood and persist only due to a practical knowledge of their functioning.

Relations with the external world: Period of isolation and resistance to foreign threats. Civilization, economy and technologies are characterized by a clearly lower level of development compared to more evolved contemporaneous civilizations.

The Asian-Pacific Civilization is mired in feudal wars between its local lords, and its profound intellectual regression places it much behind the American Empire of Europe.

Methods of warfare: War is mostly an affair for aristocrats, armies are few and used for private wars.

War is the affair of aristocrats, who combat in small skirmishes between one another with small armies. Weaponry and technologies are inherited from the American Empire, personalized and adapted to local needs. They lose their standardized character and their adaptation to large military manoeuvers and instead are focused on small wars. The towns surround themselves with concrete walls and lords erect powerful fortresses.

2) Secondary gestational period—Normalization and reappearance of a central power.

Political institutions: Appearance, from among the aristocracy, of a structural central power.

Political entities begin to crystallize in the nebulous Asian-Pacific Civilization: Istchana[2] (new power of the Chinese coastline), Japan, California and Indochina. Cities begin to reappear.

Society/Law: Development of a bourgeoisie which stimulates trade, development of urban centers which are more secure for trade.

Trade is slowly re-established, which favors the appearance of larger political entities that are accruing power. A renaissance of law occurs, and feudal conflicts diminish. This progression forms a basis for the future developments of a merchant class.

Arts/Culture: Art begins to detach from religion. The enrichment of a bourgeois class and the establishment of a developing central power funds new forms of art, sometimes on profane themes.

The appearance of a merchant class and the accrual of wealth by the aristocracy lead to the rise of a luxury market throughout the Asian-Pacific Civilization. This market is further favored by the re-establishment of contacts with the European world, which is in decline but still shining through its culture.

Religion: Religion remains an important aspect of society, but the supernatural loses its status as the only source of explanation for the world.

The progressive rise of levels of education, notably in the clergy, leads to a drawback of superstition, and to a rationalization of faith.

Sciences: Beginning of the search for causes beyond mere observation. Birth of reason. First explanations of the world that do not directly appeal to the supernatural.

The emergence of new cities and re-urbanization favor the development of new intellectual centers, universities where science is rediscovered. New academics are trained, mostly on the coastline of the territory of the former country of China, in Korea, Japan and on the Pacific coastline of America, in centers that are most impacted by trade.

Relations with the external world: Affirmation of sovereignty and first offensive against foreign powers, first movement for colonization. The economical and technological gap with respect to other great civilizations diminishes.

Confrontation in the Indian Ocean and deep into the lands of India and Iran with the warriors of Neo-Islam. Struggle against pirate raids by Africans in Oceania.

Methods of warfare: Development of more massive armies, assembled under a senior command functioning under a traditional aristocratic system.

The reappearance of central powers leading large principalities or independent kingdoms allows mobilizing larger military forces and the establishment of permanent armies.

3) Renaissance Period—Consolidation of the State

Political Institutions: At the outset of a period of gestation, establishment of the State, a political entity that concentrates public legislative, executive and judiciary powers.

The strengthening of central powers, founded on new classes of bourgeois, merchants or well-off artisans, allows the true reappearance of the central state with an organized administration, to the disadvantage of the feudal noblesse.

Society/Law: Thanks to the safety guaranteed by a concentrated and efficient public power, trade increases, the bourgeois class grows and extends its social influence (appearance of large bourgeois fortunes). This class takes a great political weight and tends to replace the old warrior aristocracy whose protective role was taken over by the state. Beginnings of the rational organization of justice. Growth of cities.

164

The share of peasantry within the overall population diminishes constantly. Cities increase in size, fueled by the development of the middle class, small artisans and merchants. The feudal regime is combatted with even more force as the wealthy bourgeois reach a political power that is comparable to that of the great aristocrats. The Pacific region engages intensively in trading, but also in influence struggles between the great States.

Arts/Culture: Art becomes profane. Theater turns away from religion, loses its cultural aspects and becomes political, philosophical and bourgeois. Rediscovery of the classics from the previous Type A Civilization.

Theater, cinema and great holographic spectacles are impacted by the development of the entertainment market for bourgeois and aristocrats, which offers a greater artistic freedom than religious representations. The classical works of American and European cinema are rediscovered and reinterpreted in all places of the Pacific, presenting political intrigues and social satires.

Religion: Tensions between the emancipation movement and traditional beliefs. Progressive withdrawal of religion to the benefit of sciences and philosophy. Differentiation of beliefs between different states.

The rivalries between States, the appearance of large-scale wars and the fixation in time of the great States lead to the appearance of a national sentiment. The growth of the political power of the chiefs of States offers cover to those who criticize the Neo-Christian clergy and religion which brings arguments for the expansion of their powers. The central religious authority of Neo-Christianity finds itself weakened from this critique and disparities appear in how the cult is conceived within each people, leading to the rise of tensions and feeding the process of national differentiation.

Sciences: Rise of philosophy. Reason divorces from religious beliefs and becomes inquiring. Birth of schools of thought. Development of astronomy, medicine, mathematics. Decline of mythical and traditional explanations.

A new rise of sciences is favored by the immigration of Europeans fleeing the African conquest and the fall of the European Empire. Philosophy and scientific critique occurs in Universities and spreads thanks to profane art, which carries new modes of thought and mores. Cutting-edge science from the times of the American Empire is rediscovered and the scientific level of the American apogee is equated and eventually surpassed.

Relations with the external world: Decisive victory over foreign threats. The technological and economical gap is no more. Exploration movements are initiated, based on new navigational techniques, establishment of first colonies.

The surpassing of ancient technologies for space travel allows organizing great inhabited expeditions through the solar system. The Swahili Empire has been vanquished and the Asian-Pacific Civilization is liberated from any threat of foreign invasion. Colonies are established on Mars, Venus and on the satellites of Jupiter. This movement is favored by internal crises, notably religious persecutions, in the States of the Pacific.

Methods of warfare: Disappearance of private wars, development of permanent and professional armies. Caste system is abolished.

The old feudal aristocracy is still employed by sovereign princes of the Pacific to lead their armies, but those are formed mostly by men from the people who are paid, thus constituting a permanent military force in the service of the State. The wars only occur between States: Indochina, Istchana, Japan, California…

4) Classical Period—The Nation state

Political institutions: Establishment of democracy. Progressive extension of the concept of the rights to the citizenry. Development of an identity around States, supported by historical glorification and celebration of benefactor heroes from the community. Virulent and violent competition between States.

Istchana, Japan and Indochina are overturned by revolutions caused by the strong development of the bourgeoisie and the uselessness of the aristocracy. Certain kingdoms are maintained while accommodating democracy, while others become Republics that base their legitimacy in national identity and by developing a patriotic mythology.

Society/Law: Almost complete disappearance of the aristocracy. Movement for the equality of rights between citizens, priority of the law, softening of the customs (notably of legal punishment). The great urban centers reach record sizes.

The aristocracies are erased and replaced by a meritocracy based on wealth. A long political struggle is necessary to extend civil rights to the less wealthy. Cities become gigantic, surpassing the size of the agglomerations in Ancient America. These cities are provisioned by a very dynamic economy thanks to the disappearance of feudal rights and their replacement with capitalist liberation.

Arts/culture: Development of entertainment. Art loses virtually any religious significance.

Great forms of entertainment are democratized and become popular. Competitive sports reappear in colossal stadiums.

Religion: Religion is excluded from the public sphere through rationalization of the political domain. Anti-religious reactions. Intellectuals are attempting to find a rational origin for traditional beliefs.

The monarchies of great states, which were relying on the clergy and religious legitimacy, crumble. This leads to the loss of political power for Neo-Christianity. Religion is less attacked by the most radical enemies of traditional order, and its prestige is reduced.

Sciences: Development of general education and organized teaching systems. Knowledge is no more esoteric and becomes open to all.

The development of democracy and the important movement for the urbanization of society result in the establishment of a public education system, encouraged by the partisans of a new post-revolutionary order.

Relations with the external world: Explosion of the movement for colonization. Complete submission of all old enemies, control over maritime routes. Worldwide hegemony. Economic, technological and scientific supremacy. A peak of civilization is attained.

The Swahili Empire is destroyed under the attacks of the great powers of the Pacific. Dominated territories are colonized. Colonization is extensively managed and encouraged by the States seeking opportunities for expansion of their industries and extraction of raw materials. Similar interests also underlie the drive to colonize space.

Methods of warfare: Massive armies, highly disciplined infantry. Development of conscription. War becomes increasingly costly in terms of human lives lost.

The new democratic order is accompanied with the re-emergence of the citizen-soldier and the spreading of conscription, establishing armies that take part in major confrontations, motivated by nationalist fanatism. The great wars between States exhaust the economies and populations of the great powers of the Pacific.

5) Late period—End of sovereign nations

Political institutions: Durable peace under foreign control between the States. Weakening of democracy to the profit of an oligarchy which follows orders from the dominant foreign power.

Mars extends its protectorate over the Pacific.

Society/Law: Loss of dynamism. Control imposed by the foreign powers favors stability and therefore the stagnation of society.

Mars limits the ambitions of the great States of the Pacific and favors a pro-Martian oligarchy as leadership for these democracies.

Arts/culture: Importation of the entertainment of the dominating power, influence of its standards.

The great Martian forms of entertainment invade the screens and holographic projection areas of the Earth. Local productions begin to seek inspiration in Martian productions.

Religion: Development of religious syncretism, relativism, as well as the appearance of new spirituality movements to the disadvantage of traditional beliefs.

The cults and spiritualties of the south of Africa progress within the Asian-Pacific Civilization, where traditional Neo-Christianity has been weakened by the attacks of post-revolutionary radicals.

Sciences: End of technological and scientific supremacy.

Mars becomes the central pole of scientific research.

Relations with the external world: Decolonization, loss of influence to the benefit of foreign powers. Unification attempt in order to resist to foreign powers. Switch toward a foreign tutelage model.

The Asian-Pacific Civilization loses control of the Earth as well as its suzerainty over space colonies.

Methods of warfare: Interventions alongside the power in charge of the tutelage, with their agreement and participation.

Subordination to Mars, operations for peace and order are led under the control and leadership of Mars.

We have also observed that A contained a subcycle ω. It could be interesting to hypothesize what such a subcycle would look like in the future. We will not locate this new entity ω randomly. Let us again attempt to identify the repeating patterns. Sparta was founded by the Dorians, invaders of the Mycenaean Empire, and Prussia was a Germanic State, a people that had invaded the Roman Empire and that had never lived under its direct domination. It thus seems logical that a people at the periphery of the future Asian-Pacific Civilization will become ω. Thus, we surmise that India, specifically in the valley of the Ganges, would be a probable location for ω.

In **bold**: stage of Cycle ω
In upright: corresponding Indian predicted fact

1) Establishment of a warrior aristocracy in the lands where the original population is subordinated. They form the nucleus of nation ω.

Indochinese Lord-Warriors invade the Bangladesh and acquire a sizable domain in the valley of the Ganges.

2) ω, a nation belonging to Civilization A, structures itself into a military nation.

The domain defended by the Lord-Warriors becomes the Great Kingdom of Gangaride[3], based extensively on the aristocratic and warrior values of its founders. Native people are economically exploited by the Gangarides who refuse to engage in any production activity, solely relying on military control.

3) Formation, through war, of a federal hegemonic system of ω, led sovereignly, with a certain autonomy left to some political entities. Annexation and subordination of others.

The Gangaride Kingdom becomes an Indian Empire by subordinating the valley of the Indus River and the Deccan Plateau, as well as the Himalaya. The Gangaride Empire is established as a continental fortress, controlled by the caste that descends from the initial Indochinese conquerors. This caste preserves its ethnic distinction from the Indian autochthone majority.

4) Following various crises, hardening of the regime, which becomes increasingly totalitarian and brutal. Identitarian withdrawal.

During the exhausting War of the Greats, opposing the Indian Empire of the Gangarides, allied to Indochina, to the great democracies of Istchana and Japan, a part of the Indian and Nepalese peoples revolt against the authority of the Gangarides, forcing them to accept a humiliating peace treaty in order to concentrate on troubles internal to their empire. Ratjarhu, the new Gangaride Emperor, cruelly represses the revolts, organizing the extermination of dozens of millions of Indian autochthones, as well as some Gangarides advocating for their civil rights. This shapes the Gangarides into a totalitarian and traditionalist regime, reinforcing its racialist and autarkic tendencies.

5) Great war against a maritime power from an open, democratic and maritime civilization.

After having crushed the revolts, Ratjarhu stimulates the desire of revenge in his people, and restarts the total war against Istchana and Japan, this time finding an ally in Venus colonies, an oligarchical Republic whose power is rising and who is looking to place its pawns in the Earthly game.

6) Victory of the foreign power, occupation of the territory, support for the establishment of a complacent non-democratic regime.

Istchana is vanquished, and the Gangarides impose over it an aristocratic government in accordance with their values. Japan resists, united by links of friendship to Mars, which has a negative outlook over the progression of the totalitarian regime of Ratjarhu and the risk of a Venusian control over the Earth.

7) ω establishes its hegemony over Civilization A, and becomes a champion for the fight against foreign powers to which it had previously been an ally.

The Indian Empire of the Gangarides establishes its hegemony over the lands surrounding the Pacific, but refuses to offer concessions to Venus on its ambitions for terrestrial domination and declares war against its previous ally.

8) The war against the foreign power leads to a situation of a war over two fronts; weakening of the position of ω and defeat in the external war.

The Gangaride Empire, relying on the industrial power of the subordinated Pacific, pushes back invading forces from Venus, and succeeds to bring the war to Venus itself. However, constantly constrained to monitor Japan, which maintained independence, and facing other economic difficulties, the Gangaride Empire is forced to withdraw too many forces from the Earth.

9) This initial weakening allows another power, in alliance with the formerly-vanquished enemy, to defeat ω.

Mars benefits from the mutual weakening between Venus and Ratjarhu in order to intervene and establish its own hegemony over the Earth. The Gangaride Empire is vanquished by the Martian Landings.

10) ω loses its hegemony and falls into a state of crisis. Rise of a confederate alliance of the other powers of the same Civilization A.

The forces of the Gangaride Empire are destroyed and it loses its dominant position. The forced establishment of a new democratic regime by Mars gives, through dominance by the numbers, power to the Indian autochthones who erase any trace of the old Gangaride order. The countries from the Pacific West form, together, the Asian Community.

B) TOWARD THE STELLAR EMPIRE

In **bold**, Cycle B. In upright, its next iteration.

1) A human community is founded by a pre-existing civilization, under the influence of Civilization A.

Asian colonists establish on Mars during Stage 6) of Cycle A.

2) Rejection of the suzerainty by the mother-civilization under the leadership of the aristocracy.

The colonists reject the suzerainty of one of the political entities of the Asian-Pacific Civilization which controlled Mars. They name themselves the Martians, by opposition to the colonies of other Asian-Pacific Powers who are referred to as the Asians.

3) Establishment of the Republic with limited democratic mechanisms, conflicts over political rights.

The monarchic or autocratic system in place in the Asian-Pacific Civilization is rejected. The model of the Ancient USA, with a constitution, is preferred.

4) Conquest of the natural territory by the historical center of the civilization.

Mars is progressively colonized and terraformed, in order to ease life for the colonists. Tensions appear with the Asians. The Martians consider that the Manifest destiny of their free nation is to extend over the whole planet and they want to subordinate these secondary colonists to their power.

x) Civil war: the nucleus of the civilization faces a desire of separation from its allies due to inequalities. The allies secede and form a confederation imitating the institutions of the nucleus, but in opposition to it. This secession concludes with the victory of the nucleus of the civilization and the imposition of its model to the other parties as well as the unification of the nation.

A war occurs between Martians and Asians who refuse to be subjected to the Martian State. All the Asians, colonists from different nations of the Earth, unite into a confederation in order to oppose Martian hegemony. The Martians triumph in this war but must concede the equality of rights to Asians. All inhabitants become part of a unique Martian nation.

5) Confrontation to a powerful conquering nation. A fight for survival and supremacy leaves Civilization B without rival and able to dominate the world.

After the Asian-Pacific Civilization was exhausted by a terrible internal conflict, Mars finds itself face-to-face with the Venusian power. The distrusting equilibrium turns into the "Venusian Wars," which lead to the final triumph of Mars and its imperial domination over the Solar System.

6) The states of A become dominated by B.

All of the states of the Asian-Pacific Civilization pass under Martian control.

7) Absolute hegemony over the known world, absence of rivals (it is at this step that Stage 1 of the next Cycle A occurs).

Mars reigns as a master over the solar system and all of humanity. The satellites of Jupiter, based mostly on a very dynamic mining economy, with an important growth of population, pass under the control of Martian powers.

8) The Empire, a militaristic and autocratic regime, succeeds to the Republic.

The democratic and liberal Martian power mutates toward an autocratic, socialist military regime.

9) Decline and dismemberment of Empire B (corresponds to Stage 2 of the next Cycle A).

The Martian Empire crumbles. The satellites of Jupiter are ready to pick up the burden…

Let us now have a look, through the centuries, at the predicted internal evolution for this new Civilization B:

In **bold**: stage of Cycle B
In upright: corresponding predicted Martian fact

1) The Foreign Monarchy

Political institutions: Domination of a foreign monarchy.

Mars is under the domination of Japan.

Society/Law: Society is mostly rural and based on agriculture. Local communities are governed by assemblies that organize security under the control of the foreign power.

The Martian society is mainly composed of agricultural exploitations in domes, terraforming installations and mining colonies. The colonies are either led by governors named by Asian princes, by assemblies of local colonists, or by managers mandated by Earth-based mining companies.

Arts/culture: The culture is identical to that of the dominating foreign power.

Art is based on the Asian-Pacific model.

Economy: Agriculture by small farmers, beginnings of the development of commerce.

Agricultural exploitations in domes, terraforming installations, mining of resources and exportation back to the Earth. Interplanetary trade is based around the perpetual topographic changes of the solar system, since the planets are moving with respect to one another according to their specific period of revolution around the sun.

Religion: Specific religion that is not dictated by the foreign influence.

A religion, founded on a syncretism of various heresies having attacked the Neo-Christianity of the Asian-Pacific Civilization, was excluded from various territories of this nation, which motivated the colonists to leave for Mars, where this religion dominates.

Sciences: Mostly acquired from the suzerain civilization.

The technologies for constructing domes, foraging the Martian soil, and for terraforming are the result of research in the Asian-Pacific Civilization.

Relations with the external world: Foreign suzerainty.

Mars is under the suzerainty of the Asian-Pacific States.

Methods of warfare: Based on the model of the civilization in charge of the tutelage, warrior militias that are more or less voluntary.

Private militias of colonists, armed in the Asian-Pacific fashion, constituted mostly for the purpose of maintaining order and combatting theft and piracy.

2) The Heroic Republic

Political institutions: Independent republic, citizenship, suffrage, individual liberty.

Mars becomes a Republic whose colonists are free citizens with civil rights.

Society/Law: Individual rights and liberties are guaranteed by a written system of Law, and magistracy is based on suffrage. Puritan morals.

Writing of the Constitution of the Federated Martian States and of a Bill of Rights. Martian society is pious, moralizing, austere and animated by the feeling of a sacred mission: to allow life to extends to Mars by making it viable, for the glory of God.

Arts/culture: Profound influence of Civilization A, which is the most advanced civilization of the time.

Martian culture is characterized by the architecture and clothing styles of the Asian-Pacific.

Economy: Peasant exploitation by small owners, artisans, and trade.

The Martian economy remains based on small exploitations by colonists in domes, but the rupture of certain commercial links with the Asians stimulates local manufacturing at small scales. The terraforming of the Planet progresses and even allows to extend a part of agriculture outside of domes, which become increasingly reserved for habitation.

Religion: Development of a civil religion, the ensemble of beliefs and behaviors are not exclusively but significantly tied to a view of good citizenship and founded on the religion of the original dominant ethnicity.

While civil rights protect the freedom of religion, most of the Martians share the same faith, or some variants of it, founded on the most fundamental dogmas of the Asian-Pacific religion, but without its clergy and decorum. The institutions are placed under the protection of the divinity, and this religious culture has a strong influence on mores.

Sciences: Progress of production techniques, beginning of great innovations in the military and transportation domains.

The terraforming tools improve, and agriculture adapts to Martian conditions. Such new independence leads to the development of military forces and lower-orbit tools of defense to protect against terrestrial landing. Development of magnetic fields as a tool of defense (thanks to developments in the use of large magnetic fields as part of terraforming activities). Infrastructures for the control of transportation become common in great population centers and form a network allowing safety in aerial transports which is becoming increasingly denser.

Relations with the external world: Creation of a protection glacis by the subordination of neighboring peoples and the conquest of a strategic space; persistence of isolationism with no real imperialistic will.

Martians, in order to completely ensure their safety against an invasion, want to become masters of the whole planet. The independent Asian colonies or those still controlled by the Asian-Pacific Civilization are subordinated one after the other through force or integrated to the Martian military system through treaties. The empty Martian spaces are subject to a voluntarist colonization policy by the Martian government. The satellites of Mars are annexed and bases are installed on them.

Methods of warfare: Armies of conscripted soldiers developing an organization that is rational and adapted. Extension of the recruitment pool to non-citizens.

The army is an army of conscription, but its organization becomes extremely detailed, based on the model of Earthly armed forces. Asian neighboring colonies are, through treaties or force, invited to join the Martian effort for the defense of the Martian orbital space.

3) The Imperial Republic

Political institutions: Extension of citizenship outside of the historical nucleus, appearance of a macro-Republic extending to the protection glacis.

All of the inhabitants of Mars become Martian citizens. The Martian constitution applies to all of the Martian colonies. The Federated Martian States end up identifying with Mars as a planetary identity.

Society/Law: Industrialization, appearance of an urban society. Rapid growth in wealth destabilizes the mores, which become more permissive. Appearance of contestations of the ancestral sociopolitical consensus.

The progresses of terraforming lead the domes to become increasingly useless, and technological progresses make any protection that remains necessary to be scaled down to individual housing units or big buildings, favoring a real estate boom, as well as the appearance of gigantic and cosmopolitan cities. The new cultural diversity breaks the homogeneity of the society and threatens the original social consensus. This also increases inequalities and, despite the general increase in the standards of living, leads to increasingly strong social demands, even when such demands compromise the concepts of liberty defended by the foundational Martian ideals.

Arts/culture: Appearance of mass entertainment. The culture of Civilization B becomes a dominant reference and an imitated model in foreign places.

With the demographic and economic boom, Martian culture becomes sufficiently wealthy to develop an independence from Earthly influences, and develop its own standards.

Economy: Replacement of the network of small exploiters by greater entities, favored by the lowering of the cost of labor. Establishment of an economic domination founded on force.

The privileged access of Martians to raw materials of the Asteroid belt of the Solar System favors the development of the extremely robotized Martian industries, including robotization that takes over administrative duties, and the quantity of human labor in many fields becomes negligible. The structures that humanity can build reach a degree of complexity and size that are unimaginable today, and this ingenuity leads to the floating cities of Jupiter. The monetary and financial system dominates the world, able to impose the Martian will unto foreign governments. The Martian economy dominates all markets. Governments that refuse to partner are overthrown.

Religion: Diversification of religious beliefs, importation of foreign beliefs as the population residing in Civilization B becomes more cosmopolitan.

The earthly Neo-Christian cults spread over Mars, as well as other forms of spirituality.

Sciences: Apogee of the creativity of Civilization B. Multiple and important technological innovations. Reflections are undertaken about the organization of human activity.

The mastery of artificial intelligence reaches new heights. A spectacular leap is made in our understanding of physics, gravity, energy and antimatter. Development of antigravity, as well as artificial gravity fields for spaceships. Application of these technology to the military domain.

The practice of terraforming has made Mars a leader in environmental technologies and climate control, as well as in the generation of large electromagnetic fields (protection of spaceships against toxic radiation, weaponry, etc.). Progresses in telecommunications become the first to avoid the barrier of the speed of light, making possible instantaneous exchanges from one part of the Solar System to another. This breakthrough provides a glimpse into future possibilities for extremely fast travel outside of the Solar System, toward other planetary systems.

Relations with the external world: Hegemonic position, multiplication of foreign interventions. An imperialistic attitude is adopted and justified by the appearance of a new discourse divorcing from traditional isolationism. There is a desire to assume the role of world police.

Mars becomes the police of the Solar System, subordinates Venus, and establishes its protectorate over the terrestrial Asian-Pacific Civilization, by intervening following troubles provoked by Islamic syncretism in Europe, Asia and Africa.

Methods of warfare: Professionalization of the army. Acquisition of a strike force over sea. Strong organization and technological superiority.

The army becomes entirely professional, equipped with the best combat systems in the world, largely robotized. As is the case in the economy, human labor becomes negligible and the armed forces are composed mostly of drones and robots, keeping men away from combats. Mars becomes the first space power, equipped with an unequaled float, a vector guaranteeing its hegemony.

4) The Empire

Political institutions: any form of democracy is abolished to the advantage of a central dictatorial power whose control grows, up to totalitarianism.

The Martian government becomes dictatorial, under the control of the army. An autocratic and dirigist culture develops, whose grasp over society reinforces progressively in a vicious circle. The socialist dictatorial central power is at the root of this problem. The grasp of Martian centralism over the ensemble of the Solar System becomes increasingly burdening.

Society/Law: The Empire appears as a remedy to the break of the ancestral sociopolitical consensus. Individual liberties and judicial protections against the power disappear as the central power is reinforced. We observe a reappearance of castes with judiciary-political disparities and social mobility disparities.

The rise of the Empire puts an end to social conflicts affecting Martian society through an excess of authority. Legalism progressively disappears from the priorities of governments, which becomes increasingly authoritarian and autocratic. The new statist system favors corruption, and a true fracture of castes appears between the people and imperial officials, members of the state apparatus and dignitaries of the regime, who benefit from a special judicial status. Social mobility only exists due to a love affair here or there, but largely the old Martian virtue of individual success leaves place to a generalized demoralization, and integrity and honesty become devalued.

Arts/culture: Official art supporting the power of the State. Art is marked by the absolutism of the central power and its increasingly totalitarian structure. Disappearance of the individual to the benefit of a symbolic and typical imagery. This systematic art, fixated and sterile, does not respond to universal sensibilities and loses its reference status in the Empire, provoking the reappearance of local sensibilities.

Official art appears as an instrument of propaganda exalting the glory of the Martian Empire and its leaders, making an apology for subordination to authority and for blind obedience to an omniscient and benevolent government. Disappearance of the old archetype of "one against all," replaced by a hero that is integrated to the group and acting in the name of the collective good.

Economy: The system evolves toward totalitarianism. The economy declines until complete crumbling, paralyzed by the authority of the central power and the control over production to the satisfaction of the needs of the State and the army.

The economy is almost fully planned, at the service of the army, the administration and the state. Individual economic liberty disappears, and the state imposes the distribution of employment. Shortages reappear, as well as a black market which is severely repressed.

Religion: Traditional civil religion becomes a unique cult imposed in order to favor central power.

The moral superiority of the Martian power is pushed unto the people with propaganda and its successive leaders are exalted in line with the Soviet model. After power takeovers, the propaganda literally erases the existence of the previous emperor and suddenly starts exalting the eternal value of the new one. The emperor is a quasi-divinity and is the subject of a personality cult. Traditional monotheistic religions are reticent to enter that cult, and, as a result, they are subjected to persecution.

Sciences: Stagnation of technological progresses, innovations are not used.

The dirigist and planned economy stifles entrepreneurial liberty and prevents the innovative use of very advanced scientific knowledge: no interest is given to technologies for interstellar travel circumventing light speed.

Relations with the external world: Transformation of the hegemony into an empire. Domination of vassals without further extension, except for punctual interventions. The more authoritarian character of the central government is felt in the way the power of B is expressed outside of the nation, leaving less autonomy to local governments.

Mars and its provinces are governed with a similar, increasingly weighty authority, by the imperial government. Martian military governments are imposed to various terrestrial and Venusian districts, as well as colonies of the Jupiter orbit.

Methods of warfare: Professional imperial army, important weight in the State apparatus, auxiliaries are employed.

The imperial army is organized according to the distribution of local districts. The difficulties in combat against anti-imperialist local guerillas require the use of human mercenary commandos, recruited locally.

2. C and D: between post-Islamic syncretism and the African Black Empire. The New Orient

A) NEO-ISLAMIC CIVILIZATION

In **bold**, Cycle C. In upright, its next iteration.

1) Civilisation C is born in a nomadic community: a prophet, leaving his place of origin, delivers a politico-religious law to his people based on a more ancient tradition and guides them toward the appropriation of a territory.

In the valleys of the Caucasus, heir of a form of Muslim faith, among a community of merchants and shepherds that developed between Chechnya and Azerbaijan, an individual in the XXIIIth-XXIVth centuries claims to have had a revelation and carries his people guide by a divine message, which takes the form of a syncretism between Ancient Islam and the old Orthodox Christianity of the neighboring regions, toward a new religion, Neo-Islam. He flees his place of origin and brings his people to conquer the plateau of former Turkey and the plains of former Russia in the North.

2) C establishes into fertile lands outside of the desert, by benefiting from the weakening of the Civilization B of the previous cycle.

The new Neo-Islamic Civilization benefits from troubles caused by the implosion of the American Empire, which impact the whole of North Africa and the lands between Eastern Europe and the Ural, including Persia. These troubles led to the persecution of the proponents of Ulemic Islam. On its western front, the civilization is blocked by resistance from the resilient American Empire of Europe[4].

3) Civilisation C undergoes a golden age of political and religious unity. Appearance of a single power.

The Neo-Islamic Civilization reigns from the Arctic Ocean down to the Sahara Desert, bordering the American Empire of Europe, under the leadership of a prophet.

4) Divisions weaken C.

Difficulties related to the succession of the Prophet-Chief and cultural as well as ethnic differences in this vast empire divide the Neo-Islamic world into distinct political entities.

5) After centuries of decline, C is dominated by the powers of a foreign civilization, which come under different successive identities. The first identity of this foreign civilization does not dominate the historical center of C, but the second one attains it.

Internal divisions weaken the Neo-Islamic Civilization, which is strongly impacted by vast population movements affecting the south of Africa. Millions of individuals from Black Africa migrate toward North Africa and in the lands surrounding the Mediterranean Sea, overthrowing the American Empire of Europe and forming a new African-European Empire, extending from the Cape of Good Hope to the Ural. The first African Empire, the Bantu Empire of Congo, only penetrates the Neo-Islamic world up to Turkey, without succeeding at subordinating Armenia, the Caucasus and the Russian plains, the historic heart of Neo-Islam. The second African Empire, the Swahili Empire, subordinates this historical center and extends up to the Arctic Ocean.

6) After the fall of the foreign civilization, C is dominated by powers of Civilization A.

With the final defeat of the Swahili Empire against the Asian Civilization, the Asian Civilization succeeds at dominating over the Neo-Islamic Civilization.

7) Nationalist uprising. The structures of the new independent State are inspired by those of the states of Civilization A, secularized and hostile to the partisans of a political application of religion.

The ethno-cultural entities forming the Neo-Islamic Civilization rise against the Asian colonial powers and restructure into independent political entities, adopting the secular principles of Asian life, and showing hostility toward the adepts of traditional Neo-Islam.

8) Interventions of Civilization B. Its power is increasingly present.

The Martians enter the terrestrial game, wanting to ensure access to its great planetary market.

9) Radicalization of the defenders of a politico-religious view of the State, birth of violent groups and rise in power with respect to the presence of Civilization B.

The presence of the Martians in the Caucasus, a strategic point of communication for the sizable Eurasian-African group, provokes the anger of radical Neo-Muslims faced with the invasion of their holy places.

10) A limited attempt at policing the problem fails: the movement gains in strength and size and becomes more of a threat, with increasing potential for violence. The diaspora of Civilization C in the lands of A and B raises the mistrust and hostility of local populations in relation to its distinct way of life, its refusal to integrate and its vindictive spirit.

The attempts of the Martians at controlling the populations fail to put an end to the Neo-Islamic problem in Eastern Asia and America, and the hostility of the Neo-Islamic populations is growing.

11) The fanatics of Civilization C aggravate the situation through terrorism, in order to cause a war thought of as eschatological within a religious logic.

The radical Neo-Muslims, convinced that they are engaged in a holy war against the Martian enemy having lost its Earthly human blood, undertake terroristic attacks against the agents of Mars.

12) In the face of the rising provocations, which reach an intolerable degree, Civilization B, infuriated, opts for the military solution and crushes the fanatics in bloody wars, repeatedly.

Exasperated, Mars is confronted to a general uprising which is violently repressed, with the help of the Asians.

13) Confirmation of the dominance of the model of Civilization B. Civilization C is eradicated as a political power.

The Neo-Islam power is definitively broken and forgotten. It joins the club of the three other great pacific monotheisms: Judaism, Neo-Christianity and Ulemic Islam.

B) THE GLORY OF AFRICA

In **bold**, Cycle D. In upright, its next iteration.

1) A nation begins to develop at the margins of neighboring, stronger powers.

A nation of Central Africa develops within other great powers of Southern, Western and Eastern Africa. This nation could be the Congo, bordered by great powers such as Nigeria, South Africa and Ethiopia, although as far into the future as we are, it is likely that the borders will have changed.

2) The nation takes over a part of the territories of the Empire to which it belonged until then, and enters an expansionist dynamic.

The Congo benefits from its position and from the decline of its neighbors in order to impose itself as a dominant power over the southern two thirds of the African continent, and federates a large Bantu Empire.

3) The nation establishes an empire which integrates a part of the lands of Civilization C, sparing its historical center.

The progression of the Congolese power leads the Congo to extend its empire to the African continent as a whole, and to penetrate the Arab Peninsula up to Turkey. It hits an obstacle with the resistance of the American Empire of Europe.

4) The nation begins a phase of decline and decomposes, leaving a fragmented political space.

After a period of domination and prosperity, the Bantu Empire of the Congo fragments into multiple principalities.

5) A population at the margins of the old empire rises to power.

The Swahili populations are growing in the remainders of the Empire and eventually subordinate all principalities.

6) The new population establishes an empire which takes several elements from the former one, and takes over all of its lands, including the historical center of Civilization C.

The Swahili populations pick up the remainders of the Bantu Empire of the Congo and become masters of Africa. The Swahili Empire extends over all of the Neo-Islamic world between the Ural and the Indus River. They overthrow the American Empire of Europe and become masters of the Mediterranean Sea and of the continent up to the Arctic Ocean.

7) The progression of the empire threatens Civilization A, and absorbs a part of its territories.

The Swahili Empire wants to extend toward South America, as well as in the Orient in India and in the rest of Asia. Their fleet invades the Indian Ocean, and their armies progress in South America. The Asian-Pacific Civilization courageously combats them, thus engaging them in a two-fronts war.

8) Defeats on land and on sea against A. End of the progression.

The Asian-Pacific Civilization stops the African fleet in the Indonesian straits and triumphs over the Swahili armies in Central America.

9) Recoil of the empire, weakening of the central power and important losses of territories.

The defeat against the Asians and their turning away to the materials of the new world in space, in which the Africans had little interest, marks the beginning of the decline of the Swahili Empire in History.

10) Complete crumbling against A, the Empire is conquered by Civilization A.

The Asian-Pacific Civilization, reinforced by the wealth of its colonies and its spectacular economic and technological progresses, leads to the fall of the Swahili Empire, which is soon reduced only to the Eastern African Coast, the remainder of the former Empire becoming an Asian-Pacific possession.

C) BEYOND THE SOLAR SYSTEM

At the end of the Martian Cycle B, we have imagined that the following supercycle ABCD would start in the satellites of Jupiter dissociating from distinct and rival Planet-Nations. The great political entities of the fourth cyclic age would all be celestial bodies such as Ganymede, Titan and Europa. The next iteration of Cycle A would, beyond this leap of scale, bring a qualitative technological leap allowing men to free themselves from the limit of the speed of light, which would allow humanity to colonize exoplanets within travel times that would approach those of the Antiquity between Greece and space, and later in the XVIIth century between Europe and America. We would thus pass from the scale of Planet-Nations to nations establishing over entire planetary systems. As for what will happen after that, this would bring us more than four thousand years into the future. We have said enough for this prospective essay.

---

1. We could as well say Venus or some exoplanet of another planetary system if Man succeeds at solving the problem of the speed of light earlier. But, since we have to choose, we choose Mars!
2. A name that could come from East China, the name of a province in the time of the American Empire. Imagining future names is another interesting prospective exercise but while it may be intellectually entertaining, it relies on separate mechanisms underlying the evolution of names. We know that numerous European designations come from Roman names: Zaragoza, in Spain, takes its name from the Roman town named like the Emperor, *Caesar Augusta*. Similarly, since Emperor comes from *imperator*, that is, the "commander," it is possible that in future languages, the important term "Emperor" becomes a deformation of, for instance, the leader of the American State: *Commander in Chief*. In Asian languages, this could lead to deformations of words like Komandrinchi, Komanchi. It could also be the deformation of the name of an important character, turned into a title, like *Caesar*, which became *Kaiser* or *Tsar*.
3. I hope that my borrowing this expression from Voltaire will not offend anyone.
4. Thus here I take the side of the survival of a united European entity based on the model of the Byzantine Empire, and my naming of it is a wink to the Roman Empire of Orient. This could also very well be simply an extension in time of the current European Union.

Recommendations for action

The interest of what we have called Historionomy is not only in improving our understanding of the past but also our anticipation of the future. As we have said, History is not only deterministic, but it is partly so, with some amount of randomness. This randomness is the space of liberty, the margins for historical manoeuvers that we can effectively impact. In other words, while we cannot change the overall scheme, we can push its realization into the best possible scenarios. We can accelerate the darkest periods, and make the periods of enlightenment last longer. We can reduce the size of the inevitable violent episodes and increase the gains made in periods of peace. After having predicted what will come, I would like to end on a couple of notes on what we should do.

I have said that, for many situations for which we have anticipated what was to occur, and that are destined to evolve toward a given conclusion, various scenarios are possible. Some are hard, others are soft. I think that while it is impossible to go against Necessary History, which seems to be formed by movements that are too broad, too deep, by trends that are too heavy to be countered, we can act on Contingent History and make it so that the soft scenarios occur before the historic path toward the hard ones is taken.

That is why we must, for instance, hope that Europe and the USA will remain strong allies and will remain attached to the state of rights and liberal democracy. For Europeans, this means not to let the divisive manoeuvers of Vladimir Putin and to avoid creating opportunities for an unstable situation to develop, which would come with new risks of war in Europe, just like those that affected Greece after the cities had taken the side of Macedonia against Rome. Such a war would certainly lead to a victory of America, and the situation of Europe, under their domination, would be as undesirable as how disloyal Europeans would have been to America. On this point, knowing in advance the inevitable result of a war could help us make less adventurous decisions.

Inversely, from the American point of view, if Europe were to defect and side with Putin's Russia, the USA would find themselves in a delicate geopolitical situation, and once the victory would be attained, America would have to show itself capable of restoring liberal democracy in Europe, instead of punishing it with submissive oligarchical regimes, since a recoil of democracy in Europe would mean an accelerated crumbling of the American political system. This was the case for Ancient Greece which, once transformed into a province by Rome, was subjected to the predation of corrupted Roman governors, who used the money they were gaining through corruption in order to fund their career in Rome, importing into Italy the degraded political mores of the outside.

Concerning Islam, the patterns we have identified must show to our contemporaries that there is indeed an Islamic danger, based on the model of the Kitos War, but that the worries against this danger should remain limited, notably by keeping in mind that the danger is not an existential one for European Civilization, no more than it was for Greek Civilization. Underestimating the danger, just like overestimating it, is risky in and of itself and can lead to inappropriate actions that aggravate the problem rather than solve it.

I hope that my contemporaries will be able to take away a better understanding of the world from the explanations I have developed here. Such an understanding will allow preparing historical transitions with appropriate measure, common sense and objectivity.

I invite the readers who wish to engage in a dialogue on the subjects covered in this book, and specifically to get updates or additions that I may make to my theories in light of developing news, to visit my blog: www.historionomie.com

www.ingramcontent.com/pod-product-compliance
Lightning Source LLC
Chambersburg PA
CBHW062106080426
42734CB00012B/2768